fake
perfection

My Journey from Broken Trust to Trust Broker

Linda Ginac

Ginac Publishing
Austin, TX
www.fakeperfection.com

First Edition: June 2011

Cover design by Kristie Langone with www.2faceddesign.com

ISBN: 0-9834561-0-0
ISBN 13: 978-0-9834561-0-0

To my husband, Frank
You have been my source of inspiration and guidance since the day I met you.
I love you completely and wouldn't be the woman I am today without you.
I am blessed to be married to a man as wonderful and caring as you.
I am the luckiest woman in the world. ILUA

To my children, Andrew and Vaughn
I love you with all my heart.
Every day I wake up, I thank God for bringing you into my life.
A mother could not ask for better sons.
Hugs and Kisses

Contents

Part 4   Trust Broker

Acknowledgments

First, I want to thank my husband, Frank, for his unconditional love, devotion and support of my career and dreams. I'd also like to thank my children for making me feel like the best mom in the world; my parents, Gloria and Simon, for giving me life and teaching me that life is full of surprises; and Frank's mother, Patty, for accepting and loving me like a daughter.

I want to acknowledge Debbie Woodward for inspiring the title of my book. I would like to express my gratitude to Frank Ginac and Wendy Nolin for reviewing the book and giving me candid feedback. I would like to give thanks to Kristie Langone for working with me to perfect the cover art.

I wish to thank Jeffrey Dinsmore for editing my book. I would also like to express my love and appreciation to Jamie Armstrong for her encouragement through the production of this book. She took on many roles, including reviewer, editor, writer, and designer. Without her, this book would not be where it is today.

I want to give special acknowledgment to Adriana Hook. Her efforts were instrumental in growing The Ginac Group and building the foundation for TalentGuard, and I appreciate the personal and professional sacrifices she made to make that happen.

Finally, I want to thank my investors for believing in me and my vision, my many friends and coworkers for always encouraging me to move forward, and lastly my clients, who helped me along this amazing journey.

Introduction

I am perfect. I am an accomplished entrepreneur and successful business owner. I live in the best neighborhood and own a luxury home and drive a German luxury sedan. I belong to the finest country club and count among my many friends the elite of our society. I am blessed with a loving and devoted husband and two handsome and gifted sons. I am inspiring, resourceful, creative, and have a wicked sense of humor. I am positively stunning. Many people envy what I have and wish that their lives could be more like mine.

❈❈❈

I've spent most of my adult life carefully crafting and refining that story, then bringing it to life. This is what I wanted everyone who entered my life to think of me and nothing more, until a life-changing event altered me forever. On the surface, I had the perfect life, and the backstory I'd created was equally impressive. *I was raised by a carpenter and a mother who had a successful career in the fashion industry. I had the perfect childhood. I was a cheerleader, an A student, and one of the most popular girls in school.*

The truth, however, is not nearly that glamorous and will surprise and sometimes astonish you. It may even inspire you. If nothing else, I hope to convince you that behind the veil we all wear—that veil of fake perfection—lies the true story of each of us—who we are, how we came to be, and what we really want. Facing that truth, and being honest about who and what you are, is the first step to removing that veil and finding the success that you deserve, the success that I ultimately found, and to begin your own odyssey of inspiration.

My story begins where everyone else's does—childhood. You have to grow up somewhere and somehow, right? Where my story might be different is that I wasn't allowed to grow up, I was forced to. My parents were too young to be married, and unsuited to be married to each other. Add to this combination penny-pinching, unintended kids, and a debilitating disease, and you've got a recipe for a very unhappy home. My parents coped early on with alcohol, drugs, and endless parties, and later on by escalating their habitual violence. Amid my volatile surroundings, I learned to use hatred and anger to cope, and it eventually permeated every crevice of my soul, hardening my heart in the process. The anger eventually grew to indifference, and my desensitization to violence became such a natural part of my life that it no longer bothered me, and finally stripped me of any feelings altogether. (This is why I can still—when necessary—go from sweetheart to bitch in no time flat.)

It's amazing that I came out of my childhood unscathed and in one piece—well, at least physically. According to everyone and everything around me, I should've ended up addicted, pregnant, and jobless by the time I turned eighteen. However, despite all the ruffians surrounding me, there were some treasures who encouraged me to face reality and finish school. One in particular made me realize that I was better than my surroundings and that it was time to leave and start a new chapter, which is exactly what I did, in the end creating a new life for myself.

My shining light throughout those dark years was that despite the life I was born into, I somehow made good choices and was able to break the cycle of addiction and violence. I also had a few things going for me. I was very smart and excelled in school. My knack for picking incredible boyfriends who offered me something that I couldn't get at home—stability and unconditional love—saved me from a life of ruin. Lastly, I loved television, and many popular programs, such as *The Brady Bunch* and *Happy Days*, taught me fundamental life and social skills (imagine that—TV being a positive influence!). I gained other skills by observing and analyzing the interactions of my boyfriends' families.

Over the years, I committed to a few important relationships with men who were filled with love, self-esteem, and patience. Delving into the emotional world of my relationships would be akin to the thrill of riding a roller coaster. One moment I would be feeling the exhilaration of being in love only to plunge into the depths of my fear because people were getting too close. It was through these experiences that I began to understand myself, forgive my family for their past mistakes, break free from anger, and rediscover my innocence.

My life took great leaps forward when I met my husband Frank. Frank gave me the courage to live without shame, the guidance to pursue everything I wished for, and the patience to teach me how to love. His love, strength, and confidence allowed me to reach goals that I never thought possible, such as working my way up to a vice president role, earning my master's degree, starting my own business, and most importantly, becoming a loving and caring mother. Beyond giving me the most amazing gifts on earth—two children that I love with all my heart and soul—he helped free me from my lifelong servitude to humility and shame. I no longer allowed them to drive my behavior.

As far as I've come, though, there are moments when I feel like a visitor in my life. Even though I didn't cause or create any of the dysfunction of my family, it's difficult for me to completely eliminate the shame I feel having come from it. I look around me sometimes and feel like an imposter, because really I should be knocked up, hanging out in a bar, shooting up heroin or smoking a crack pipe, drinking myself into a stupor every night, and married to a man who abuses me. The few people who know my true story have been shocked to find out about my background, and equally surprised at my ability to withstand so many setbacks as a kid and still turn out to be so "normal." I am not a screwed-up junky or raving alcoholic for one reason only—I had people who believed in me, and I believed in myself, and those were the voices I chose to listen to.

Most people I've met assumed that I'd always had a perfect life because of the way I dressed and the lifestyle I maintained. I understand that mentality because we were all taught from an early age that the achievement of the American Dream is to have the nice house and cars, great kids, holiday vacations, and happy lifestyle. Those people weren't necessarily wrong, though, because I had wanted and needed them to perceive me a certain way. However, learning to love and trust others has freed me, allowing me to break the veil of fake perfection that I'd cultivated since childhood. It took me a long time to realize that my mask had robbed me of the opportunity to be human and grow from my mistakes, but I'm so glad I did.

Today, I operate two very successful businesses in the southwest, a career management firm called The Ginac Group and a talent management firm called TalentGuard. My success is not a result of me being the best business-person in the world, or the smartest, but because I understand people. The one trait I proudly carry away from my childhood is empathy. What I once considered my biggest shame has actually armed me to achieve success. I know how to read people's pain, remove insurmountable barriers, broker their trust, and eliminate their veils of fake perfection so that they can achieve greatness.

The reality is that I am here today to share this story with you thanks to a few people who helped me break a vicious cycle of hatred and self-doubt and to live a life filled with authentic friends and loving relationships. Find that person in your life who gives you the courage to find your truth and path to happiness, comfort, and hope.

PART 1
BROKEN TRUST

Chapter 1 Broken

I woke to the sound of freezing sleet pitter-pattering against my bedroom window while the wind whistled through the cracks and blew splints of chipping paint across my room like pixie dust out of a scene from Peter Pan. The frost-covered window pane appeared beautifully etched by snow fairies who'd worked until the break of dawn. As the sun began to rise, it cast orange hues across my room and onto the handmade quilt my grandmother had made for me.

My eyes slowly began to play peak-a-boo with the morning light as the sun made its way up to my face. The cold air lurked just outside the quilt, waiting for the opportunity to invade the warm haven I had created underneath the covers. As I began to stir, my thoughts were consumed with making a mad dash downstairs into the kitchen where the huge black grate awaited me. The grate took up a four-by-four space in the kitchen floor and blew hot air up from the giant oil-burning furnace below in the basement. It was my favorite spot in the house and I always started the morning sitting cross-legged on the grate until I shook the deep chill from the core of my body.

As I slid my head out from under the blankets, the smell of fire filled my nostrils. It wasn't the usual musty smell from the furnace and hundred-year-old wood that kept my red, two-story, saltbox house standing strong in the small town of Fitchburg, Massachusetts. My mind connected with the foreign smell and I was sitting up in an instant. I pushed the blankets off my legs and put my feet onto the chilled hardwood floor. Mumbling voices could be heard in the background as I made my way downstairs. When I appeared in the kitchen, tiptoeing out from the living room, my parents weren't where I expected them to be. I envisioned them making breakfast for us near the stove, which was the typical routine.

Instead, my father stood three feet away from my mother, pointing a silver gun at her head. Tears streamed down his face. He looked so vicious that I almost didn't recognize him. My mother was against the wall between the two windows in the kitchen, with only the kitchen chair separating her from my father. I stood frozen in shock over the black grate as the heat blew my nightgown up like a balloon. They both screamed at me to go upstairs. Oddly, the screams didn't scare me; rather, they encouraged me to walk straight into the line of fire.

I still remember the rush of adrenaline flowing through my body as I heard my little brother coming down the stairs calling for me. My only thought was, *I have to protect Steve from this sight.* I ran to the stairs, grabbed my little brother's arm, and rushed him upstairs to his room where I asked him to stay put until I came back. My heart pumped so hard I could hear the blood rushing through my ears.

My parents continued shouting at one another but I had no idea what they were saying—all I could hear was my heart beating furiously. As I moved in slow motion into the kitchen toward my father, I had a split-second recognition that my mother was begging my father to put the gun away. Just then, I heard the explosion of the gun being fired, followed by a thud, and then silence. When I opened my eyes I expected to see my mother slumped to the ground. Instead, she stood plastered against the wall, head dripping with sweat. Beside her, the bullet had carved a medium-sized hole in the wall.

Everyone stood silent for many minutes staring at each other. My legs were shaking so uncontrollably I thought I was going to fall. My entire being altered at exactly the same moment the gun went off. I went completely numb, void of any emotion. I stood wide-eyed, wondering what would happen next.

"What are you doing?" I demanded.

My mother cried hysterically and my father stood in shock. There was never a point during my childhood that I could pinpoint as the "good old days." My parents had what I would generously call a "marriage of obligation." They had gotten married when my mom was only fifteen and my dad was twenty-one, shortly after he'd gotten out of a rocky nine-month marriage to a woman who had been cheating on him. My dad had been the best friend of my mother's oldest brother. He had also been very popular and a bit of a wild child who loved to drink and get rowdy. My mom had been a stifled artist and high school dropout who viewed marrying my father as a way to get away from her mother's second husband, whom she'd hated. It hadn't taken my parents long to realize that their marriage wasn't the storybook romance they'd envisioned. In fact, as I learned at far-too-young an age, they had been on the verge of getting a divorce until an unfortunate accident named "me" had come into the picture.

That was twelve years ago, but right now I wished for the thousandth time over that I had been born into another family. Only then, as I looked around the house, did I notice the burned clothes on the floor. In a panic, I scrambled to pick them up and the soot got all over my hands.

My father turned from the kitchen and walked into his bedroom to sit on the bed. His expression surprised me. Instead of looking angry, he looked horrified and sad.

"Dad, what the heck happened?" I asked as I followed him into the bedroom.

"Your mother had an affair. It's over. She needs to go."

"Why did you burn her clothes? That was stupid."

I walked over to the bed to put the clothes down, but noticed that the floor was covered in warm water. "Dad, what did you do to the water bed?"

Tears streamed from his eyes and he was sobbing uncontrollably. "Your mother and I slept in this bed. I need a new one now."

I hugged him but he didn't move. "Why did you burn her clothes though?"

"Because I don't know which ones she wore when she met him."

I struggled to get a grip on myself as I took in the situation. Despair filled my veins and I was worried sick that Steve would come down any minute and see our parents in this horrible state. Only 18 months separated us, but I already had a very strong protective older-sister instinct toward my brother. I moved swiftly to pick up all of the clothes I could find and then put every towel in the house next to the bed to sop up the water, thinking to myself, *How did it come to this? How did it ever get this bad?*

Despite the fact that my parents' marriage was stressful, they had always been hardworking and struggled every day to provide the basic necessities for their young family. My dad worked as a skilled craftsman, and my mother worked in the sewing factory she'd been at since the age of sixteen, making ten dollars an hour. We'd never had much money, but that had never bothered my parents because they had gotten by. In addition, nearly every night of the week you could hear the sounds of laughing, bottles clanking, and music blaring through the open windows. A close group of family and friends regularly came to our small house with a desperate need to escape reality, and reveled in the poker games, drunken partier antics and smoke clouds. The group always started off small but always ended up big, and it just became the norm. It was during these parties that I learned how to roll the perfect joint and pour beers with perfect heads for twenty-five cents a glass.

Roughly five years prior to this fateful morning, my father and mother had come home from yet another trip to the doctor's office with cataclysmic news. Dad had been going to the doctor's office on and off for years because he kept losing feeling in his fingers, arms and neck. He always felt very weak and he was constantly dropping simple items such as spoons and plates. Specialist after specialist couldn't figure out what was wrong with him because the symptoms weren't consistent—they'd come and go with no apparent pattern. Most of the doctors thought it was a pinched nerve or stress, but after years of tests and endless worry, they were finally able to come up with a diagnosis. The truth was worse than any of us had feared—my father had multiple sclerosis.

Around the time of the diagnosis, my dad had dropped a tool into a machine at work, causing it to break. His boss, who was also a good friend, had told him that he was a danger to himself and others and that he had to let him go. Dad was only twenty-nine years old at the time. He knew he would never work again and it hit him hard. The burden for providing for the family fell on my mother, an unskilled, low-wage earner who was only twenty-three years old, essentially still just a kid. During the ten months it took for Dad's social security benefits to kick in, the shit really hit the fan.

My dad was devastated by the news about his disease and the loss of permanent work. He couldn't cope with the idea of being confined to a wheelchair for the rest of his life. At the same time, my mother's anger and resentment grew in parallel with the financial stress of being the sole provider for her family. Alcohol consumption increased for both of my parents, and each night would end the same way, with my dad ranting to my mother that he wasn't a man anymore because he couldn't work, that he'd be a crippled person, confined to a wheelchair, and dead by fifty. He'd say that he would rather die than become a welfare recipient, and actually tried to kill himself with booze and drugs many times over.

My mother's lack of sensitivity made things much worse than they should have been, but she was learning how to be a mature adult while figuring out how to raise two children and a sick husband. Her inability to back down from a fight was both her biggest strength, because she never let anyone take advantage of her, but also her worst liability, because she could quickly rile my father up to the point where he lost control. Looking back, I realize how helpless and trapped she must've felt, but her actions didn't help the situation at all.

Even after we started receiving the disability benefits, Mom grew increasingly furious with my father because the mortgage was often very late, the electricity was regularly shut off, the furnace would run out of oil in the middle of winter, and my brother and I looked like refugees in our tattered and undersized clothes. As a result, their violence grew more volatile than it had ever been. Their fights transitioned from simple arguments over who would grocery shop with the food stamps and pick up gifts from Blue Santa to their throwing things at each other and tearing stereo systems from walls over jealous rages.

It was no wonder that this day had arrived. *How could my father have ever expected to be loved when my mother told him so many times that she didn't sign up to be married to a cripple?* Perhaps the only curious thing was that it hadn't happened before now. A voice snapped me out of my reverie and back to the very unpleasant present.

"Linda, come in here and help me please." The sound of my mother's voice made my stomach cringe in pain. I walked into the kitchen and noticed three garbage bags packed with clothes.

"What are those? Where are you going?" I whispered, horrified at what would happen next.

"This is what is left of my clothes. Dad burned the rest." I had known my mother was cheating, having caught her myself. It was a secret I had kept hidden from both parents.

As she stood in the kitchen, three garbage bags full of clothes at her feet, she asked me one question, "Are you coming with me, or are you staying?"

At that moment, my brother walked into the room. He didn't hesitate. "I'm staying."

I didn't like my mother very much at that moment, but I couldn't let her feel that both of her kids had rejected her. "I'll go," I said quietly.

As soon as the words came out of my mouth, I knew I'd made a mistake. It hurt my father terribly, but I didn't feel like I had a choice. I threw some clothes in a bag, joined my mom, aunt, and uncle in the car, and drove away from the only life I'd ever known.

✿✿✿

My brother eventually joined me and my mother in our new home in Waterville, Maine. As is common in broken families, he and I spent the next several years bouncing back and forth between our mother's home and our dad's.

There were brief periods of time when we managed to live together in relative peace and harmony, but no one would have confused us for the Waltons.

At that point, though, my expectations for a nice, normal home environment were pretty low. I couldn't find my groove with either parent, but now they lived 400 miles apart. As I matured and developed into a teen, a deep rift began to develop between my mother and me. When my parents had separated, I had expected her to spend her time with me, but she was young and wanted to sow her wild oats. Her insecurities about having a blooming teenage daughter in the house around her boyfriends were catalysts for constant conflict between us. Like most young teenage girls, I viewed my mother as the enemy and everything she recommended was old-fashioned and stupid, or so I thought at the time. The more I challenged her authority, the more enraged she'd become. She simply couldn't back down. We clashed on every level.

On one particular occasion, shortly after I'd turned fifteen—and on Christmas Eve, no less—one of our confrontations escalated to the point where it became a physical contest. Fortunately, we both walked away without physical injuries, but the emotional damage ran deep. I knew then that I had to leave and decided to make my dad's home my permanent residence.

With two suitcases in hand, I boarded a Greyhound bus with a one-way ticket to freedom. My mother stared at me coolly from the sidewalk as my heart crumbled. My brother's face was whiter than newly fallen snow as he hugged me before I boarded the bus. I watched her smug face and listened to her muted voice as she shouted to me that it was entirely my fault that I was being sent to live with my father. Again, I was the mistake.

Chapter 2 Shocked

A brilliant stream of moonlight shone in through the open window, illuminating the darkened bedroom. For a late-autumn night in Austin, the weather was warmer than usual. I lay in our king-sized bed with one leg caressing the surface of the handmade, gold-silk duvet, and the other leg tucked under the 600 thread count, Egyptian cotton sheets. I was wearing my favorite Oscar de la Renta "Sweet Surrender" black babydoll nightie, which had spaghetti straps, black lace, and ribbon accents. After a stressful day at work, the silence of the bedroom was a welcome relief.

In an area west of Austin proper, there was a small community known as Barton Creek where million-dollar homes lined the streets, kids attended the best private schools, and nearly everyone drove a luxury car or a fancy SUV. More people in this small community had founded new start-up technology companies than in any other area of the United States, with the exception of Silicon Valley. It was the place I had called home for nearly ten months, and there was no other place I'd rather be. It was the only place where I truly felt at peace.

I lived in Barton Creek with my husband Frank and our son Andrew in a private neighborhood that ran along one of Barton Creek's many tributaries. It was a dream come true when we had moved into this neighborhood the past February, where elegant Mediterranean-style homes presided over verdant manicured hedges, grand shade trees, and brilliant kaleidoscopes of flowerbeds. Prior to living in Barton Creek, the three of us had lived in a modest home in Pflugerville, a small town just northeast of Austin. Frank and I knew that we'd eventually want to build our family, though, and the home in Barton Creek seemed like the perfect place to do it.

The neighborhood was completely secluded and nearly everyone who came to visit missed the turnoff from the busy main road. There was only one way in and out of this gated community. The neighborhood had been plotted as a condominium complex by the builder to avoid strict city policy regarding streets, drainage, and easements. It was composed of twenty-four custom-built homes that surrounded a cul-de-sac, and the homeowners maintained the acres of shared interior courtyards. Everyone shared the same address, with the exception of our unique house numbers. The neighborhood was nearly perfect, with the only potential problems coming from the narrow, serpentine roads that were unwelcoming to large vehicles, such as fire trucks, in the event of an emergency.

Quietly nestled under a massive, 200-year-old oak tree at the highest point of the neighborhood's hill, our two-story Mediterranean-style home was both stunningly elegant and cozy. The golden-colored stucco exterior was complemented with a red barrel tile roof. In the back, a huge patio surrounded a pool and spa. A portion of the yard was dedicated to the well-cared-for oak tree and low-maintenance landscaping. To the west of the pool was a grassy play yard. With its magnificent archways, columns, cast stone exterior, oversized verandas, massive windows and three-car garage with wood paneled doors, it felt like we were living in a palatial estate.

Frank finished his pre-sleep routine and crawled into bed next to me. Where I was petite, dark-haired, and graceful with a feminine frame, my husband was built like a Roman warrior. His well-kept salt and pepper hair, athletic build, and fair Irish complexion were still undeniably attractive to me after six years of marriage.

"How was your day, love?" he asked when he'd settled under the covers. It was the first real chance we'd had to talk all evening.

"I've had better," I sighed. "I don't know what's worse—being in a company that drives you nuts, or staying in a career you don't like. I need to submit my layoff recommendations tomorrow and I still have no clue who I'm going to put on the list."

Work had been especially stressful lately. When the company I worked for, Trifinity, had failed to close a number of key accounts, the board had decided that the only way we could stay afloat was to reduce our workforce. As Vice President of Product Management, I was expected to eliminate between twenty-five to thirty of the positions of my friends and coworkers. At the moment, I didn't know who those people would be. HR had been no help—they'd given us no instructions about how to approach the process. My boss had been useless, too. When I asked him for advice, he just told me he trusted my judgment and I'd figure it out. The decision was weighing on me heavily—I felt torn between doing what was right for the company and doing what was right for my team.

"What do you think you're going to do?" Frank asked.

"I don't know," I said quietly. "I don't really want to think about it right now. How was your day? I called you at work a couple of times in the afternoon but you didn't answer the phone."

Frank looked at me with an expression that I couldn't quite place. "Oh, you did?" he asked, concerned. "I must not have heard the phone ring. Maybe my ringer was accidentally turned off."

"Just admit it," I said, feigning sorrow. "You were avoiding me. You think I'm a . . . a monster." I buried my head in my hands in a melodramatic display of distress.

Frank wrapped his arms around me in a bear hug and rested his head on my stomach. "Never. I love when you call me."

I moved my hand to his head, stroking his hair and playing with his earlobe in a way that never failed to soothe him. He stared into my eyes with a focused look that told me he was in processing mode.

"Stumped on an engineering problem, again?" I asked. "Stop thinking about it. You'll wake up in the middle of the night with the solution. I can read your mind. It's one of my monster powers," I joked.

"I wish it was that simple. I was actually thinking about a meeting I had with Ken." Ken was Frank's boss at work.

"Oh yeah?" I asked. "What did you guys meet about?"

"Well," he said, hesitantly, "it was more of a disagreement than a meeting."

The information didn't strike me as anything unusual—Frank's team was, to put it mildly, a bit dysfunctional. Frank was the Vice President of Software Development for NomaSoft, a hot dot-com start-up company that was experiencing explosive growth. The founding team had extensive broadband industry expertise but no senior leadership talent and limited start-up experience—a common situation during the Internet boom. His coworkers had never run a company before. Most of them had never even managed a team. Frank, on the other hand, had extensive senior leadership experience and a solid track record of releasing successful and commercially viable products to market for giants such as Digital Equipment Corporation, Convex and Data General.

When Ken, the company president, had approached Frank about joining the company, he initially offered him the role of Director of Development. After numerous interviews and discussions, they realized that Frank wasn't interested in taking a step down from the VP of Product Development role he held at Dazel, another Austin start-up that had been acquired by HP a few months before. Instead, they offered him the position of vice president. At the time, Frank was torn because he would have been guaranteed an excellent income if he'd stayed on at Dazel.

In the end, however, NomaSoft made a competitive offer and Frank joined up. He viewed NomaSoft as his opportunity to work on new technology that could very well change the world. In spite of the occasional office flare-ups, it seemed like everything was going pretty well—which was why what Frank said next took me completely by surprise.

"Linda," Frank began, choosing his words carefully, "I resigned."

"What?"

I bolted upright in bed, pushing Frank's head off my lap. "What happened?" I asked, my voice becoming frantic. "You've only been there for a year! Not to mention the fact that they practically begged you to come on board. What the heck did you do?"

"What did I do?" he protested. "I didn't do anything!"

Thoughts careened around my head as I stared up at the ceiling, feeling completely dumbfounded. As I replayed the last year of Frank's career in my mind, the outlines of a previously hidden pattern began to emerge. Since he started at NomaSoft, we had spent countless nights discussing the company's problems. Although Frank was a pussycat at home, when he got into the office, he was a much different person. He often spoke out about tough issues that no one really wanted to address. It was one of his traits that was both intensely admirable and completely frustrating. When Frank noticed a problem or an injustice, he couldn't rest until it was fixed. And when he perceived someone as incompetent, he couldn't help but challenge that person directly—even if that person was his boss. The combination of his insatiable need to win and his sense of righteousness sometimes made him blind to the finer points of work relationships.

For Frank, failure was not an option. He expected a lot from people—at times, it seemed like he expected too much. There was no question to me that he was often the most competent person in the office. The issue was one of self-confidence. It wasn't enough for him to know he was an authoritative voice, he needed other people to know it, too. This sometimes made him a difficult person to work with and for. He set high expectations for his coworkers and had trouble giving them enough space to make mistakes. Anyone who ever worked for Frank would tell you the same thing. He challenges each one of his employees to be better at what they do, how they think, and what they provide. The analysis was not always comfortable, but it was always meaningful and necessary to achieve growth. Under his leadership, both technical teams and creative teams flourish and deliver a better product while keeping the business constraints in mind. Frank was someone who challenged himself and his team members to be a better leader each day, and he always succeeded.

"Things like this don't come out of left field, Frank," I said. "Why do you have to be the one to take on all of the tough issues at work? It seems like you're on a mission to prove that Ken is wrong and you're right."

"I just can't stand by and watch Ken destroy the company, Linda. If something isn't right it's important to raise attention to it, because it affects other groups. It could affect the value of my equity and it's putting all of us at risk."

"I understand, but if your boss asks you to drop something, you need to back off," I lectured him. "How many times have we talked about this?"

"I just think he's an idiot. He's a self-centered, egotistical, neophyte suffering from only-child syndrome. He's an idiot!"

"Yeah, an idiot with a job," I quipped.

I recognized that this was not the most supportive thing I could have said, but it's hard to remain sympathetic when suddenly faced with the possibility that the life to which you have become accustomed could quickly crumble into dust. As soon as Frank said something to puncture a hole in my sense of security, the doubts began pouring in . . . *Is my husband a failure? Am I stuck in a marriage with a guy who can't get along with anyone? Why do people keep telling me this person is different at work than at home? I should tell him to get the heck out of this bed and never come back. Heck, I should get out of this bed and tell him I am leaving—that I don't want him and I don't love him anymore!*

If my reaction seemed somewhat severe, you only have to look to my background for cause. To an outside observer, I didn't appear that different from any other upwardly-mobile young professional working in Austin's booming dot-com industry. If you met me at a networking party, you might have thought that you knew who I was—a child of doting parents, straight-A student who sat on the homecoming court, a go-getter who earned a business degree from a reputable college and easily transitioned into the workforce, a young woman who moved to Austin, got married, and had a kid to pursue the American Dream. You might have taken one look at my clothes and my mannerisms and listened to how I spoke and assumed that I'd never had to struggle for anything in my life, that my only real accomplishment had been hanging onto the silver platter upon which everything in my life had been handed to me.

If you were to think all of those things, you would be completely wrong.

To describe my childhood as *chaotic* would be an understatement. One of my earliest memories was my dad using a knife to peel the skin off of my arm after I received a third-degree burn from a boiling teapot. Considering my childhood, that actually counted as one of the more pleasant memories. Some of the not-so-pleasant memories included being fondled by my uncle and grandfather when I was eight, and then having my mother accuse me of lying when I brought it to her attention; growing up in an environment that was rife with drug and alcohol abuse and was marked by regular bouts of violence; shuttling back and forth between Maine and Massachusetts after my parents decided to part ways; moving in with Dad for good after getting into a fistfight with my mother on Christmas Eve because I was fifteen minutes late coming home; and, caring for my father and being subjected to his endless partying lifestyle, making it almost impossible for me to get any sleep during my high school years.

By the time I was in high school, my father was confined to a wheelchair due to his multiple sclerosis. Our house had become an "open house." He literally opened the house up to street people, including thugs, drug addicts, alcoholics, and more. Seven days a week you could find someone shooting up heroin, smoking crack, snorting cocaine, and drinking alcohol, with people sleeping everywhere from atop the kitchen table to the corner of the living room. But endless screaming at the top of my lungs fell on deaf ears.

Because my father's lifestyle was so open to drugs and alcohol, I went through almost my entire middle- and high-school days without inviting a single school friend over to my house. I was ashamed of the way he lived and didn't want anyone to discover that he did drugs for fear of my friends' parents hating me. My father's parties made it nearly impossible to get up in the morning and go to school. As a result, I had dropped out of high school and had moved into my own apartment at age seventeen with little ambition, no focus, and no idea where my life was headed.

My childhood and adolescent experiences had filled me with an unshakeable inability to keep a sense of perspective during moments of distress. The minute I began to feel out of control, all those memories of being a helpless child came roaring back into my mind and the wall that kept my emotions in check came crumbling down. I was living in the present, but reacting from the past. More often than not, my reaction took the form of explosive anger. It became easy for me to say heart-stopping, hurtful things and not blink twice. Given time to process, I could always come back to reality and find that shred of hope that kept me going. But if you caught me during those moments when I was feeling vulnerable, the best advice I could give you was: stay out of my way.

As the reality of our situation sank in, tears began streaming down my cheeks. I threw the covers off of me and walked into the bathroom to grab a tissue. This couldn't have come at a worse time. Frugality was not exactly one of our strong points, and we hadn't even been in our $850,000, brand new, 6,000-square-foot house for a year. We were expecting over $20,000 worth of custom-made furniture to be delivered that we couldn't cancel. On top of that, we had just spent several thousand dollars on an upcoming trip to New England for the holidays. Two new cars, expensive vacations, gourmet restaurants every weekend . . . our lifestyle was the kind that required a lot of upkeep. With one fewer source of income, it wouldn't take long for us to be underwater.

I took some deep breaths and returned to the bedroom. In my hand I held a Kleenex that was covered in black mascara and tears. I got back into bed, turned off the lamp on my bedside table, and squeezed my eyes tight to stop myself from crying. If my upbringing had taught me anything, it was to bury my feelings deep inside. Frank was the only man who ever got close enough to understand why I responded this way, and as a result, he was the only man I've ever loved. Well, as much love as can be felt by someone who's spent most of her life hiding her emotions behind a veil of indifference.

I held my breath tight to hold back the whimpering and to control my body from shaking the bed. My mind was buzzing with so much fear about all of the money we'd spent lately that I couldn't fall asleep right away. We had some savings and investments to hold us over, but that wouldn't last more than six to nine months. Unless I suddenly doubled my salary, we weren't going to last long as a single-income family.

Next to me, I could tell that Frank was lying on his back staring at the ceiling, wondering if he should say anything to me or not. As much as he tried to put on a positive face, he had clearly been deeply wounded by his experience at NomaSoft. But if I knew Frank, concerns about his decision to leave and the affect it would have on his career were nothing compared to his fears about what this news was doing to me.

Even after years of marriage, he still woke up every morning with the fear that I could walk out at any moment (and indeed, I didn't help the situation by constantly telling him that I would). This concern had some positive side ef-

fects—I certainly didn't feel taken for granted, and he remained a die-hard romantic after all our years together—but at other times, his lack of confidence in
our relationship unwittingly filled me with the same kinds of doubts.

At the moment, with the possibility of my life crumbling before my eyes, I
was in little mood to make him feel better about himself.

"Linda, are you all right?" he whispered.

"Leave me alone. Don't talk to me."

"Come on. Can you give me a little slack here?" he pleaded. "I'm in a funk
and I don't want to worry about losing you, too. You and Andrew are my life."

"I said don't talk to me."

"Honey," Frank said in a whisper, "we can make it through this." He put
his hand on my hip and rubbed me softly.

I expelled a deep sigh of exasperation over the never-ending complexity of
married life. One minute I wanted to pummel him for the pain he was causing
me, and the next minute I wanted to squeeze him tight to make the pain in his
heart go away. I knew he needed to be nurtured, but so did I. At the same time
that I was telling him to get his hands off me, what I wanted most was for him
to embrace me in his arms, making me feel protected and reassured that everything was going to be okay.

As my anger began to subside, I started to feel bad for thinking all of those
terrible thoughts. This poor guy was suffering. NomaSoft was a company he
had poured his heart and soul into to make it something big, to put another
trophy on the wall, to prove that he could do something bigger and better than
anything he had achieved to date. This was a guy who never quit, and quitting
hurt him more deeply than failing.

"I love you," he whispered as he hugged me closer.

This time I didn't shake him off me and actually let his arms envelop me.
The heat from his body surrounded me in a comforting cocoon. His body was
always so warm.

"You love me?" he asked with playfulness in his voice.

"Yes," I sighed. "Don't be such an idiot."

I blew my nose into the shredded tissue and turned around to face him,
nuzzling my head under his chin because I didn't want him to look at my face. I
was sure that my eyes and nose were swollen and that I had red patches all over
my cheeks. My vulnerability made me feel exposed in a way that made me
deeply uncomfortable.

"So tell me more about what happened," I said.

"Well, you know how much tension there's been between me and Ken lately," Frank said. "He never wants to hear the word 'no,' and I'm the guy who says 'no.' I just finally realized that this relationship is never going to change. As long as we're in business together, I'm going to be fighting with him about things that I consider common sense. And I just don't think I have it in me anymore to fight."

"Could you just agree with him on whatever it is that bothers you and move on?" I asked, already knowing the answer.

"It doesn't work that way, Linda."

I pulled my head out from under his chin and looked him in the eyes. "I can't believe you turned in your notice before telling me about this," I said.

"This isn't exactly something I was planning for, it just happened. The only thing I've ever wanted was for the company to be successful so that everyone would benefit."

"I know," I said. The earnestness of his response made my heart go out to him. "Frank, you've had a great career. Don't let this experience make you feel otherwise."

"I don't feel like I've had a successful career. It seems that every time I stretch beyond engineering, someone is always there to push me back down. I enjoy running development but I can do it in my sleep at this point. The challenge is gone. I wanted this to work so badly, Linda. For both of us," he said despairingly.

"I know you did," I said, rubbing my hand along his back.

Frank's oversized pillow hung above his head, casting a shadow over his topaz-colored eyes and making them look unusually ominous. Normally, Frank's gleaming eyes contain a playful glint that broadcasts his good-natured personality to the world. I, on the other hand, have a stare so piercing that people feel like I can look right through them.

"Well, I'm sure it will be all right," Frank said. "Tomorrow, I'll reach out to my network and see what kind of opportunities are out there. Everything is going to be fine."

I knew he was trying to make me feel better, but I could sense the worry behind his words. It was the year 2000 and the dot-com bubble had just burst. The market was in the tank and people throughout our industry were being downsized. Everyone was having layoffs—my own company included. Even in the best of times, Frank had a hard time believing in himself. I sensed that his words of reassurance were as much for himself as they were for me.

I lay in Frank's embrace for a long time, listening to the rhythm of his breathing. He hugged me tightly from behind until he finally fell into a deep sleep. I lay with my head on the pillow, watching lights play across the bedroom ceiling from car headlights as they passed by the house. I was tired. But mostly, I was terrified.

Despite my intense fear of what was about to happen, I knew deep down that I loved Frank. He had never disappointed me. I knew he would do what it took to provide for his family. We worked so hard to keep the house together and to see that Andrew would be provided for in life, but as much as I trusted my husband, I didn't have a lot of faith that the universe was looking out for us. The unstable economic state I grew up in was not anything I ever hoped to return to. Frank worked hard, without question . . . but who cares if you're a hard worker if you don't have a job?

With Frank's resignation, we had both just been thrust into a new phase of our life. We were about to embark on the most stressful period of our lives, punctuated by pain, sacrifice, and an unshakable sense of impending doom. I knew that it wasn't going to be easy. I just prayed that we would make it through this period together—if we made it through at all.

I rolled over and cried myself to sleep.

Chapter 3 Displaced

I felt oddly disconnected as I walked up Wallace Way along the stone-white stairs leading up to Fitchburg High School, which was built in the 1830's. It wasn't because of all of the memories that I had prior to abandoning my friends in the middle of the night in a Bonneville heading for Maine, though I'm sure that had something to do with it. Maybe it was the suddenness with which my life had become unsupervised, and the knowledge that I'd have no limits or restrictions put on me. It could have been that I knew I'd have to go into self-preservation mode again. Or it may have been the inevitable stigma that would be tied to me, a young teenage girl living in a home known as "an open house" in every way imaginable, with street people roaming freely in and out of the house with alcohol and drugs for non-stop partying.

Walking into the school gave me more pleasure than it did most students. I suspect it was partly because it was my escape from everything in my life that was wrong. I was an excellent student and it was the one area where I felt the smallest form of accomplishment.

The registrar's office was dimly lit with a small wooden desk in the corner of the room. The same lady, Ms. Butler, worked in the office from as far back as I could remember. She peered at me through her bifocals and gestured her hand for me to sit in the chair just beside her desk.

"Are you enrolling in school again?" she asked.

"Yes, I just moved back from Maine." She had yellowish hair pulled into a bun that appeared to have been stained by cigarette smoke.

"Where is your father?" Her glasses were sliding down her nose and I could see the makeup caked around the frames.

"At home. He can't make it in the building in a wheelchair. Call him at home if you need to speak to him."

She gave me a little bit of a hassle about the fact that I was enrolling myself in school at fifteen, but when I explained that my dad was just unable to make it in, she reluctantly made an exception. I'm sure the school administration had a lot more pressing problems to worry about than kids trying to sneak into school.

She sighed and pulled out the enrollment forms and a course schedule for me to complete. I provided all of the necessary details and picked mostly AP (advanced placement) classes on the schedule. "I'd like to start today if that is okay."

"I don't see a problem with it." She handed me a green slip and asked me to present it to the second period English teacher. I picked up my bag and headed for the door.

"Linda, if you need to talk to anyone, our new counselor is great."

"There is no point, really. I have everything under control," I said smiling.

Being back at Dad's house, although an improvement over having to put up with my mom, was no picnic. My dad's MS had left him confined to a wheelchair, but he always had a lot of people around to help him out. He had rented out the extra rooms to lodgers and he had lots of friends and admirers who were constantly stopping by to party. Unfortunately, as Dad's disease worsened, his home gradually turned into a crack house. The never-ending party that swirled inside our house had started as a way for Dad to have a good time and stay social, but it took a darker turn as the neighborhood began to crumble around us. It also steadily became more and more difficult for me to keep it together.

During the time I lived with Dad, new people I'd never seen before started showing up for the parties. They brought with them harder drugs and a propensity for disturbing the peace that attracted the attention of the police on more than one occasion. I didn't like it, but it was my only home—I wasn't about to move back with my mother. I woke every day to the scene of strung out bodies strewn over the floor. Occasionally, I would trip over a dead body on my way out of the house because someone had overdosed on drugs or alcohol.

It was painful to watch the effects my dad's illness was having on him. Inside his head, he was still as sharp as ever, but his body was incapable of doing the simplest tasks. He was miserable living like that, and around this time, he actively started trying to overdose to make his pain go away forever. On several occasions, I'd hear him having seizures in his room, on the verge of death, and I'd think, *If I just lay here for one more minute, this can all be over.* But every time, my conscience would take over and I'd end up calling the paramedics. For a guy with a life-threatening illness, he was remarkably resilient. Before I knew it he'd be back to his old self, playing cribbage in the kitchen and partying with his friends until the next wave of depression hit.

It was during those years that I perfected the art of hiding who I really was from my friends. I was so embarrassed by my dad's behavior that I never allowed my friends to come over. The one time I did, we walked into my house to find one of my sixteen-year-old friends giving my father and his best friend a blow job in exchange for a few lines of coke. Everyone was cheering and thought it was hysterical, but I was humiliated beyond words and couldn't show my face at school for almost three months.

When my friends would ask about my dad and why they couldn't come over, I would just tell them that he was sick and didn't like having people around. Most of my friends didn't even know where I lived. They knew nothing about my background or about the drugs, alcohol, and violence that had surrounded me as a kid, and I was convinced that if they ever did find out, they wouldn't want to have anything to do with me. I kept my pain locked up deep inside and greeted the world with a plastic smile and a mask of complete confidence.

Dad provided me with no parental supervision while I lived with him, giving me complete freedom to come and go as I pleased. Despite this, I was hardly in the best of spirits myself. I'd taken a job at a bank so that I could afford to buy the clothes I needed to keep up with my rich friends. Between my job, school, my boyfriend, and the all-night parties at home, I was hardly getting any sleep. One night, around 2:00 A.M., my dad's coke-addict friend Nancy cornered me in the hall, wanting to have a deep conversation about her boyfriend, my half-brother Mark. I told her I had to go to bed because I had school in the morning, and she went ballistic. She started banging on my bedroom door and screaming at the top of her lungs. I wasn't scared of much in life after all I'd been through, but the way she was acting that night scared the piss out of me. She was clearly out of her mind on some kind of drug. I had no idea what she might do to me.

She literally kicked my bedroom door in half and pulled me into the hallway. We stood at the top of the staircase. In her hand she held a butter knife, which she slashed into the air between us. It would have been laughable if she weren't so totally out of her mind. The blade might not have been sharp, but it still would've hurt like hell if she managed to hit me in the chest with it. Luck-ily, her reflexes were slow enough that I managed to knock her off her balance before she could get a good poke in. She tumbled down the staircase and landed at the bottom with a heavy thud, knocked-out cold. She woke up seconds later and walked back up the stairs. I was shaking so hard I could hard-ly stand. My mind was racing with thoughts about what to grab to protect my-self. I could hear my father yelling in the background but couldn't make out what he was saying. I stared at her ready for a fight, but she walked right past me toward her room.

It took me hours to stop shaking. I sat in the corner of my room until day-break, waiting for her to kill me. The next morning, when I woke up, I walked down into the living room to find Nancy sitting on the couch. A giant, purple bruise covered the part of her face where she'd fallen. My dad sat across from her in his wheelchair, talking to her sternly.

"You have two choices, Nancy," he said. "You can either pack up your stuff and get out of here, or I'm going to call the police right now and have you ar-rested for attempted murder."

She left, of course. It wasn't too hard a choice to make.

When she was gone, I sat down with my dad and had a long talk with him. I told him that I was getting scared about the changes I'd seen around the house and it was having a negative impact on my life.

"I don't want you to feel like I'm abandoning you, Linda," he told me, "but it is not safe for you here any longer and you have to go. I don't know who some of these people are, what they're on, or what they're capable of doing. One of these days someone could show up with a gun and go on a shooting rampage. I don't care about what happens to me, but I do care about you."

To my surprise, my dad started crying. "You deserve better than this." At heart, he wanted what was truly best for my brother and me. He wrote me a check with enough money to cover a few months' rent in an apartment and to purchase some furniture. He was able to do this for me because, in addition to receiving his disability checks, he had also remortgaged the house and had got-ten equity loans.

That week, I found an apartment close enough to my dad's place that I could check in on him and my brother pretty regularly. I wanted my brother to come with me, but he wouldn't leave my father. I felt no joy at being out on my own, though; instead, all I could think was, *What the hell am I going to do now?* I was only a few months away from graduation, but I suddenly felt like there was no point to any of it. All my friends from the neighborhood and my cousin had already dropped out. I now had adult responsibilities that required the support of a full-time job. Besides, who was I kidding, thinking I could escape my destiny? Girls from my kind of background didn't grow up to be successful people with happy families. They got pregnant at an early age and settled into abusive relationships that ended in unhappiness and divorce. So, just a few months shy of graduation and with grades that put me in the top ten percent of my class, I called the school and informed them that I wouldn't be coming in any longer.

The next year was one of the darkest periods of my life. At the same time I dropped out of school, I broke up with my boyfriend. We had been drifting apart for awhile, anyway, and being around him was just a painful reminder of the path my life could have taken if I'd been brought up in different circumstances. I started working full-time at the bank, where I made just enough money to get by. I'd go out drinking with my friends and act like I was having a good time, but I was living under a cloud of perpetual hopelessness.

Fate intervened in the form of a new boyfriend named Brian. When I was at my lowest point, Brian convinced me that I needed to go back and get my high school degree. "You're better than this, Linda," he told me. "If you give up, you're going to regret it for the rest of your life." I don't know if he was particularly convincing or if I was just finally ready to hear it, but his words had a tremendous affect on me. With his support, I reenrolled in high school and finished the three classes I needed to get my degree, graduating in 1988—one year later than I was supposed to and one hundred years wiser.

With graduation behind me, the ambition that had been such a huge part of my makeup since I was a kid came roaring back to life. I moved on to a much better job at Digital Equipment Corporation, which prepared me for a life of working in technology. Working at Digital was a dream come true because I knew I would have opportunities that would enable me to change my life. One of the biggest opportunities was a fully-funded college education. Digital offered a 100% tuition reimbursement program and I took full advantage of it by enrolling in Norwich University to pursue my Bachelor's Degree. I worked full-time and carried a full course load in the evenings, but it didn't matter because within four years, I would be the first person in my family to have a college education.

Over the next four years, I got promoted from Administrative Assistant to Executive Assistant to Marketing Specialist at Digital. I was exhausted from the intense schedule of work and school, but I persevered despite wishing that my personal life were more fulfilling. It was quite difficult to date since my nights and weekends were consumed with classes and hours of homework.

My next promotion took me to Nashua, New Hampshire, where I secured a job as a Business Operations Manager for a growing business that was focused on a corporate-wide, international technology standards initiative. I was terrified to move away from my home and friends, but knew that it was the right thing to do. This move would offer me a fresh start in a place where no one knew me or my history. For the first time in my life, I would be working from a blank slate and could build my story without any historical baggage.

Within a few weeks of receiving the formal job offer, I packed up my belongings and moved without hesitation. Well, maybe I hesitated a tiny bit because I was moving in with a male roommate. My former boss had introduced me to his best friend who was searching for a roommate in New Hampshire, so we met and I liked him instantly. Things would not be complicated in the romance department because he was not my type.

After weeks of decorating my new place, getting familiar with the new job, and working tirelessly on term papers, I decided a night on the town with my pals was desperately needed. When I say town, I'm referring to the energizing and beautiful place along the Charles River called Boston! I planned an outing for Friday and my best friend, Maura, drove up to my place from Fitchburg for a sleepover.

Maura wore off-white, silk gaucho pants with a matching top and gold heels. She looked like a goddess with her golden hair flowing down her back. I wore a one-piece, fitted, blue jumpsuit with tapered legs. The top part of the jumpsuit had a plunging V-neck and hugged my plunge, push-up bra perfectly. I could have done without the large polka dots covering the silk, but Saks Fifth Avenue promoted the style as the newest fashion trend. This fashion-forward design was completed by my 70's-inspired wood clogs with glossy navy blue leather and walnut-colored platform soles, and a white fedora with a navy blue ribbon. We looked like models who had just completed a Cosmopolitan magazine photo shoot.

We drove twenty minutes to Lowell, Massachusetts, and picked up the Amtrak train for the remaining trip into Boston. We met up with the rest of the gang at Cheers for a few drinks before heading over to Zanzibar. This dance club and lounge was where the rich and famous would come out to play. The club had three levels with three dance floors, seven bars, and a large stage for live performances. The place was so packed that I had to press my body against other people's bodies to get through the crowd. We danced until we were soaked with sweat, and around 11:30 P.M. we called it a night because we had to catch the train back to town.

When we arrived back in Nashua, Maura still wanted to dance so we went to the Bahamas Beach Club for a nightcap and a bit more dancing. Even at 1:00 in the morning, the casual nightclub was buzzing with excitement. This was Nashua's only dance club so it was easy to see why the modern venue attracted so many hot singles. As we walked through the door, all eyes were on us. We liked to imagine that our beauty was so stunning, but we giggled knowing that our outfits were over-the-top for this lounge. With heads held high and shoulders straight, we strutted past the gawkers (and snickerers) straight to the bar. "Maura," we heard through the chatter of people trying to hook up. We looked around to identify who was calling her name and noticed a large man with salt-and-pepper hair. He looked like a glam-rock cowboy in his black leather jacket, blue jeans, black cowboy boots and pale gold dress shirt.

"Frank, how are you? Wow, it's been a long time," Maura responded.

"Who is that?" I whispered into her ear. "He looks old enough to be your father."

"He was two years ahead of me in school," she said.

"He must have stayed back a few years, then," I responded jokingly.

She turned to face me as we walked toward him. "Be nice, Linda. He is a really great guy. We used to work the roller coaster together at Whalom Park."

"You are kidding me!" I exclaimed, just as we got to where Frank was standing.

"Frank, this is my friend Linda," Maura said, introducing us.

We exchanged pleasantries and Frank introduced Maura to his friend, Chuck. It was getting late, so they invited us to breakfast at Denny's, another popular hangout after a night of drinking.

"Maura, I don't want to go out to breakfast with these guys. They are not my type," I whispered to her.

"Chuck is cute! Come on . . . you can hang with me. It's only for an hour," she pleaded.

"Arg! If Frank hits on me, I'm outta there," I warned her.

"He's cute. Give him a chance," she replied.

"Not on your life" I asserted.

Breakfast was stress-free and I was pleased that Frank didn't hit on me. We had a great conversation and I learned that he worked at Digital, too. Maura was forming a crush on Chuck, so I knew that only meant one thing—she'd be inviting them over to my place. Frank lived close to me so he recommended that we stop at his place to pick up a cold bottle of Sambuca because I didn't have any alcohol. We waited in our car while he ran into his condo. When he came out, he had a fifth-sized bottle of alcohol and three VHS video cassettes.

I turned to Maura and said, "If that is porn in his hand, I'll literally freak out. What kind of guy would do that?" Maura looked as shocked as me but said nothing. Within minutes, we were at my house and had to tiptoe up the stairs because I rented the converted second floor apartment from an old couple. I liked the security of knowing that *grandparents* lived downstairs. Frank poured us all a shot of Sambuca and we moved into the living room to watch TV. I turned the channel to *Silk Stalkings,* my favorite late-night TV show, but no one seemed interested in watching it.

"I brought some videos for us to watch," Frank announced, obviously bored with my selection. My heart started skipping a beat. *Should I say something? Should I give him a prewarning that I'm not interested in watching porn with complete strangers? What if I'm wrong? Oh, jeez.*

"What movies do you have?" I asked innocently enough.

"Let me put one in. I guarantee that you will laugh," he responded with a smirk.

I think he knows that I'm worried about what's on those VHS tapes. Hopefully, the laugh was an indicator that it's not what I think it is.

Within minutes, I was watching a hot-tempered, malnourished Chihuahua being squashed by a fat, stupid cat with red fur. The cat was holding the Chihuahua by its neck as violent farts exploded from the cats backside. Everyone was laughing hysterically, except me. "What the heck is this?" I asked.

"It's *Ren and Stimpy,*" Frank replied.

"A what?" I asked as Maura and Chuck laughed a bit harder at my ignorance.

"It's an adult comedy cartoon with lots of off-color humor," he explained. "It came out a year ago."

"I guess I don't watch enough TV. I've never seen this cartoon before. It's very dark," I admitted, as giggles tried to escape my mouth in response to more antics by the cat. "Okay, now I've seen everything. I'm just thankful that it is not porn."

"What? You think I would bring porn over to your house? Are you serious?" Frank could hardly contain himself and his laughter was contagious. Soon, we were all laughing so hard we were crying.

By 3:00 a.m., I couldn't keep my eyes open any longer and asked the guys to leave. Maura went to bed in the spare bedroom and I walked through the house one last time to shut off the lights. When I strolled past the kitchen counter, I noticed a man's watch sitting on the counter. It was the same watch that Frank had been wearing on his left arm. *Interesting. He is sneaky, I'll give him that. He's trying to open the door for another exchange.*

Thanks to that fateful evening, we'd wind up having many more exchanges, maybe more than he bargained for.

Chapter 4 Resigned

The morning after Frank told me about his resignation, I woke up at 6:00 A.M. I was feeling dazed and confused, and for a brief moment I didn't know where I was. I rolled over to say good morning to him and discovered that he was already out of bed. Suddenly, the discussion from the night before came flooding back to me. The last thing I remembered was Frank telling me that everything was going to be okay before falling asleep; however, now that it was morning, I hardly felt like the situation had been resolved. All the anxiety that had been spinning through my mind before I fell asleep was still there just waiting to be stirred up again. The thought of leaping back into the discussion with Frank made me feel sick with panic.

Come on, Linda, I thought. *Be courageous. You have to talk about it sometime.* Heaving a deep sigh, I rolled out of bed and walked downstairs to the kitchen.

I found Frank leaning against the kitchen counter, sipping a cup of coffee. "Why are you up so early?" I asked. "I didn't hear the alarm clock."

"I thought I'd get up and make you some coffee," he said.

I walked over to the couch and sat down. Shivering, I pulled my nightie down over my legs. No matter how warm it was, I tended to be cold in the mornings. Frank followed behind me and handed me a cup of coffee. "Here ya go, love," he said, smiling.

I raised the cup to my lips. "Mmmm, it smells good. Is this hazelnut?"

"No, I bought something new called Snickerdoodle."

I took a sip. The coffee was both sweet and mildly bitter, with hints of maple syrup, hazelnut, caramel, and cinnamon.

"Yummy. I like it."

"Yeah, it's good," Frank agreed, sipping his coffee next to me.

We sat on the couch in silence, focusing our attention on the coffee. Neither of us wanted to break the ice, and I didn't know how to start the conversation without lashing out at him. As what always seemed to happen in moments of potential confrontation, Frank seemed to be waiting for me to get the ball rolling. I could sense that my silence concerned him—he knew how much difficulty I had dealing with anything involving finances.

Frank rubbed my arm affectionately. I was still cold, so I pulled my favorite purple chenille blanket off the back of the couch and wrapped it around my lower body.

"How did you sleep?" he finally asked, half-smiling as he moved his hand to rest on mine. "Did I snore?"

"Yes," I answered, curtly. "I shook the bed a few times to get you to roll over. You seemed to sleep very well."

"I don't feel like I slept at all," he said, biting his lip. "I woke up several times during the night and couldn't fall back asleep."

"You could have fooled me. I was up for hours and you snored the whole time," I snipped.

We sat in silence for several minutes. I gazed out the bay window at the pool in the backyard. Frank stared straight ahead at the double doors that led to the entryway. A million thoughts ran through my mind, most of them too mean to say aloud. The night before, as I had tried to fall asleep, I had rehearsed over and over in my mind exactly how I would behave. In my late-night vision of the morning, I was going to wake up, transformed into a rock of encouragement for Frank. Now that the morning was actually here, however, the encouragement wasn't coming quite as easily as I'd imagined.

To my surprise, Frank was the first to broach the subject of his employment situation. "I'm going to call a few people today to see if they know of any opportunities in Austin," he announced.

Rock of encouragement. Rock of encouragement, I thought. "That's a good idea, Frank," I said. "Who are you going to call?"

"Just some people I know at a few venture firms I've worked with."

"Great! Like . . . who, exactly?" I asked. I could feel the panic beginning to creep into my voice.

"Do you remember Joe White at ATX Ventures? I heard he recently funded a couple of start-ups, so he may have some opportunities for me to explore."

"And ... when do you think you'll be able to meet with him?" I asked sharply. I could see from Frank's body language that he didn't want to answer this question.

"Well, Joe is a very busy guy and I hear he's travelling right now—maybe a few weeks."

"A few weeks?" I gasped, perplexed. "But you just said you were calling him today. Which is it, today, or a few weeks?"

"I'll put in a call with him today and probably meet with him in a few weeks."

"We don't have a few weeks," I said, beginning to feel cold. This rock of encouragement business was harder than it seemed. "You need to get in to see him sooner."

"Hon—" he began.

"Frank, we can't afford to put all of our eggs in one basket. You need to talk to everyone you know. We can't let one day go by without talking to someone."

Frank looked at the ground sadly. "I'll see what I can do," he sighed.

I took a deep breath and attempted to switch gears. "Listen, Frank," I said, "I believe in you. You're a brilliant technologist who is worth five times the amount you make at these upstarts. Anyone would be lucky to have you on their team. You would be an asset to any company ... you just need to find the right one. And that's going to take a lot of hitting the pavement and talking to everyone you know."

"Really, Linda, we are going to be fine. I know I'm one of the top technology executives in Austin. If opportunities exist, I'm sure I'll at least get an interview."

"Maybe you're right," I hesitantly agreed, wanting to give him the benefit of the doubt. "I'm just worried that you're not going to find many opportunities out there right now. The economy's in rough shape, Frank, you know that. Just yesterday I was talking to a girl at work whose husband is in engineering. He's been out of work for six months. Six months! I mean, I have to lay off a bunch of people today myself. It would be ironic if it wasn't so depressing."

We sat in silence, feeling the weight of our situation hanging on our shoulders. I could hear our five-year-old son Andrew stirring upstairs, getting ready to greet another day, free of stress and anxiety. I envied his innocence. He hadn't yet had the chance to develop the kinds of expectations that make being an adult a struggle at times.

Frank stared straight at me with an inquisitive expression. "You know, Linda," he began tentatively, "I've been thinking ... this might be the perfect opportunity for me to make a change. I've wanted to get out of engineering and high-technology for quite some time. It might be a good time to start my own company or do something different."

For years, Frank had been tinkering with different career ideas. When he was younger, his real passion was to become a surgeon, but his parents talked him out of it because it cost too much and took too long to achieve. In several of his former jobs, he had tried to break out of engineering and get into sales or some other role, but someone was always there to shoot the idea down. "Frank," they'd say, "you're too good of an engineer and we can't afford to lose you." He was just an engineer, and engineers are paid to "do." He hadn't let it get him down, though. Over the years, he had developed a few software applications on the side, written some technical books, and never stopped thinking about how to break out of engineering.

I eyed him warily. "I don't know if this is a good time, Frank," I said, carefully. "The market is so unstable. I think you'll have a lot better shot at getting a job if you stick with what you're good at. And as for starting your own business, hardly anyone's getting funding right now. You know as well as I do that most new businesses don't turn a profit for years. We don't have enough money to last us more than a year in our current lifestyle. And who even knows how stable my job is?"

"Well, that's true . . ." he said, "but it might be the perfect time for me. I might not get another chance to live my dream."

"What is your dream?" I asked, growing frustrated. "I never once heard you tell me that you were not pursuing your dream. As a matter of fact, I thought you were living your dream. You told me you love working with technology and building teams."

"I do like working with technology. It's all the other crap that goes with building a product that I'm sick of. People complain about the most trivial things, put up barriers for no reason at all, and make mountains out of molehills over the most insignificant of things."

"People? You mean Ken? Is that what this is about? You're going to turn your back on something you like to do because of one big asshole with a chip on his shoulder?" I stammered.

"I am not turning my back. I just want to pursue something new. I want to be excited about work. I'm sick and tired of being stressed all the time."

I took a deep breath and tried to calm myself. "I truly want you to be able to do what makes you happy, Frank," I said, "but we need to be practical. Not

just for us, but for Andrew. Staying the course is the fastest path to employment. We just can't afford to start something new right now."

Frank nodded and let the conversation drop. It did not feel resolved, but
we had to get our day started. I went into the bedroom to figure out what to
wear for the day with a heavy feeling in my chest and tears welling up in my
eyes. I couldn't believe I had to go to work today and put other people through
the same thing we were going through. I shuddered at the thought of spending
another day sitting in our stuffy conference room with a bunch of aging jocks
making inappropriate jokes that were intended to make me feel like "one of the
guys," but really just made me feel embarrassed for the entire male population.

Why am I being so hard on him? I wondered as I halfheartedly rifled
through my closet. *Who am I to tell him that he must find a job, rather than pursue his dream? If he really wants to pursue a new path he should be allowed to. He
has always supported me and my career choices. No other man even comes close to
being as supportive as Frank. He offers encouragement and love to me even when I
don't believe in myself. My income isn't enough to pay the bills long-term, but I certainly make enough to keep us afloat for a while.*

I walked into the master bathroom and was startled to find Frank leaning
on the sink. Normally, he'd be shaving or fixing his hair, getting ready for work.
Today, he had his head bent down over the sink with his elbows resting on the
countertop and his hands gripping the back of his head. Tears streamed down
his face, which had turned a faint red. His nose, like his eyes, was swollen and
puffy.

Seeing Frank in such a state, I was overcome with a combination of dread,
fear, sadness and guilt. I wanted to wrap my arms tightly around his waist in
comfort, but I froze. It was one of those moments that I will never forget, the
scene of a movie being played in slow motion to emphasize the drama. Something I loved was being destroyed before my very eyes, and I felt powerless to
do anything about it. Frank's definition of self—his identity—was now unclear.
The jobs, the people, the connections he'd made as he climbed the corporate
ladder all defined him, as they do for most of us. Here he was without a job,
uncertain of what he wanted to do, and feeling condemned to repeat a pattern
that made him miserable.

It was frightening to think about the future when we were in limbo. In our
minds, Frank and I were in a safe zone where we'd remain until we chose to
climb up the next rung of the ladder. Other people had to deal with job losses,
sure, but we weren't "other people." We were the type of people who could not
and would not fail, no matter how many obstacles life threw at us. Everything

that Frank believed about himself and his value to society, the years he spent defining what type of executive he would be, they were all shaken by the doubts he harbored about his own destiny.

I touched him gently on the back. "Frank, are you okay?" I asked.

His voice shook as he stared into the basin of the sink. "I am so sorry to do this to you and us," he said, sniffling. "I wanted to tell you three days ago but I was a wreck."

I looked at him, puzzled. "Three days ago," I said, carefully. "What do you mean three days ago? I thought you left yesterday."

"I was hoping that I might have some good leads before I worried you sick."

Only moments before my heart had gone out to Frank—now I felt as if he'd just slapped me across the face. Frank and I had always agreed that no matter how bad things got, we'd always be honest with each other. For the past three days, he'd been waking up and going through his morning routines, leaving at the normal time, pretending as if everything was just fine. Meanwhile, he'd been hiding a gigantic secret that affected our entire family. It made me feel like a tremendous fool.

"You've been out of work for three days and you didn't tell me?" I asked. "What the hell have you been doing with your time?"

He stood up from the sink and looked at me. I could feel that it was taking everything in his power to look me in the eye. "Sitting at the Kileynon coffee shop on Bee Caves, getting my résumé together and organizing my contact list."

"I can't believe you've been lying to me for three days."

"I didn't lie," he mumbled. "I just needed some time to sort this out."

"What happened to telling each other everything . . . good and bad? The minute you encounter a real problem, the deal's suddenly off? How would you like it if I withheld something this big from you?" I responded angrily.

"I'm sorry, Linda. You know that I would never intentionally hurt you."

"Oh, I see. You didn't *intentionally* keep this a secret for three days. You just forgot that you were sitting in a coffee shop instead of going to the office. Well, that makes me feel much better," I replied sarcastically.

"Linda, I don't—"

Before he could finish, I put my hands up in surrender. "Please stop," I said, shaking. "I don't want to talk about this. I'm done. I am about ready to pass out from all of the stress."

I knew the conversation was just leading up to a huge argument that was only going to make things worse. It wasn't even seven o'clock and I felt like my entire day was already shot. As upset as I was in the moment, I knew I'd feel

guilty about my angry reaction later. There are no winners in this type of situation. I wanted to encourage my husband to pursue his dreams, but truth be
told, I was scared. I knew the practical route was for him to leverage his expertise and get right back into another job for the stability, even if it meant that
one more year down the road, we'd be right back in the same position. It re-
quires a great amount of dedication and energy to probe into the emotions and
fears that surround your career to find your calling—and I just didn't know if
Frank or I had the strength to go through that struggle. Could I get beyond the
fear I had about maintaining my lifestyle and allow Frank to dream, one step at
a time, about a new future?

My fear was definitely exacerbated by the fact that lately, there seemed to
be no end of unemployed professionals in Austin. As the economy worsened,
people were leaving the city because they couldn't find work. Many of Austin's
workers moved here from other states, so they didn't have family close by to
help them out when times got rough. We were in the same boat. If we hoped to
stay in Austin—and I, for one, did not want to go back to New Hampshire—
we were on our own.

I forced these worries out of my head and tried my best to give Frank the
support he needed. "Frank," I said hesitantly, "we will figure something out."

He nodded and forced a pathetic smile. I put my arms around him and
gave him a consoling hug, and then he left me alone in the bathroom to get
ready for the day. I sensed that it was hard for him to leave, but I appreciated
his recognition that I needed some time alone. Frank has always had a hard
time letting me be alone when he knows I'm upset about something. He tends
to solve problems by talking them through, while I like to work through issues
in solitude. Thankfully, this morning he knew when to leave well enough alone.
I was glad to be by myself, to have a moment to wallow in my own fears instead
of having to consider Frank's feelings. With the relief that the only one looking
at me was my reflection in the mirror, the pain I'd been feeling all morning was
finally released in a stream of tears. I felt like being even more vocal, but I
stifled my urge to scream out loud, fearing it would bring Frank rushing back
to try and make things better.

After a few moments of solid sobbing, I managed to compose myself. I
styled my hair and applied my makeup, then left the bathroom and headed toward the kitchen.

The large kitchen was one of the house's biggest selling points, and I had
decorated it myself to be elegant but homey. The walls were a beautiful combination of faux finish and Italian tile. Set into the walls was a multitude of dark

honey cabinets that gave us more storage space than we could ever use. The countertops were made of coal-colored granite, and the floor was covered with tasteful cream-colored travertine flooring. As I walked over to the coffee maker, I tried not to think about the possibility that our days in this kitchen might be numbered.

Andrew and Frank were seated at the round breakfast table eating cereal. I glanced at Frank as I poured the coffee into my favorite mug, a white mug with a picture of Andrew and me hugging. Frank looked pale with dark circles under his eyes. The pale skin set against his white hair gave him a ghostly appearance. My heart sank.

Coffee in hand, I walked over to the round breakfast table and sat down. I looked out the door to the patio and stared at the beautiful Texas sky. I could see our reflection through the glass and I felt the anxiety wash over me again. I couldn't help but see a family on the brink of failure.

"What are your plans for the day?" Frank asked.

"Mom, mom, mom, mom," Andrew interrupted, tugging on my sleeve.

I ignored Andrew and shot Frank a look of annoyance—he'd known for weeks that today was D-Day at my office. "I have the executive team meeting," I said drily.

"Mom, mom, mommmmmm," Andrew persisted, "can I play the computer? I want to play Scooby Doo." And then, with a cartoonish rumble, "Scooby Dooby Doooooo!"

I gave him a tired smile. "Wait a second, Andrew. Let me finish my coffee and then we'll set up the computer," I responded.

"I want to play now. Can I play now?"

"In a minute, Andrew."

From the time he was old enough to speak, Andrew has been incredibly tenacious at getting his way. He was always a considerate and well-behaved kid, but he turned into a bulldog when he wanted something. "The apple doesn't fall far from the tree," Frank always said, although it's up for debate which one of us was the tree in that analogy.

Frank slid his chair away from the table, dragging it across the travertine floor with an obnoxious screech. He got up, swooped Andrew into his hands and said, "Let's go play on the computer, my friend."

After they left the room, my eyes wandered over to the pictures that lined the counter near the oversized breakfast nook. To the left was a family picture of Andrew's baptism at St. John's Cathedral in New York, then one of Frank and me in Aspen, followed by a host of happy family pictures spanning the years. Amid the stress of the morning, these glimpses into our past suddenly didn't seem real. Everyone looked too happy. I briefly considered hiding them in a drawer so I wouldn't have to be reminded of better times. My anxiety was starting to get the better of me. I decided I needed to get outside for some fresh air before work.

I returned to the bedroom and grabbed a pair of shorts and a spandex top from the custom-made bureau, my favorite item of furniture in the house. When I opened the sock drawer, it came off its rails and spilled onto the beige carpet, sending socks all over the floor. This wasn't the first time it had happened—although I loved the look of the bureau, the rails on the sock drawer were slightly out of alignment. Gritting my teeth in irritation, I grabbed a pair of running socks out of the pile. The rest of the socks were thrown back into the drawer, and then I lifted the drawer off the ground and slammed it back into the bureau. I stared at the bureau for a moment, lost in thought. As beautiful as it was, it was full of flaws. Unless you began examining it closely, you'd think it was perfect.

I reached for my sneakers, which were usually sitting by the reading chair in the corner, but they were nowhere to be found. I left the bedroom and did a quick search of the rest of the downstairs, to no avail.

"Frank!" I shouted up the stairs. "Have you seen my sneakers?"

"No," he yelled back from the game room. "Why? Where are you going?"

"I'm going for a walk to get some fresh air before work," I replied. "Is that all right with you?"

"Hang on a minute," he yelled back, "I'll go with you."

I knew that was coming. "Can you just look upstairs for me?" I shouted, trying to stifle my irritation.

"Of course," he said. I could hear him walking around the game room and down the long hallway into the media room. "I don't see them, love. Are you sure you took them off up here?"

He walked back down the hall and down the stairs. "I'd like to go for a walk with you."

I pursed my lips. "I would rather be by myself right now, Frank. If I talk to you I might blow up and say something that I'll regret later."

"We can just walk in silence," he promised.

I clenched my teeth and released a loud exhalation of irritation. Frank followed me as I walked back to the bedroom, hovering as he often does when he feels like I'm mad at him. Apparently the period in which he decided to stay out of my way had reached its time limit. *Where the hell are my sneakers?* I thought. All I wanted to do was get out of there and be by myself. Behind me, Frank was droning on about what a great idea it would be for him to join me on my walk. While he talked I threw the duvet onto the bed, kicked his clothes around on the floor and pushed the mountain of pillows across the room.

I threw my hands up in frustration and left the bedroom to retrace the areas Frank had searched. Thankfully, he didn't follow me. I finally found the sneakers in the game room sitting under the black coffee table. I scooped the sneakers up and slumped down to put them on.

The game room was my favorite spot in the house. The dark orange venetian plaster with a hint of bronze gave the oversized room a warm, friendly feeling. Arranged around the room were two camel-colored matching couches, an oversized chair and a big, square, antique, black coffee table with a matching armoire. A bright light streamed in through the nine large windows that had been custom-fitted with plantation shutters. An octagonal-shaped wooden table was nestled in the corner of the room surrounded by four matching chairs. Andrew sat at this table playing his Scooby Doo game on the computer, oblivious to the tension filling the air around him.

I skipped down the stairs to find Frank lacing up his sneakers in the kitchen. "You're not going with me," I said assertively.

He smiled. "Did you find your sneakers?"

"Yes. They were in the game room. Right where you said they weren't," I shot at him.

"Oh, good," he said, smiling sweetly.

I headed toward the door, intent on leaving Frank behind, but I was stopped in my tracks by a trail of Lego pieces scattered around the kitchen floor. "Andrew," I yelled upstairs, growing more irritated by the moment, "if you can't keep these Legos in your Lego box, Mommy is going to throw them away. I need you to pick them up right now."

"Can you bring them up, Mom? I'm playing the computer," he shouted down.

"I am walking toward the trash can."

"No, don't throw away my Legos! Can I just finish this one game?"

"I am going to count to three. One . . . two . . . two and a half . . ."

"I'm coming, I'm coming," he said in exasperation. I heard his footsteps on the floor above as he scurried across the game room and down the staircase.

"Andrew, please put your toys away," I said when he stepped into the kitchen. "I don't like stepping on these things because they hurt."

"I knowwwww," he said in a boyish voice filled with attitude.

"When you're done with that, go put your shoes on," Frank said. "We're going for a walk with mommy."

I clenched my fists. *Just walk out the door and go for a walk. Ignore him.* I did a quick pivot and walked out the kitchen door and into the garage, slamming the door behind me. Seconds later, Frank was right behind me, struggling to put Andrew into his gray and green jogger. I bolted out of the garage and down the driveway, desperate to leave them behind. I could hear Frank's feet hitting the pavement behind me.

"Hey, Linda, wait up," he yelled.

"Mom, wait for Dad," Andrew yelped.

It didn't take long for them to catch up to me. Frank gently touched my shoulder. I stopped, heaved a sigh, and then turned around to face him. As he looked into my eyes, my face flushed a cherry red, and I felt a moment of regret for having rejected him. Even in our worst moments, there was still something undeniably comforting about his presence. My eyes moved down to the jogger where Andrew grinned back at me. It was hard to be upset when looking at his adorable, chubby cheeks.

We walked briskly around the cul-de-sac that runs in front of our house. All around us, our neighbors went about their normal routines, reading their morning papers, getting the kids ready for school, and envying one another's lawns. Although the news of Frank's unemployment had yet to become public knowledge, I had the paranoid feeling that they were all judging us from the comforts of their outdoor kitchens.

"It is a great morning, huh?" Frank offered.

I stared straight ahead, trying to focus on the walk. "Very nice."

"I wish the weather would be like this year round."

"Not likely."

"What are you thinking about?" he asked, tentatively.

"Can we just walk in silence, like we agreed to?" I asked.

"Oh," he said. "Do you want me to stop talking?"

"Yeah."

He looked away and we continued the walk in silence. At first it felt like a welcome relief from the incessant chatter of the morning, but soon my mind drifted back to our prospective money woes. In the jogger, Andrew rode along contentedly. He was used to blocking out the boring adult-speak that constantly surrounded him.

"We should cancel our trip to New Hampshire and Killington," I suddenly announced. For months, we'd been planning a vacation to celebrate the holidays back home. Both sides of the family were planning to come because we would be belatedly celebrating Andrew's fifth birthday, too. It would be the first time that both sides of the family would be together at the same time with Andrew.

Frank's brow furrowed. "Why? Everyone's excited about it. Everything is booked."

"What do you mean, why?" I whispered. "Frank, you don't have a job. We can't just pretend like this didn't happen. Spending $10,000 on a vacation right now doesn't seem like the wisest decision."

"Come on, don't be like this, honey," Frank said. "We really need this right now."

"Shhh!" I hissed, glancing around me to make sure no one could hear us. The last thing I wanted was for the entire neighborhood to learn that Frank was out of a job. "Don't be like what? Responsible? Conservative? Worried? How can you be so nonchalant about all this?"

"You know what I mean. Can we just go on this trip and try to have a good time?" he asked hopefully.

I started to reply but bit my tongue. As much as I wanted to be cheerful for Frank, I was continuing to struggle with my emotions as I walked around the neighborhood. Inside, I felt nothing but despair.

I looked down at Andrew, who was playing with a Buzz Lightyear action figure in his jogger. The sight of him sitting there quietly, his round face beaming with happiness, made my heart melt. As I observed the pure joy he got from the simple, two-dollar plastic toy, my hopelessness began to be replaced by awe. After everything I experienced growing up, it was hard for me to see the world through his eyes—a world in which parents were dependable and it was okay to just be a kid. I wondered if he sensed the tension between Frank and me.

After taking a few moments to calm down, I knew Frank was right. We couldn't spoil the trip that we'd all been looking forward to just because we'd hit a rough patch. Who was I fooling? I needed this trip just as much as he did. I was just scared out of my mind and looking for someone to blame—and since his resignation was the catalyst for my anxiety, he naturally took the brunt of my anger. The real test of a relationship was how well it survived during the moments of greatest difficulty. If the last twelve hours were any indication, we might be in for a rough haul.

After completing six loops around the cul-de-sac, we came to a rest at the end of our driveway. To Frank's credit, he seemed to be dealing with my mood swings rather well. He reached for my hand and I knotted my arms in front of my chest so he couldn't touch me, teasing him. I was feeling better, but I still wasn't quite ready to give up the fight. He grabbed for my hand again eagerly while tickling me to release my grip. I swatted his hands away, playfully. He tried one more time, and this time I gave in, letting my fingers interlock with his. I gave his hand a soft squeeze and held it gently. Knowing that he had broken my mood, he grinned in triumph.

I lifted Andrew out of the jogger, gave him a huge hug and carried him into the house. As we walked in the kitchen door, I lowered him to the ground and gave him a kiss on his forehead. He was so big now, standing up to my thighs. He looked up at me with a grin that made me want to burst into tears.

"Mom, will you play with me?"

I looked at the clock. It was 7:00 already. "Not right now sweetie. I need to get ready for work."

Andrew thrust out his lower lip. "You're always at work," he complained.

"I know, sweetie. It's just something adults have to do," I said, sighing. I looked at Frank, who was pouring himself a fresh cup of coffee. "Maybe Daddy will play with you."

"Sure, I'll play with you," Frank said, smiling. "Let's go get some toys."

I watched them walk toward the toy room with a mixture of pride and envy. Andrew turned around to look at me, and I blew him an exaggerated kiss with both hands. He laughed and turned back around. Then I headed to the bathroom to get ready for a day of work that I knew was going to take the life out of me.

Chapter 5 Terrified

Before leaving for work, I chugged some orange juice from the carton and put it back in the refrigerator. The kitchen would have been clean by anyone's standards—except mine. There were a few dirty dishes sitting in the sink. I pulled them out, placed them in the dishwasher, and began scouring the room for other items that needed to be washed. Two empty coffee mugs sat on the kitchen table. I stepped over the dishwasher door and grabbed them. Remembering that Frank had left a mug in the bathroom, I cut across the living room and headed that way. Along the way, I found a bowl that Andrew left on the floor, so I grabbed that too. With full hands, I went back into the kitchen and loaded the dishwasher.

I had been delaying going to the office all morning. As anxious as I was to get away from my domestic turmoil, the alternative of going into the office to decide which of my coworkers were going to get the ax was none-too-motivational. As I stood in the kitchen, paralyzed with indecision, I noticed that there were fingerprints on the countertop. I grabbed some paper towels and a bottle of Windex and began spraying. One counter led to the next. And now the table looked dull in comparison, so I wiped that down, too. And then the sink . . . the patio door window . . . until every surface in the kitchen was gleaming.

While I cleaned, I thought about the twists and turns that had brought my company, Trifinity, to this point. It seemed like only yesterday that we were at the top of our game, closing multi-million dollar deals with huge financial institutions. Now we were on the brink of failure, burning through cash faster than we generated it. Just last week, I had pitched our product strategy to four venture firms to try and raise another round of funding. The prognosis was grim. We had to slow the cash burn and the only way to do it was to fire people, and lots of them. This would be my first time letting people go for reasons other than performance, and I was sick with guilt about it. Some of the people on my team had followed me to Trifinity at a time when it was brimming with potential. How had things gone wrong so quickly?

As I moved from the window to the walls, I suddenly realized that I'd be there all day if I didn't force myself to stop. I put the Windex and paper towels away and grabbed my bags. "Honey, I'm leaving," I called out.

"Give me a second, love . . ." Frank shouted, "I'm in the bathroom." One thing you can say about Frank, he's as regular as they come. That man was always in the bathroom. I've never met anyone who spent as much time sitting on the toilet. It's like clockwork. He's in there before he leaves the house, as soon as he comes home from work, and right before bed. I wouldn't be surprised if he snuck in a few sessions at work, too.

"Hurry up," I said impatiently. "I want to get to the office before everyone else arrives so I can prepare for the meeting." I usually arrived at the office between 8:00 and 8:30. This morning, even with all the hustle and bustle, I wanted to get there by 7:30.

"Just one more second," he chirped.

"You need to go to the doctor, Frank. You spend far too much time in the bathroom. It's not healthy," I responded, irritated. I looked at my watch, tapping my foot against the floor. "Are you almost done?" I shouted with growing impatience.

The toilet flushed. I could hear the sink running, and then the bathroom door squeaked open. "I'm coming, I'm coming," he said. "Jeez, you're impatient," he walked toward me to give me a goodbye kiss.

"Are you going to keep Andrew home today from pre-k since you'll be home?" I asked, trying to keep the snideness out of my voice.

"You know what? I think I will," he said.

I rested my head on his chest as we embraced. For a brief moment, the tension between us melted away. It was time to leave, and I was finally feeling the closeness I'd been longing for all morning. It took every ounce of my willpower to break away and head for the door.

"I gotta go," I said. "I'll call you later to let you know if I can do lunch."

"Okay, have a great day. I love you."

"I love you, too."

"Bye, Andrew," I shouted up the stairs. "Love you."

"Bye, Mom," his voice chirped from the game room.

I walked out through the kitchen and settled into the driver's seat of my black BMW 745iL, the smell of new leather filling my nose. The car was still fairly new. There were only 2,000 miles on the odometer. I pushed the square electronic key into the ignition and pressed the start button. Frank and Andrew stood in the doorway waving goodbye—for all observers, the picture of domestic bliss.

The drive to my office was only about two and a half miles door-to-door. Even though it was a short distance, it could take several minutes if the traffic was bad. Today, we were bumper to bumper. I looked around at the people in the cars adjacent to mine, wondering where they were going and what stories they were hiding beneath their veils of fake perfection. *Who is that hottie dressed in a dark blue suit driving a Porsche 911 and talking on his cell phone? Is he speaking to his wife? A business colleague? A mistress? Is he on his way to work or is he faking it like Frank had, pretending he was on his way to his fake job? Will he spend his day in an office, a gym, a coffee shop? Or will he sit at a bar drinking beer until it's time to go home and face his life?*

In front of me, a woman was staring into her rearview mirror applying mascara. I found this unbelievably irritating. *She couldn't have spent sixty seconds more at home to do that? Or waited until she got to work? She's going to kill someone one of these days!* I had the urge to nudge her bumper and make her smear her makeup. My luck, though, and she'd poke herself in the eye and sue me. What if I honked instead? Maybe she'd smear her mascara just enough to satisfy my sudden need to teach her a lesson.

I sighed. *Linda, pull yourself together.* This woman and her makeup routine were the least of my worries. In just a few minutes, I'd be at the office, deciding the fate of my team. I wondered how the rest of the executives would react to the session today. From what I gathered, most of them had never laid anyone off either. Until now, we had been a bunch of hardworking executives riding high on the dot-com wave with all the perks that went with it—expensive dinners, fancy hotel rooms, and first-class airfare anytime we traveled. All over Austin, however, the halcyon days were coming to an end, and we were now faced with the hard reality of managing a struggling business. Just thinking about what I was about to do made my stomach burn and my eyes well with tears. I suddenly envied the woman with the mascara, with seemingly no greater concerns than getting her face put together before work.

From the conversations I'd had with the guys at work over the last few days, they didn't seem nearly as affected by this process as I was. "It's just business," they'd say whenever I expressed concerns about letting people go. I mean, who were they trying to fool? Anyone with a heart would have to recognize that it was not just business. Anything that involves people was not just business. I guess this was what Dan, the CEO of the company, was talking about when he said I needed thicker skin. "Screw him," I said aloud. "I like my skin just the way it is."

I envisioned myself calling up Dan and telling him that I didn't want to work for the company any longer. If I only had the guts to do it, it would have felt so good. I picked up my car phone and put it to my ear, just to see what it would feel like. "I'm not coming back, Dan," I said aloud. "I'm finally going to follow my dreams and there's nothing you can do to stop me. Have Ravin pack up my office and Fed Ex me my belongings. . . . I'm sorry, what's that? . . . No, I won't stay. I simply can't. . . . Why? It's a matter of principal, Dan. These people are my friends. I don't care how much you offer me, I can't be surrounded by you yahoos any longer. You heard me—yahoos." That felt good. If I could only do it for real. I placed the phone back in its cradle and stared out at the unmoving traffic.

My thoughts drifted back to Frank's resignation. Maybe things weren't as bad as they'd seemed earlier. After all, we had enough in the bank to last us a while. We had invested wisely in our 401(k)s and they seemed to be growing. We had money socked away in different mutual funds and other investments. We could definitely stand to cut back on our expenses, but we were hardly on the verge of bankruptcy. Frank might be unemployed for a few weeks, but something was bound to pop up. As far as I knew, my job was safe. Still, no matter how irrational it felt, I couldn't shake the daunting feeling that something terrible was about to happen.

It was hard to think about our situation without my ego getting in the way. Pride stood in the way of acceptance. Throughout my life, I'd protected my pride at all costs. Even the people who thought they knew me only got to see what I let them see. I had a constant, unshakable feeling that the people in my life would no longer like me if they knew my background. I tried to forget my past, to lock it away in a box, but it followed me around like a raincloud, forever hovering over my head like a character in a comic strip. *Is it even possible to escape your past?* I wondered. *Why do I always seem to be surrounded by job and money issues? Is God testing me? Did I fail some test somewhere along the line and now I am being forced to retake it until I get it right?*

Just as I was on the verge of a major psychological breakthrough, the traffic started moving again. Being close to work has its advantages and disadvantages.

The advantages were that I was close to home, close to my son's future school, and I saved tons of money on gas. The biggest disadvantage was that the short commute didn't allow for much alone time to unwind before and after work. More often than not, I'd reach my destination just as I started getting to an interesting train of thought. Today was no exception. In moments, I had reached the driveway into my company's parking lot. As I turned into the parking lot, I was temporarily blinded by the reflection of the sun off the black-tinted windows of my company's headquarters. I narrowed my eyes into slits as I slowly navigated to my favorite spot directly in front of the entrance to Building II.

I climbed out of the car with my computer bag and purse in hand, shut the door, and darted toward the entrance in my usual brisk fashion. Midway to the entrance, I stopped abruptly; something didn't seem quite right. I turned around and noticed that there were more cars in the parking lot than would be typical at 7:30 on a Thursday morning. My throat suddenly felt constricted as anxiety overtook me. Most of the cars belonged to members of the executive team . . . but we weren't supposed to be meeting for another hour. Why would they have come in so early? Was something going on that I didn't know about? Maybe it was nothing. Maybe Dan had invited members of the Board in to discuss the layoffs. I sure hoped that was the case. The alternative—that the rest of the team was purposely meeting behind my back—was just too disturbing to consider.

Feeling shaken by the possibility that things were worse than I knew, I headed into the building and entered the elevator. As the elevator ascended to the second floor, I leaned back against the elevator wall, sighed deeply, and stared at my reflection in the full-length mirror. *Nowhere to go but up*, I thought.

The elevator doors opened and I stepped into the office suite. The room was dark, save for the low pulse of the security lights. In light of the changes that were to happen that day, the effect was creepy. It felt haunted. Soon enough it *would* be a ghost town, filled with rows upon rows of empty cubicles—we had to let go of more than half the company. I made my way to the end of the hallway and turned the lights on, suddenly feeling thankful for the artificial fluorescent glow, which usually made me feel like I was walking into a prison.

To get to my office I had to walk through a row of eight cubes. My feet felt heavy as I passed by my coworkers' desks. I imagined the faces of my staff staring at me as if I were a fanged monster as they packed their lives into the company-provided boxes.

The first two cubes, situated directly across from one another, belonged to two of my managers, Janet and Steve. Janet had followed me to three different companies. When she interviewed with me for the first time, I liked her instantly. She had moved to Texas from Canada to be with her Russian fiancé, Vasil. I hired her on the spot and we became close friends. Not long after we began working together, she broke it off with Vasil (a decision I approved of wholeheartedly—he was a real jerk) and really started to bloom. She was no longer the shy and timid gal she had been when we first met. Once Vasil was out of the picture, she finally let her independent spirit shine. There was only one hitch—Janet had been so eager to settle down that she and Vasil had bought a house together in one of the nicer areas of Austin. Now that he was out of the picture, the entire mortgage fell on her shoulders—a situation that was already putting a strain on her finances. If I chose to let her go, there was a good chance she'd no longer be able to afford the house. Losing her fiancé had been difficult enough . . . how would she react if she lost her job and her house, too?

At least Janet didn't have to support a family. Steve's case was even more unfortunate. He and his wife, Susan, both worked at our company, and they could *both* be let go. What would become of them? Or their coworker Kari, who sat just behind Steve? She was the breadwinner of her family while her husband stayed home and took care of the kids. How would they pay for their children's college educations, their mortgage, the bills, or even food? The thoughts started to converge and echo within my head, wildly spinning out of control. I could almost feel their eyes staring through me and see their heads shaking in disapproval. "It is not my fault," I whispered to the cubes as I continued on to my office. "It's just business." I started to feel dizzy.

I made a sharp turn at the end of the cubes and walked to my corner office on the opposite side of the building. I was not in any mood to sit in a meeting deciding who would stay and who would go. Troubled, I opened the door, tossed my computer bag on the round gray table and turned on the lights. I settled at my desk and pulled the black laptop out of my bag.

Why would the board be here on the same day as the layoffs? I wondered. *It doesn't seem right. It seems more likely that they'd meet off-site so as not to raise suspicion. So then, what's going on?*

To calm my nerves, I picked up the phone and dialed Frank's cell phone. He picked up after two rings. "Hi!" he said jovially. "Miss me already?"

"No," I whispered, even though there was no one around to hear me. "When I walked in this morning, everyone's cars were already here. I think all of the executives are meeting upstairs."

"Are you late? Did you mess up the time?" he asked.

"No, I got the same invitation as everyone else." I flipped to the invitation on my computer to double-check. "Yep, 8:30 A.M. on Thursday. It was sent to the entire team."

"And you didn't get a message or an email or anything that the time had changed?"

"No! Frank, something weird is going on."

"Hmm," he said. "Well, why don't you just go upstairs and see what they're doing?"

"Oh sure, just voluntarily walk into the fire? Nuh-uh, I don't think so. They're probably planning my assassination up there," I said.

"Oh, you're being silly. Go ahead."

"I haven't been sleeping well for days. Last night, I thought I couldn't sleep because I was upset about your resignation. But maybe it was because of this meeting. Maybe it was a premonition. My gut instincts are never wrong, you know."

"Yeah, I know. You're like the princess and the pea."

I took a determined breath. "All right," I said. "You're right. This is ridiculous. I'm going up there. I'll call you back later."

"Good luck, honey. Love you."

"Love you, too."

Steeling my nerves, I hung up the phone and made my way to the third floor. When the elevator doors opened, everything seemed peaceful. The lights had not yet been turned on and I couldn't hear any voices. It was quiet. Maybe even a little too quiet, I thought.

Although the executive conference room was directly across the hallway from the elevator, it suddenly seemed miles away. I could feel the beads of sweat forming under my arms and on the back of my neck along my hair line. When I finally got my feet to move, I walked over to the thick, wooden, conference room doors and put my ear against them, listening for movement on the other side. I reached down to place my hand on the chrome handle when all of a sudden, the conference doors swung open. I jumped back in surprise. Ravin, our executive assistant, stood in the doorway of the conference room, looking at me with a puzzled expression.

"Ravin!" I said, flustered. "Hi, Ravin! What a coincidence! What, uh . . . what's going on?" I crossed my arms in an awkward attempt to look calm, cool, and collected.

Ravin had bleach-blonde hair and always wore a cute headband, which I thought was somewhat quirky for a fifty-something-year-old woman. It suited her pretty face and petite frame though. If I'd had to draw a picture of what the ideal executive assistant would look like, she would be it. She was attractive, attentive, and friendly, and she always had a welcoming smile for you no matter what was going on in the world.

"Good morning, Linda," she said brightly. "Would you like some coffee?" If she knew I had been eavesdropping, she didn't let on.

"Morning! Sure, I'd love a cup of coffee." The day hadn't even officially started yet, and I was already on my fourth cup.

Ravin opened the door wider to reveal the entire executive team sitting around the large conference table. "Dan, Linda is here." Then, giving me a pleasant smile, she brushed past me and hurried off toward the kitchen.

Dan didn't bother to stand up. "Linda!" he said. "Come in here. I was wondering where you were."

I pushed the door open hesitantly. The other executives stared at me, as if I were some exotic species of butterfly in a glass cylinder. I felt like a child being summoned to the principal's office. I looked around the room and noticed that there was one other executive absent—Jason, the guy who designed our technology infrastructure. Jason was the newest executive on the team. He had only been to two or three prior executive team meetings and he didn't say much unless specifically asked. If I had to choose anyone to ax from the executive team, he probably would've been at the top of my list. *Last hired, first fired*, I thought nervously.

"What do you mean, you were wondering where I was?" I asked, trying to keep my cool. "I wasn't aware the meeting time had changed."

Dan looked confused and turned to Glen, our Vice President of Business Development. "Glen, I asked you to call Linda to let her know about the meeting change."

"That's right, Dan, you did," Glen said in an affectless tone. "My apologies, Linda, it must have slipped my mind."

"Hmmm. Okay," I said skeptically.

"Well, never mind that, you're here now," Dan chimed in. "Have a seat, Linda. We have a kit here for you to review. Don't worry, you haven't missed much. We've just been chitchatting."

All eyes in the room remained focused on me. "Where is, uh . . . where's Jason?" I asked.

"Oh, he should be here shortly," said Eric, our Vice President of Technology. As he spoke, he tugged his shirt repetitively and rubbed his elbow. It was a dead giveaway that he was uncomfortable. Now I knew for certain something was up.

"I'm sure he will," I said. I walked around the conference room table and sat down next to Dan. He always sat with his back to the window, facing the conference room door so that he could see everyone that entered the room. It was the power position.

Dan was a fifty-year-old, 5'6", stocky male with a year-round suntan and short, curly, salt-and-pepper hair. He was a good leader who enabled everyone to have a voice, but he was the epitome of the classic smooth-talking, deal-making sales guy. It was because of Dan that I got my first vice president role and for that, I had always felt an allegiance to him. He took me under his wing and coached me along the way on how to be an effective leader. A big part of his mentorship centered on how to deal with the competitive nature of men with big egos. He made sure that my voice was always heard and that my ideas were implemented. Having Dan on my side was a blessing. He was one of the few executives I worked with who understood how difficult it was to be a woman in a male-dominated culture. He was always there to calm things down when the guys got out of hand with their crude jokes or inappropriate remarks.

"Okay, now that everyone is here, let's get started," said John, the president and founder of the company.

"Everyone except Jason," I offered.

John shot me a bemused glance. "Right. Well, I'm sure he'll catch up quickly. Now, did everyone have a chance to rank their employees on the spreadsheet?"

Eric, Glen, Ted, Dick, and I all nodded in agreement. I wished I knew what was going on inside their minds. I glanced across the table at Ted, our Vice President of Marketing. He sat with his legs crossed and arms stretched back holding tightly onto the chair handles, looking like a man ready to take flight. Next to him was Dick, our interim Vice President of Sales who was filling the position for the former VP who had been fired a few months ago. Dick was a foul-mouthed lone ranger who seemed to have little interest in being a manager. He rocked back and forth in his chair with a bored expression that told me he couldn't care less about any of the people he was about to fire.

Come to think of it, none of them seemed to be too uneasy about the exercise we were about to engage in. Was it really so easy for them to dispose of people as if they were getting rid of old furniture or used computer equipment? Or were they, like me, trying like hell to appear professional while this whole thing was tearing them apart inside?

In disgust, I turned my gaze away from them to the Excel spreadsheet before me. For days, I'd been studying this sheet of paper as if it were the Bible. The names of all one hundred and twenty employees at Trifinity were on the list, divided into groups according to department. My section had forty-two names. Forty-two names of forty-two different employees, each one with his or her own personal story. Each of them would be affected in a different way if I chose to eliminate his or her position from the company. Christine was on an H1-B visa and would have to leave the country within days of losing her job. Mark had just gone through a terrible divorce and was already in a funk—this could be the push to send him over the edge. Jason's daughter's illness was so severe that, despite his wife working, too, they struggled to pay the medical bills. Did his wife have insurance? If not, would he even be able to afford COBRA?

Every name on the paper represented a real human being whose life would be permanently, unalterably affected by my decisions. Personal matters were not supposed to sway our decisions, but how could I just ignore the reality of my coworkers' situations? I knew these people. They had given up vacations, school plays, and countless weekends to help the company hit its goals. According to our mission statement, Trifinity's leading value was "employee loyalty." But where was the company's loyalty to its employees?

"Are you sure there are no other alternatives available to us before proceeding with this workforce reduction?" I blurted out.

Steve, the CFO, sat straight up in his chair and glared at me. "No," he replied firmly. "We've already reduced budgets in every area and streamlined where possible. It is our only course of action to keep the company afloat and to get another round of funding from our investors."

"Linda, we didn't close several key accounts, which would've enabled us to navigate through this economic downturn. You know the next round of funding was contingent on us getting those deals. We have no choice but to shrink the team. It's the only way to minimize our expenses," explained Dan in a matter-of-fact voice.

"I am well aware of the lost deals, and I know we were counting on them," I retorted. "But I heard about another company in a similar position that reduced hours and cut salaries across the board before resorting to layoffs. I didn't hear anything about those types of options being discussed."

John, the company founder chimed in, "Dan, Steve, and I reviewed these options and decided they wouldn't work for us."

"Why not? No one asked me if I would be willing to work fewer hours or take a pay cut. Was anyone else asked?" I asked as I scanned the room. I didn't see one head nod in agreement.

"Linda, I know you're new to this and that you care about everyone and you get high marks for that," John responded. He had an irritatingly condescending manner that came out whenever someone challenged him. "But we've done our homework. This is the best option."

"I understand the reasons, but I was hoping there was some other way," I said. My voice sounded sharper than I intended, but I was having a difficult time controlling my temper in the face of such unabashed apathy. John stared back at me, blankly, having said his final word on the matter. Finally, I shook my head in disgust. "Let's just move on."

I looked at my spreadsheet, which was covered with red circles, black "X" marks and blue scribbles. When we were first informed about the layoffs, I was told that I needed to remove more than half of my team—at least twenty people. With the exception of development, I had the largest team in the company, which meant that Eric and I had to lay off more people than anyone else. Over half of the employees being laid off would come from our teams.

Even though I'd been thinking about it almost nonstop for the last few weeks, I had put off making decisions until the night before the meeting. Last night, I had sat at the kitchen table for hours staring at the list of names. We had been offered little-to-no guidance on how to go about eliminating people, and I was terrified of making a mistake when the stakes were so high. Our Director of HR, Haley, was little help. Not only had she never been through a downsizing, she wasn't even certified to be a human resource manager. We were all operating in the dark. The only words of wisdom offered up were to be careful with employees over forty and pregnant women. As I was learning, the downsizing process was a minefield of potential litigation. If any employee felt he or she was being let go strictly because of the amount of money it cost to keep them employed, the law was on their side.

With that in mind, I had begun by scrolling through my list to assess how many of my employees were forty and older. It was a pure guessing game for many of the employees because I didn't have access to employee records and their birthdates were not on the spreadsheet. I could only assume birthdates were excluded to mitigate any potential wrongful discrimination suits . . . ironically, if birthdates had been included, it would've actually helped the older employees keep their jobs. A few of the employees were close friends, so I had made a note of their exact ages. For the rest, I had marked their names with a minus or plus sign to indicate whether I thought they were older or younger than forty. It didn't surprise me that only four employees were over forty, equally split between two women and men. I didn't think either woman was pregnant.

After I'd guesstimated the ages of my team, my gut told me to take stock of employee contributions and how their work impacted current projects. Due to a recent acquisition, I also oversaw some employees who worked in Boston. Some of my team members had been with me for two years and others, like the employees in Boston, only a few months. Was tenure important in a layoff? I had no earthly idea.

If this layoff had been based on performance, I would have been in big trouble. All of my employees were stars or rising stars. We had let go of the underperforming employees a few months earlier. The first reduction (which was not supposed to be called that in public) had not been terribly difficult because we simply eliminated anyone who hadn't received excellent scores on their previous performance review. Only two employees had been terminated from my group. They were both on "performance improvement plans" at the time and I had been contemplating letting them go for weeks. Frankly, I had been happy to be rid of them. No matter how much coaching and training they had received, they simply had not improved.

This time around, the decision making wasn't nearly as easy. We were supposed to be objective, but I had struggled to figure out what the objective criteria should be. I needed some kind of system that could encompass everyone, that way I couldn't be accused of favoritism. What if I made my choices based on skill level? Or was seniority a better way to go? Every time I'd come up with a new system, I'd have to start over from the beginning because the names I crossed out on my previous list no longer fit the criteria. I had worked and reworked my list so many times that it looked like the scribbling of a lunatic.

"So, what do we think?" asked Dan, snapping me back to the present.

My coworkers were silent, so I spoke up first. "Honestly, I had trouble figuring out whom to put on the list. I'm not even sure what our company priorities are going to be moving forward. Are we continuing to build out the new broker-dealer product, the consumer product, or both? Or are we going into maintenance mode?"

"I had the same problem with my list," said Eric. "If we continue to build new product then I need a completely different team than if we simply maintain what we already have."

"It's a good point," Glen echoed, matter-of-factly. "We've been so focused on cutting costs that I have no idea what the company even plans to do after this."

"Okay, guys, let's stop before we get off track," Dan interjected, always the peacemaker. "It's clear we're going to have to modify our go-forward strategy, but let's continue with this exercise assuming that we still want to release the new collaborative product. You need to base your decisions on that strategy."

Glen stood up and walked over to the whiteboard at the front of the room. He grabbed a blue marker and created two side-by-side columns with the headings STAY and GO. As he turned back to the group, he said, "I'd like for each of us to go around the room and share our recommendations on which employees are critical to your group and which ones should be laid off. Once we have a completed list we can have a group discussion of each of the lists. Good?"

No one responded.

"Great," Glen responded, nonplussed. "Okay, who wants to start?"

No one volunteered to go first. I deliberately kept my mouth shut because I wanted to see how someone else approached it first. The room was dead silent. Glen stared at each of us individually, hoping someone would break the silence. I felt like we were in a corporate version of *High Noon*, each of us waiting for the others to fire the first shot. As Glen scanned the room, he spent extra time glaring at Eric and me because we had the largest teams in the company. It didn't work. Neither of us budged.

"All right, I'm trying to figure out a way to temper all this enthusiasm," Glen finally said. It broke the silence and everyone chuckled in relief. "I'll go first to get this started, even though my team is the smallest."

He turned back to the whiteboard and wrote three names on the GO list—everyone on his entire team. I looked at the list in puzzlement. If Glen was letting his entire team go, what was he going to do all day? As if in answer to my question, he moved his marker underneath the final name and wrote his own name on the board.

I stared at the board in shock. I've heard of taking one for the team, but I've never known anyone who fired himself. I suddenly realized why Glen had seemed so distant all morning. How was he managing to keep it together, knowing that he was offering himself up for the slaughter?

"I love my team and I love working here, but we don't need a business development group. We will not be acquiring another company anytime soon, nor will we be establishing any corporate partnerships. The company doesn't need me any longer, so we should eliminate the group."

John was the first to speak. "Glen, I agree with the three employees on the list but don't think you should be on it. Everyone in this room is key to turning around the company—yourself included." His voice was steady and a bit muted.

Glen remained at the board, a determined look on his face. I desperately wanted to know what was going through his mind. "I appreciate the thought, John," he said, "but I want to make sure we do the right thing. Let's keep going through the exercise and we can discuss it in further detail once we've made it around the room. Who's willing to go next?"

Eric volunteered to go next, followed by me, and then the rest of the team. Over the next two hours, we managed to get through everyone's lists. When we'd all exhausted our suggestions, there were eighty-two people in the GO list and a handful of people in the STAY column. To Glen's credit, he managed to lead us through the exercise with relative ease and few interruptions. I admired his focus and lamented the fact that he might not be with the company for much longer.

"All right, now that we have a solid GO list, we can start talking about each employee. I recommend that we break for lunch and regroup at 1:00 P.M. to move on to the next part," Glen proposed.

I looked at my watch. It was 11:40 A.M. The process of going through our lists had left my stomach aching and my palms sweaty. I felt an incredible urge to kick something or break a vase into little pieces with my bare hands. The feelings were frightening—normally I'm not a violent person. I couldn't help but think of how good it would feel to have some kind of relief for the tension of the morning, but I knew I had to maintain my composure. I got out of my chair, gathered my papers and walked toward the conference room door, the picture of calm energy.

Chapter 6 Anxious

"Wait, Linda," Dan called. I stopped in the door of the conference room and turned to face him. "Are you going to your office?" I nodded my head yes. He caught up with me and together we walked out of the conference room. "I'll walk with you," he continued. "I want to talk to you about something."

"Okay, what?" I grumbled. I was hoping to have some time alone to collect my thoughts.

"I wanted to talk to you earlier this morning, but I didn't want to disrupt the meeting," he offered.

"Is everything okay?" I asked, irritated by his caginess.

"Yes, everything is fine. Let's just wait until we get to your office."

I sighed. "Fine." We walked down the hall and stepped onto the elevator. "So, how do you think the meeting is going?" I asked, making an attempt at small talk.

He smiled pleasantly. "I don't think it could be going any better. We have a great list already and I suspect we'll have the entire list done by the end of the day."

"It couldn't be any better?" I interjected. "Seriously, Dan, that sounds so cold." I felt a sense of disgust at his callousness. It seemed like the human dimension of the layoffs wasn't affecting him at all.

He looked back at me with empty eyes. "Linda, you are too sensitive," he said. "But I like that about you."

I clenched my teeth and squeezed my papers tightly against my chest. I pinned my hands under my armpits to stop myself from winding up and knocking him on the head. I was sick and tired of people telling me I was being too sensitive. I wasn't an overly sensitive person, despite what my callous co-workers might think. Caring and empathetic, yes. Sensitive, it depends. Someone who was too sensitive flipped out and cried at the drop of a hat over trivial things—and that wasn't me. It's a sad world in which having compassion for anyone but yourself gets you labeled "too sensitive." If I were so sensitive, then why did I have no idea what was about to happen to me?

We had reached my office. I walked in first with Dan trailing closely behind, shutting the door behind him. I leaned against my desk and he leaned against the wall, attempting to appear casual.

"What's up?" I asked, feeling a bit confused.

"Remember the lunch discussion we had a few weeks ago at the restaurant?"

"Yes," I said cautiously. A few weeks ago, when it became clear that the company wasn't in great shape, Dan and I had gone out to lunch. There was nothing particularly unusual about this. We had gone to lunch many times in the past.

"Do you remember the discussion we had about the team?"

"What specifically about the team?" I asked, unsure of what he was leading up to.

"Well, not just the team," he said. "We were talking more specifically about you and your goals. Do you remember?"

"Yeah," I said, a cold feeling beginning to crawl up my arms. "What about my goals?"

"You said that you didn't want to be in product strategy or business development forever and that you had aspirations to pursue something new."

"I remember," I responded as I crossed my arms in front of me protectively.

"I also asked you for your opinion on who from the executive team should be let go," Dan continued.

"Yup," I said defensively, "and I gave you my honest opinion, based on what I believe the company needs going forward."

I leaned heavily against my desk. My heart was beating a hundred miles a minute. My throat felt dry. I closed my eyes and braced myself for the other shoe that was about to drop.

"John and I have talked with the board several times about the executive team and we are going to make some changes."

"Okay," I said. "And what exactly does that mean?"

Dan readjusted his position and stared into my eyes. "John is no longer going to be with the company and neither am I," he said.

"What?" I responded, stunned. That was unexpected. I felt a brief moment of relief. *Maybe I'm safe after all*, I thought.

"The board has asked us to step aside." He spoke slowly, as if he were speaking to a child. He seemed to be holding something back.

"If you're being let go, then who's going to run the company?" I inquired.

"Eric is taking over and we're working out the details," he responded. "But there are more changes. You, Jason, and Glen are also being let go."

There was that other shoe. I stared at him with a blank look on my face, too shocked to speak. The cold feeling turned to heat as my fear began to transform into anger. I took a deep breath and forced myself to tamp my feelings down long enough to respond.

"I understand Jason," I croaked, "and you're a little late with the news about Glen. But why me?"

"Why you?" he asked, as if the answer should have been obvious. "We didn't put you on the list, Linda. You did."

"What are you talking about? I didn't put myself on the list."

"Sure you did," he insisted. "During lunch you said that you wanted to pursue other endeavors. You said that if you had the choice you wouldn't be doing what you're doing now. Remember?"

I felt as if my words were being twisted. "Okay, sure . . . that's one of the things I said," I answered frantically, "but I also said that I didn't know what I wanted to pursue and I've struggled to figure that out for years, remember? I told you that information in complete confidence, Dan! I was hardly volunteering to be fired!"

"Well, be that as it may, Linda, this is the perfect time for you to go figure out what you really want out of life," he said.

"Actually, it is not the perfect time for me to go figure this out," I said sarcastically. "Frank is no longer with NomaSoft and doesn't have anything lined up."

"When did that happen?" he asked.

"End of last week."

"Why didn't you tell me?"

"I would have told you but I just found out last night. I didn't realize my job depended on what my husband was doing."

I felt a chill go through me as I thought about the repercussions of Frank and me both being unemployed. I walked around the desk, running my fingers through my hair, and fell into my chair. Dan eased into the chair near the door.

I just stared at the desk, shaking my head back and forth, unable to say anything.

"What happened with Frank?" Dan asked, still probing.

"It doesn't matter," I responded, my voice deep and cold.

As a salesman, faking empathy was Dan's bread and butter. For this reason, I had a hard time trusting him when he put a somber spin on his usually chipper voice.

"Linda, I don't know what to say. I thought we were agreed on this point," he said. "When we talked about who should stay with the company, you told me Ted's role was more important than yours. You said it would be easier for you to move on than Ted because he had to support his whole family, and you had Frank to help you out."

"I know what I said, Dan, but I thought we were talking in generalities," I said, irritated. I could tell he was trying to guilt me into taking responsibility for this mess and I wasn't biting. "It really pisses me off that you manipulated me."

"Linda—"

"Dan," I interrupted, "don't you dare tell me I am being overly sensitive!"

"I wasn't going to say that," he commented quietly.

I could hardly think straight. I kept picturing Frank sitting at the coffee shop with his laptop, terrified to tell me that he'd left his job. What the hell was I going to do now?

My face flushed as tears began to well up in my eyes. *Don't do this, Linda*, I told myself. *Don't let him see you cry.* I tried to hold back the tears by holding my breath and blinking quickly, but it didn't work. I reached up and wiped away the first few drops, but it quickly became impossible to staunch the flow.

"Crap, I didn't want this to happen," I said halfheartedly. I simply could not believe my luck over the past twenty-four hours. My mother always said bad luck comes in threes. If that were true, I still had one left. Even as the tears streamed from my eyes, I felt an urge to laugh hysterically over the dark humor of it all. *What could possibly come next?* I thought. *Is Andrew going to be rejected from the kindergarten program that we'd applied for?*

Dan handed me a Kleenex from the box on my desk. "I know how you feel," Dan said with compassion in his voice. "I feel the same, but I don't have any tears left. I stopped tearing up years ago. To tell you the truth, I am worn out from these start-ups and the constant bullshit from 'vulture' capitalists."

"Who else knows about this?" I asked, wiping my eyes with the Kleenex. "Were you guys talking about it in the conference room?"

"The team knows about you, Jason and Glen. We haven't told them about me and John yet. We planned to do it later today."

"I feel like an idiot," I said, wincing. "Everyone in the room knew I was getting fired before I did. How pathetic is that, Dan?"

"There is no reason to feel like an idiot." I looked up at him and he caught my eye. "Linda, there is no reason to feel like an idiot," he repeated, more slowly this time, as if speaking more slowly gave his point more gravity. A salesman to the end.

"Why did John say that everyone in the room was key to the company's survival?" I persisted. "Why would he lie through his teeth like that?"

"John is going through his own issues, Linda. He invested all of his money and ten years of his life to build this business. Now he's being asked to step aside by the board. He is not in the right frame of mind either, understandably so."

"This is a friggin' nightmare. How did we get in this mess? I know how we got into this mess. It was that acquisition that put us on the path of chaos. I knew we should have passed on the deal the minute I heard about it."

"All right, Linda, let's not go there again," he said gently. "What's done is done."

"Easy for you to say. You probably have a huge nest egg. Mine is limited."

"Frank will find a job in no time, Linda. He has an excellent reputation. You have nothing to worry about."

"Yeah, that's what he says, too. But a lot of people with awesome reputations are out of work right now, Dan. The competition is stiff."

"Well," he said, looking at me awkwardly, "I understand if you don't want to come back to the meeting."

We sat in silence for a few moments, neither of us knowing what to say. It was uncomfortable because I hated the quiet, but I could barely focus enough to think, let alone speak.

"So, how long do I have? When is my last day?" I finally asked.

"Well, we haven't decided that yet. The executives will have a different plan than the others. We have to figure out the timing and everything before the end of the day."

"Do you know if we'll be given any severance?" I asked hesitantly.

"Severance? I'm not sure. It will be up to the board."

"This really stinks," I muttered. "The timing couldn't be worse."

"I know," he responded. "If there was another way around this I would make it happen, but we don't have any options but to let people go. I know this is difficult, but we've got no other choice."

I looked at my watch. Only fifteen minutes had passed since we stepped into my office. I wasn't sure what to do next. Should I go to the meeting or hide in my office for the rest of the day? I contemplated staying put and riding out the rest of the day, but then I had a flashback to my earlier vision of my team staring at me from their cubicles. Regardless of what was happening in my life, I had to think of them.

"If it's all right, I am going back to the meeting," I told him. "I want to make sure that my team is represented and that decisions are made the right way."

Dan breathed a sigh of relief. "Of course it's all right. I want you at the meeting. You've been a huge contributor to this company." He stood up and held out his arms for a hug. I hesitated to get out of my chair, knowing that if I hugged him I was likely to start crying again. "Are you going to keep me standing here with my arms open or are you going to give me a hug?" he asked.

"I'm coming, I'm coming. Give me a second." I stood up and rounded my desk, holding my face tight to keep my emotions trapped inside. Dan pulled me in and wrapped his arms around me in a consoling hug. As we moved out of the hug, he grabbed my shoulders and looked into my eyes.

"Everything's going to work out, you know," he said, smiling.

"That's what they all say," I replied.

"You're a fighter, Linda. I'm going to give you a few minutes to collect your thoughts . . . just come upstairs whenever you're ready."

He opened the door and started to walk out, but turned around when I called his name.

"Dan, there's one more thing I think you should know."

"What's that?"

"I'm pregnant."

Dan stood in the doorway, staring at me in shock. I could tell he didn't know what to say or do. The word "lawsuit" couldn't have been far from his mind. I had no intention of suing, of course, but I couldn't help but take a secret pleasure in watching him squirm.

"What?" he asked when he found his voice. "How far along are you?"

"I'm not sure yet. Maybe eleven or twelve weeks."

"When did you find out?"

"I suspected it last week, so I took a pregnancy test. Frank doesn't know yet."

"Well," he said, clearly at a loss for words. My announcement really seemed to have thrown him for a loop. Finally he said, "Congratulations. Andrew will enjoy being a big brother." He forced a smile.

"I'm sure he will," I said. "And Dan—please don't say anything to anyone upstairs. I will tell them when I am ready." He nodded and headed back toward the elevator. As he walked away, I looked down the hall to make sure that no one else could have heard me. Thankfully, the coast was clear. I took a deep breath and closed my door for privacy.

I leaned my back against the door, closed my eyes and let the tears flow. *So, that's that,* I thought. *Frank and I are both unemployed.* In spite of my tears, I felt nothing. No anger. No sadness. No pain. Nothing.

As I stood there, the room started spinning so quickly that I had to sit down. I dropped into my chair and rested my cheek against the cool desk, breathing slowly through my nose to calm my nerves. *Maybe I just need something to eat,* I thought, as I moved my hand to the right-hand bottom drawer. I never had time to go out to lunch so I tried to keep healthy snacks in my office. I pulled a cheddar cheese rice cake out of the drawer and took a bite. It was a bit stale, but I ate it anyway, suddenly famished. I wasn't sure if it was the stress of the day getting to me or pre-baby sickness.

I picked up the phone and called Frank again.

"Hey, it's me," I said.

"Hi love, can you do lunch? Want me to pick you up?"

"No, I can't meet for lunch."

"What's wrong?"

"Everything is wrong."

"Did something happen in the meeting?"

"No, the meeting is fine. Dan just left my office."

"What did he want?"

"To tell me that I no longer have a job."

There was a brief pause on the other end of the line as Frank took in the news. "What?" he finally said. "You're kidding me."

"Oh no, Frank, I'm not kidding. I wish I were kidding."

"Are you okay? Want me to come and pick you up?"

"No."

"Are you sure? I'll come right now. It will only take me a minute to get Andrew ready."

"No," I sighed. "I'm going to finish the meeting. I have to make sure they don't throw everyone on my team under the bus."

"You don't have to do that, Linda."

"Yes, I do," I said firmly. "No one else at this company seems to care about employee loyalty, but I owe it to my team. Besides, I'm not about to let these guys think they got to me. Before I even walked in, they all knew I was on the chopping block, yet they kept me in the dark the entire morning. I feel like a complete idiot."

"Linda, it's not your fault. They're clearly choosing the quick fix over the long-term strategy, and it's going to blow up in their faces. They just lost the best talent they have."

"Doesn't feel that way," I said, struggling to hold back my tears.

"Did he say how much time you have?"

"No. He said we would work it out later today. I have no idea if it will be a day, a week or a month."

"Well, no matter when it is, hon, we are going to get through this," Frank said brightly. "Everything is going to be fine. I promise. This is just a bump in the road."

There it was again. That unwavering optimism, but rooted in nothing, I feared. I appreciated that Frank was trying to stay positive, but neither of us knew what the future held. I hoped he was right. At the moment, however, I couldn't quite share his faith.

"Okay, well, I have to go," I said brusquely. "They're reconvening at 1:00 and I need to freshen up a little."

"Okay, love. Call me when you get a break."

As I hung up the phone, my eyes landed on the picture on my desk of Frank and Andrew in our backyard. A picture paints a thousand words, but it can mask a thousand, too. The foundation of my life—everything that made me feel protected—was falling apart around me. My worst nightmare, that my life would follow the patterns set by my parents, seemed to be coming true.

I shook off the image as quickly as it came and went to the bathroom to freshen up my makeup. I was so stuck in my own head that I almost leapt out of my skin when I opened the bathroom door to see Kiley standing at the sink.

I'd met Kiley through a mutual coworker a few years back. To say that we hadn't hit it off immediately would've been an understatement. Although we were the same age and had worked at the same number of companies, I was a vice president and she was still a manager, which put an apparent chip on her shoulder that made her cool and aloof toward me. She was very talented but many people on the management team thought she was too aggressive. It wasn't until she had demanded a meeting with the CEO to inquire why she wasn't advancing up the ladder more quickly that we had become close. Dan had suggested to Kiley that I mentor her so that she could gain clarity on how her actions and communication style were working against her. She had approached his suggestion begrudgingly, but once we started working together, I found out that she was really a warm person at heart. For her part, she had actually adopted some of my advice and tested out new strategies to manage across and up the organization. From this pairing, our relationship had blossomed, and she ended up becoming my closest friend in Austin.

I'd been avoiding Kiley ever since I heard about the impending layoffs. If I were going to accidentally spill the beans to anyone, it would have been her. It's not that I didn't trust Kiley, but I knew how these things always went—if I let down my guard with Kiley, she'd likely tell someone else, and pretty soon the entire office would be abuzz with rumors. My best option was to keep my mouth shut and try my damnedest to fly under the radar until the whole thing blew over. If Kiley was losing her job, it might have been more difficult to keep her in the dark, but I knew for a fact that her position was safe. Still, I knew how Kiley's mind worked, and I had a feeling she was not going to be happy when she found out I'd been keeping a secret from her.

"Hey girl, how are you?" asked Kiley. "I haven't seen you all morning."

"I've been in an executive team meeting," I answered, more stiffly than I intended.

She looked into my face. I'm sure she could tell I had been crying. "Is everything okay?" she asked.

"Yes, of course," I said, feigning a smile. "I just . . . I just received a phone call from home about my grandmother. She's not doing very well." *Nice, Linda.* I thought. *Playing the sick grandmother card.* I made a mental note to call my grandmother when I got home and make sure she was doing okay.

"Oh, honey," she said, a worried expression on her face, "I'm so sorry to hear that. Is there anything I can do?" Good old Kiley. Always there to lend a helping hand.

"No, but thank you."

I felt terrible for lying to her, but I had been sworn to secrecy. It suddenly dawned on me that I was in the exact same position as the other executives had been in with me. The system made it practically impossible to do the right thing, no matter how good a person you are.

"Hey," I said, "I have to get back upstairs. Let's catch up later."

"Sure," she said with a sympathetic smile. She clasped her hands over mine. "I'm here if you need me, Linda."

I pulled my hands out of hers awkwardly. "See you later," I smiled and walked out. I was sure she already suspected I wasn't quite telling the whole truth. Kiley was not stupid and she knew me too well. When was the last time she saw me cry? Never!

When I got back to the meeting room, everyone else was already seated around the table. The eyes of my coworkers burned through my flesh like laser guns, blasting off pieces of my skin until I felt totally exposed. I tried to keep my head held high as I made my way around the table and into my seat. *Remember, Linda,* I told myself, *they're the ones who are making a mistake, not you. You're here because it's the right thing to do.*

"Linda," John said after I sat down. "Dan just told me that he gave you the news, and I must say, I'm impressed with your professionalism. It's nice that you can rise above these silly corporate politics to do the right thing for your team."

"Uh, thanks, John," I said, completely caught off guard. *Who the heck is he kidding?* I thought. *How dare he say that to me in front of everyone like this?* If he was trying to embarrass and humiliate me more, it was working. "I don't really want to talk about it right now, John," I said.

John nodded and winked conspiratorially. *Did he just snicker under his breath?* I wondered.

The rest of the afternoon went in much the same manner as the morning had. We argued back and forth about who would stay on the GO list. Some people were moved on and off the lists several times because we couldn't all agree on the level of value they contributed to the company. Some people were viewed as essential to the success of the business, while others never even received a mention. It was a grueling afternoon, but we finally developed a final GO list of seventy-five people. Once we had the list, we decided to make the cuts the following Friday morning. No matter which Friday—this, the next, or the one after that—it was still going to be a painful day that I was not looking forward to.

I spent most of the rest of the afternoon zoned out as Haley, the human resources manager, spoke at length about the downsizing process. She had created a termination checklist and distributed it for us all to review.

"Does everyone have a copy of the list?" she asked. "You will notice it's divided into two sections. The first section is called 'Terminated Employees' and the second section is called 'Remaining Employees.' We have to have a process for both groups." I drowned out her voice as I read through the first section, which contained such items as:

- Check for vacation owed to the employee
- Ensure the employee doesn't have any outstanding advances
- Take stock of the equipment the employee has outstanding
- Distribute calendar invite to your terminated employees
- Collect keys and badges
- Discuss Consolidated Omnibus Budget Reconciliation Act (COBRA)
- Distribute required state pamphlets regarding unemployment

Everything seemed fairly straightforward, except for the note to "distribute calendar invite to your terminated employees."

"What does this mean?" I asked Haley. Next Thursday, the day before the cuts were to be made, Haley explained that we would send out two calendar invites, one to the terminated employees and another to the remaining employees. The terminated employees would be asked to attend a group meeting in the boardroom, which was to be managed by Dan, Mark and Haley. As the employees were being informed that they no longer worked for the company, the IT department would terminate their access to the email server, network and telephone.

"That sounds incredibly demeaning," I said angrily. "Who came up with this plan?"

"It is the same process that other companies are using, Linda," Haley snapped back. It was the end of the day, and everyone was on edge.

"Who cares what the industry is doing?" I voiced loudly. "These are people we're talking about. That process seems like we're treating them like criminals."

"I agree with Linda," Eric interjected, "these are some of the best employees I've ever had and I don't want to treat them with disrespect. I think we can trust them not do anything heinous."

"Eric," Haley argued, "we don't know what people are capable of when they are upset or angry."

"How about if we modify the process to have IT terminate service at the end of the day?" Dan offered. "Is that okay with everyone?" His tone suggested that he was just as ready for the meeting to be over as the rest of us.

I glanced at my watch. It was nearing five thirty in the evening and I was aching to go home and see my family. Still, there was one lingering matter that needed to be addressed.

"I would like to discuss what kind of severance package we're going to offer the terminated employees," I said bluntly. "Do you plan to make recommendations to the board on what the severance package will contain?" All heads turned in my direction. I could tell they'd all been wondering the same thing but had been too nervous to ask.

"Actually," John said, clearing his throat, "actually, we're not going to offer any severance packages to the downsized pool."

"No severance?" I asked, shocked. "As in, none? We're just going to throw the employees out on the street and offer them nothing in exchange for their dedication and hard work?"

"Look, if it were my choice, I'd give everyone severance, but we're dealing with the VC's money," John protested. "We'd have to get a bridge loan from them if we offered a severance package, and they're simply not going to do that."

"It's always someone else's decision, isn't it?" I muttered.

"What's that?" John asked.

"Nothing," I said. "I guess I just didn't realize that we were in such a dire state. Maybe if I'd been invited to the meeting this morning I'd have a better idea of what was going on." I realized I was walking a thin line, but what were they going to do at this point? Fire me?

Dan turned toward me and looked me in the eyes. "Linda, John's getting a little ahead of himself. We don't know if we can do anything yet. I've asked Haley to evaluate our options to see what we can do."

I nodded, my lips pursed in annoyance. It had been a long day and I was ready to get the hell out of there.

"On that note, let's call it a day," Dan said. "What do you say we meet at 7:30 A.M. again tomorrow? At that time, we can review the information that Haley has on severance options, discuss if we need to compensate or provide bonuses to a few key employees to retain them, and finalize the details of the process."

Everyone agreed. The tension faded as we all got up to leave the room. I walked out of the room quickly, stepped into the elevator by myself, and hit the down button with brute force. Within minutes, I would be home with my family. I couldn't wait to get into my gym clothes and hit the treadmill. It was going to be a very aggressive run.

Chapter 7 Depressed

Friday didn't start off any better. The night before was another sleepless one for me, while Frank slept as soundly as a baby. The instant his head hit the pillow he was out cold, and within minutes the snoring kicked in—soft and steady at first, but gradually escalating to full-on gasps of air. Instead of shaking the bed violently or smacking Frank awake—my usual anti-snoring techniques—I gave up on trying to sleep and rolled out of bed at the bewitching hour.

I roamed around the house, peeking out the windows to make sure the neighborhood was safe and that no pesky animals were lurking in my yard. Living in close proximity to the woods gave us our share of unwanted visitors. Skunks visited regularly to snack on our flowerbeds, while our cypress trees were particularly attractive to deer. For some bizarre reason, the deer loved to grind their antlers on the trees, leaving huge, gaping holes like that of a well-groomed show poodle. Anyone driving by would think our gardener had gone crazy with the tree trimmers. Thankfully, the yard appeared safe for now.

I poured myself a glass of milk in the kitchen and chugged it down, and then headed upstairs to the family room. I thought some early morning TV might take my mind off my troubles, even though there's not much on at that time but infomercials for the anxious and depressed. Shivering, I settled down on the couch and pulled a blanket over me. I flipped the television on and landed on a semi-engaging infomercial for exercise videos. It was hardly the most productive way I could be spending my time, but it would do for now.

It wasn't just Frank's snoring that had led me to this dire sinkhole of entertainment. I was worried about the meeting today, and I was scared to death at the thought of Frank and I both being unemployed. I wished I could have just put a positive face on like the other executives, but the fact that I had been discarded as easily as so many other employees had really thrown me for a loop. I wished I could drown out all the questions that were circling around my brain. *How long would it take Frank to find another job? How long would it take me to find another job? Would we find jobs in Austin? Would we have to relocate to another city? Sell the house? And how would our relationship survive all the stress that was sure to come?* I needed to be sure I directed my hostility toward the right people and not at Frank. He sometimes got the short end of the stick because he was the only one that I shared my true feelings with, good or bad.

A soft creak in the hallway outside the family room made me realize that I'd drifted off to sleep. In a haze, I could hear Frank walking up the stairs and into the TV room.

"Linda, wake up," Frank whispered as he leaned over the couch. "It's 7:00. What are you doing up here?"

"I couldn't sleep again," I said, rubbing my eyes. "My mind wouldn't shut off."

"Aw, I'm sorry, love," he said sympathetically. "Listen, I'm going to go down and get the coffee ready. Do you want me to bring it up here?"

"No thanks. I'll come downstairs in a minute."

I lay on the couch for a moment, cringing at the thought of going to work. When I finally got off the couch and joined Frank downstairs, I lingered too long drinking my coffee and got behind schedule. My eyes were bloodshot from lack of sleep. I felt a bit nauseous so I ran to my bathroom in case morning sickness wanted to rear its ugly head. I stood over the toilet for a few minutes until the feelings passed. Standing there I realized that I hadn't yet gone to the bathroom and my bladder felt like it would explode. I pulled up my nightgown and enjoyed the morning flow. Looking down, I noticed a few red spots on my panties. *Oh crap, is that blood? Don't panic, you had spotting with Andrew.* I quickly grabbed the toilet paper and wiped to see if there was more blood. I almost passed out when I saw the volume. *Oh shit. This looks like a lot.*

"Frank, can you come here?" I yelled from the bathroom. "Frank, Frank, Frank, can you hear me?" *Oh no, what should I tell him?* I thought. I had told him the night before that I was pregnant and he had been so excited.

"Coming, love," Frank responded as he entered the bathroom. "Do you need toilet paper?"

"No, I'm bleeding."

"That's normal. You spotted blood when you were pregnant with Andrew. The doctor said that happens when your body changes."

"Not this much," I responded, as I shoved my hand out to show him the blood. "This doesn't look right. I wonder if it's all of the stress causing my body to act weird."

"I'm sure it's fine, love. Let's call Dr. Doss and tell him about it. I'm sure he'll tell us all is fine."

"I'll call him later this morning when I have a break. Can you make me something to eat cause I feel terrible."

"Don't worry yourself sick about this, Linda. You are already stressed enough."

"Easier said than done."

Frank whipped me up a piece of toast with peanut butter to calm my growling stomach. I rushed out of the bathroom and grabbed the toast and my car keys. It was only twenty minutes before my meeting started and I needed to rush if I hoped to make it on time.

"Let me drive you to work today," Frank said.

"You don't have to do that," I assured him.

"I know I don't have to. I want to. I think you could use a minute to relax."

We buckled Andrew into the car and headed toward the office, driving in silence most of the way. My thoughts were focused on today's meeting and the layoffs that would follow next week. I contemplated a few different motivational stories to use in telling the remaining employees about the layoff and their future with the company, but I couldn't seem to come up with the right words. With half the company losing their jobs, what could I possibly say that wouldn't come across as utter bullshit?

Frank pulled into the parking lot and I kissed both him and Andrew goodbye, then headed into the office for another dreadful day of layoff planning. I hopped in the elevator and went straight up to the conference room. Despite my best efforts at getting in on time, I was still running ten minutes late.

"Morning. Sorry I'm late," I said as I entered the room. Even though I was still reeling inside, I tried to sound pleasant to give them the impression that I was doing just fine with the news that had been dropped on me yesterday. The other executives grunted in unison.

"So, John," Eric began as I took my seat, "what did the board say about the layoff plans?"

"Well, they were okay with everything but the timing," John said. "They want us to move up the date to Tuesday morning."

"This coming Tuesday morning?" Haley asked in shock. "How are we going to be ready by then? What's the rush?"

I turned toward Dan, who looked pale. He stared down at his hands as he rubbed them on the edge of the conference table anxiously.

"The board wants to conserve as much cash as possible," Dan explained. He sounded like he was delivering a eulogy. "We tried to push the date we recommended, but they have all of the power right now. They're giving us a bridge loan to carry the company over until we figure out how to save Dick's deal."

Out of the corner of my eye, I could see Haley fidgeting in her chair.

"Haley," John said, "that means you'll need to work this weekend to get everything ready by Monday night."

"I can't, John," Haley answered, frustrated. "I'm going to Dallas this Saturday to see friends and I can't cancel my trip."

"Look," John replied firmly, "if it were my choice we would all be doing something we enjoy this weekend, but it is not. We need you to get everything ready for Monday, and I need you here at the office."

Haley didn't say another word. She just stared at the table in front of her with an angry look in her eyes. The tension in the room was unbearable. I decided to make it even more unbearable.

"Dan, what did the board say about severance?" I asked.

"Nothing," he mumbled.

"They said nothing?"

"No," he said, "we'll give nothing. We don't have any money to give."

Given the company's financial situation, his words shouldn't have come as a surprise; nonetheless, it felt like I'd been slapped in the face. The news of the layoffs was going to hit our employees out of left field. Finances were not openly discussed at company meetings, and we'd given them the impression that we were digging our way out of disaster. There had been a few rumblings from employees about the lack of sales and rumors of an acquisition, but I didn't think anyone knew we were so close to the edge. Now, not only did I have to tell my friends and loyal employees that they were losing their jobs through no fault of their own, I had to tell them that we couldn't afford to give them a penny on their way out the door.

I closed my eyes and rested my hands on my face, trying to erase the guilt from my mind. I couldn't bear to open my eyes for fear of bursting into tears. *This is not personal*, I said to myself. *It is just a business decision that is necessary to ensure the long-term viability of the company*. I wondered how many times I would have to repeat it to myself before I started to believe it.

As I sat there with my head in my hands, I decided that I couldn't just send my employees out into the world without any assistance. I sat up and turned to

Haley. "Haley, can you put together some recommendations on recruiters they can contact?" I proposed. "I mean, we might even want to hire some of these people back when the company rebounds, right? Helping them out a little bit would go a long way in demonstrating our commitment to them."

Haley stared at me with cold eyes, still upset over having to cancel her trip to Dallas. "I'm barely going to have enough time to put the mandatory paperwork together, let alone anything else. They can figure out how to find another job on their own time."

An intense scowl formed on my face. I expected more from these people.

"Look, Haley, I know you're annoyed about having to cancel your weekend in Dallas, but that was just about the most compassionless thing I've heard. It's bad enough that we're executing this whole plan so quickly, but we can't just slam the door on these people without giving them any help," I snapped.

Haley stared back at me with fury in her eyes. John jumped in, attempting to calm the situation. "All right," he said, "let's not get into a pissing match. No one feels good about doing this, but everyone needs to band together if we're going to turn this company around."

If I heard one more meaningless corporate platitude, I was going to throw up. John's comment felt especially useless in light of the fact that he was on his way out the door with the rest of us. I couldn't understand why everyone else seemed to find it so easy to turn their backs on all the people who were working so hard to make the company a success. I felt the need to do something, anything, to help these people.

"I can try and help them," I offered calmly.

"What kind of help are you thinking?" Dan asked.

"I'm not sure yet. Maybe I can help them network. Or I can offer to review their résumés. After all, résumés are a communication tool and I've certainly written my fair share of marketing pieces. It can't be that different."

"We need to be careful about offering help, because anything we say or do can be used against us," Haley interjected.

I whipped my head around toward Haley and gave her a cold glare. "I'm not planning on talking about the layoff with them, Haley. I just want to help."

"Linda, maybe if you help them 'off-hours,' on your own time, that would limit our liability," Dan suggested diplomatically. "Let's talk about it after the meeting." I resisted the urge to stick my tongue out at Haley. I could feel my helplessness starting to fade away a little now that I had a plan. Maybe the rest of them could just wipe their hands of their responsibility to our employees, but I couldn't live with myself if I didn't at least try to help.

The meeting ended around 3:00 P.M. with a plan established for how the rollout would happen next Tuesday. Haley had the most work to do over the weekend, but we all took on small assignments so that she wasn't overloaded.

At the end of the meeting, Dan asked me to stay behind. I told Dan that I'd meet him in fifteen minutes because I had to make an important phone call. The phone felt so heavy in my hand. Nervously, I dialed Dr. Doss's office to check in with the nurse. The receptionist answered and I asked to speak to nurse Donna. After a few minutes of holding, nurse Donna greeted me with a warm hello. "How can we help you today, Linda?"

I explained my story and she thought it best I meet with Dr. Doss in person. I had visited with him about a month ago to get a prenatal prescription so he knew I was pregnant. She scheduled me to meet with Dr. Doss at 7:30 A.M. Monday morning. Once my appointment was set, I walked to Dan's office.

"Are you okay?" he asked.

"Yes, I'm fine. Why?"

"Normally you're so friendly and polite. Today, you seem short and irritated."

"I have a lot to be irritated about," I replied, trying hard to stifle my anger.

"Listen, Linda, I know Haley isn't the easiest person to deal with sometimes, but I'd appreciate it if you weren't so hard on her. She is not happy about this, either."

I sighed deeply. "I understand that, Dan. I'll try to keep my anger in check. Is that all you wanted to talk about?"

"No, not really," he said. "I spoke to the board and we're going to pay you for three more months."

"But I thought we didn't have any money to pay severance," I said.

"It's not severance. We need you in business development to help close some deals in the pipeline."

"Business development?" I asked, confused. "I don't know how to sell."

"You're actually a very good salesperson. You just need some experience in the field. I want you to work with Steve."

Of all the employees I could have been placed with, Steve would have been at the bottom of my list. He was in his late forties and had worked in sales for his entire career. Back when guys like Steve entered the workforce, sales departments were still very much old boys' clubs . . . and if it were up to him, they would have remained that way. In my experience, the old-time sales guys had a harder time accepting women as equals than people in any other position. He was great at his job, but his intense lack of respect for women made him come across as egotistical and arrogant. It wasn't just me who found him aloof—he rarely spoke a word to anyone but Dan. Unfortunately for Steve, I wasn't the type of person to be ignored. If he had a problem working with me, he was going to have to get over it.

"Are you kidding me?" I said, laughing. "Did you mention this to him?"

"Yes. He said he didn't mind."

"Now you're really pulling my leg, Dan. I bet he had a ton of objections."

Dan laughed. "Okay, he did. But he's okay with it now."

"How did you get the board to approve keeping me longer?"

"I told them we needed you on some critical projects," he replied. "You have a solid reputation with the board so it wasn't that difficult. Two of the board members thought you'd be great in sales—they actually suggested moving you into sales a few months ago."

"Okay," I said after a moment. "I'll think about it and we can talk on Monday. Right now, though, I'm wiped and I just want to get out of here." With that, I picked up my briefcase and went outside to greet Frank and Andrew, who would gladly take me home.

❀❀❀

Monday morning came too quickly, and as always seemed to be the case, my happiness in one area of my life (being pregnant!) was offset by tragedy in another area (getting laid off). At the OB/GYN's office, the doctor listened for the baby's heartbeat.

"I can't hear the heartbeat," he observed.

"Why is that?" I asked. "Is it too small?"

"How many weeks do you think you are pregnant?" he asked.

"My guess is about eleven or twelve weeks, but I might be wrong."

"It might be too early for me to hear the heartbeat, but to be sure, I'm going to see if I can get you in for an ultrasound."

"Are you concerned?" I asked wearily.

"I just want to make certain everything is okay."

Dr. Doss had his nurse make an appointment across the hall at 8:00 A.M. for an ultrasound. My legs shook so uncontrollably that I nearly fell down. If Frank hadn't been there gripping my waist, I would have fallen to the floor in fear. I checked in and they walked me into the changing area immediately.

I heard many voices in the background, but I couldn't make out what they were saying. I sat on the bench, clasped my hands in prayer and rested my head on them. I didn't want to pray to God at that moment because the belief that something could be wrong was too overwhelming. *Stay positive. Stay positive. Stop thinking the worst.* I put on the standard hospital wrap and moved to the waiting area where Frank was sitting.

Only a few minutes had passed, but it seemed like hours. A plain looking lady in scrubs walked us into examination room four. The number four was my lucky number so I thought this was a good sign. In the room, I hopped up on the table restlessly.

"Don't worry, love." Frank said to minimize my nerves.

"What, are you for real? He sent us here for a reason, Frank. What the hell is wrong with you?"

"Linda, you don't know that yet. Don't get all worked up until we know for sure."

With that thought, the doctor entered the room and I felt a chill in my veins. He did not have a warm personality. He asked me to lay back on the table so I did. His cold hands moved the wrap away from my belly. As he squeezed the cold gel on my belly, my body began to tremble. I tried to distract myself by thinking about work, but it didn't work. All I could do was stare at the black and white image of my uterus on the computer screen, thinking, *Are you going to tell me what's going on, jerk?*

He pulled off his gloves and threw them into the wastebasket.

"There is no heartbeat," he blurted.

"It might be too early to hear it," I blurted.

"I'm not hearing it, I'm looking at it. You have a nonviable fetus," he said coolly.

"A what?" I could feel the vomit building up in my throat.

"I'm afraid the pregnancy didn't take. I estimate that the heart stopped beating a week or two ago. I'm sorry." He paused for a moment while his news sank in and then continued. "You have two options at this point. You can either wait for the fetus to naturally expel itself, or you can have it taken out. You'll want to talk to your doctor about the best option." With that, he left the room.

Beyond the shock of the news, there was no feeling. I tumbled off the table, with my arms spread wide to break the fall. Frank was quick on his feet and helped me regain my balance. Dazed and confused, I dressed quickly as I held back the panic rising in my body. A few teardrops fell from my eyes, but I wiped them away.

"Honey, are you okay?" Frank asked with tears streaming down his face.

"Yes, I'm fine. Let's get out of here. I need to get to work."

"Don't you want to go talk to Dr. Doss first?" he asked.

"No," I snapped. "I'll call and talk to the nurse later. I need to get out of here. Now."

My initial reaction was a confusing mixture of sadness and relief. Although Frank and I both wanted another child, I knew a baby would add a whole new level of stress to our lives. In a way, our employment issues had been a blessing. I'd been so wrapped up in dealing with the present that I hadn't yet become attached to the idea of having another baby. Whatever emotional trauma the loss stirred up, I simply pushed it into that part of my brain that was reserved for such things and went about my business.

❀❀❀

My face was whiter than a ghost when I stormed into the office, showing an angry disposition. I spent most of the day in my office behind closed doors. Kiley called me several times to talk, but I avoided her phone calls. Normally, I was the one in the office chatting up a storm and meeting with people, but I was afraid if I visited with anyone it would be impossible to hold my tongue on many fronts.

The team had decided to put two executives in each room to minimize liability and to ensure protection for the executives if someone didn't take the news well. Being the only female on the team, I suspected that decision was meant for my benefit. All of the other executives could certainly handle themselves in a physical manner. Truth be told, I could have handled myself just fine, too, but if one of my coworkers wanted to play the heavy, it was fine with me.

During work that day, several of the employees asked me about the topic of Tuesday's meeting. A few realized that they had been invited to different meeting rooms and questioned me about it, but I remained vague, explaining that Ravin must have made a mistake on the invite. They could sense something was up and they were, I'm sure, speculating endlessly about it. I could feel the tension floating in the office air all day.

That night, my stomach began burning as I prepared for bed. I took a double dose of Pepto-Bismol for good measure, and then sat in bed for awhile trying to read a book. After rereading the same paragraph three times, I decided to close the book—my ability to concentrate was gone. My mind was spinning with questions about how the employees would react to the news, how those who kept their jobs would feel, and how I could best offer my help to the employees we were terminating.

"Honey, you okay?" Frank asked as we rested quietly in the dark.

"Yeah, I'm okay. I'm just thinking about tomorrow." The Pepto wasn't doing much to help. Whenever I thought about the layoffs, my stomach started aching again. "I don't want to talk about it because I'll get worked up."

"I wasn't asking about the layoffs. I am asking about you and what happened today. Do you want to talk about it?"

"No. I don't. What's done is done."

"Honey, we need to talk about it," Frank insisted.

"No, I don't have to talk about anything. If you keep persisting, I'm going to leave this bed and sleep in the guestroom. Can you respect my needs?" My anger was beginning to swell and I concentrated hard on my breathing because I didn't want to break.

"Okay, love. Well, tomorrow is almost over," he said. He leaned over, kissed me on the lips and hugged me tightly.

"I know," I responded. His hug temporarily drove the butterflies in my stomach away.

He leaned back and gave me a comforting smile. "Well, I have two bits of good news."

"Oh really? What?"

"I have a meeting with ATX Ventures next week."

I smiled. "When?"

"Not sure yet. I'm still working with Ken's assistant to get on his schedule."

"That is good news! Do you think they'll have anything for you?" I asked sleepily.

"I'm not sure yet. Hopefully. If they have something in software, I'm sure I'll at least get the opportunity to interview."

I rested my hand on Frank's chest. "I pray they have an opportunity that fits with your background. I'm so skeptical because the market is bad and I haven't heard any news about ATX making investments recently. Make sure you pray to God tonight before falling asleep."

He rolled over to turn off the lamp on the side of his bed. "I do every night. I also say a few words to Grandma Sue and the rest of my angels."

"Hey, what's the second piece of good news you had for me?"

"Oh, I almost forgot. Hold on a second." He turned the light back on, reached for a white envelope on the nightstand and handed it to me.

The sealed envelope was from St. Gabriel's Catholic School. We had been waiting nearly a month for the letter to arrive. It would reveal whether Andrew passed the kindergarten entrance examination that would guarantee his admission into one of the most prestigious schools in Austin the following fall.

"When did we get it? Did you read it yet?" I asked.

"Yes," Frank said, deadpan. "I steamed it open, read it, and resealed it just so you could be surprised."

"You're joking, right?"

"I'm joking," he confirmed.

The arrival of the letter made me feel both excited and fearful. If he got accepted, we would be required to pay the $7.5K tuition bill before the start of school. If he didn't get accepted, I would be heartbroken. I wanted Andrew to have the very best that we could provide. Many of our friends thought we were crazy for wanting to enroll Andrew in private school when we lived in the best public school district in central Texas. There are very few other cities in Texas where every single school in the district received exemplary status year after year. Although important, we wanted Andrew to also have a Christian influence in his education.

"Let's open it," I encouraged. I pulled at the corner edge to get my finger under the glue and tore open the letter.

"Don't rip the letter, hon," Frank said.

I pulled out the letter and rested it on my chest. "Let's say a little prayer first."

We closed our eyes and each said our own little prayer. I didn't want to pray out loud because one part of me was hoping for an "accept" and the other part of me wanted it to be bad news. I suspect Frank felt the same way.

Slowly, I opened the letter and we began reading it together. "He's in. He got in! Oh, my goodness, he got in. I can't believe it."

Frank and I giggled uncontrollably and kicked our feet in the air in happiness. "Linda, I can't believe we're acting like a couple of school girls going to the prom. You would think he'd been accepted to Stanford!"

"With all the work we've put into this, it feels like he was accepted at an Ivy League school. Not to mention the price! Oh, what are we going to do?"

"He's going. Don't you agree?"

I paused for a moment in thought. The financial commitment might be tight, but Andrew's education was priceless. "Yes, I agree," I finally decided.

"Good," Frank said, smiling.

I gave Frank a few quick pecks on the lips and rolled over to my left side. I fluffed the pillow under my arms and placed the letter under my pillow in hopes that it would secretly bring us good luck. I yanked at the sheets until they came untucked from the bed. I'm not claustrophobic, but I despise having my body, especially my legs, constricted by anything. I can't handle the feeling of my feet being trapped in a cocoon.

Before I fell asleep, I gave one last thought to the events that would take place the next day. Tomorrow I would be responsible for stripping away several people's dreams, not to mention their ability to pay the bills. These were people who had invested heavily in their education and achieved great levels of success in their careers, just like we had always been told to do. People with husbands, wives, children. People who believed they were living the American dream. Now I was going to wipe it all away in one fell swoop, potentially destroying friendships in the process. My stomach churned as I closed my eyes and drifted into a restless sleep.

Chapter 8 Detached

Too often my dreams involved memories of decades past in which I was a tee-nager living with my dad on Walnut Street under a shroud of shame and fear. I remembered the house in vivid detail even though I had not seen it in over twenty years. In my memories, the small, red tile house looked dilapidated and abandoned. Once my dad got sick, he was no longer able to do any repairs. If I hadn't actually lived there, I would have assumed it was a crack house. Consi-dering some of the things that went on in the house, my assumption wouldn't have been too far from the truth.

On this night, I dreamt of an incident that happened when I was fifteen years old, getting ready for a party that my older cousin Debbie was throwing at her house. I sang along with "Girls Just Want to Have Fun" by Cyndi Lau-per as I blow-dried and curled my hair. When I determined that every hair was in its right place, I sprayed my lion's mane with Aqua Net, freezing it into an unshakable hair helmet. I sat in front of a mirror and tastefully applied enough makeup to alarm a Kabuki performer. It was 1984, and I looked hot.

When it was time to get dressed, I eased out of my makeup chair being careful not to let one hair fall out of place . . . not that it had much choice con-sidering the copious amounts of Aqua Net it was up against. I walked over to the dresser across the room in search of my favorite pink halter top. I couldn't find it in any of my clothes drawers, so I headed down to the cellar to see if it had been left in the washer or dryer.

It was late afternoon and the house was dark and eerily silent. I knew it wouldn't stay that way for long because my dad's drinking buddies always showed up around 5:30 or 6:00 P.M. with brown paper bags full of Budweiser and medicine bottles filled with marijuana. I had to walk through my dad's bedroom to get to the cellar. He was lying on his bed with his eyes closed, listening to music. For a second I stood over his bed, staring at him to see if he was awake. He was so still one would think he was dead. As I looked down at him, his eyes fluttered open. Reassured that he was still alive, I moved toward the door. Before I went down the stairs, he asked me to check on Fred on my way down to the cellar because he hadn't seen him upstairs all day.

Fred was a long-time friend of my dad who used to live in the house next door with his father. When his father died, Fred became a full-time drunk and drug addict who lived on the street. Although my dad had plenty of his own troubles to deal with, he could never turn down a friend in need. When he had found out Fred was homeless, my dad built a room for him in the cellar where he'd been sleeping for the past few years.

I stepped down the cellar stairs and called for Fred but he didn't answer. After a minute passed with no response, I opened the door to his room. The stench of stale beer and cigarettes wafted into my nostrils, causing me to gag. Fred lay propped up against the paneled wall, his legs stretched out in front of him.

"Fred?" I said.

I crouched down next to him and tried to shake him awake, but he didn't budge. I searched the ground around him for needles. Like many of the people in the house, Fred had a problem with hard drugs. I had been around it so much at that point that it barely even fazed me—people were constantly passing out from having pushed their limits. My first thought was that Fred had just overindulged and was nodding off, but I couldn't find any evidence of drug use. I leaned in closer and listened for his breath: nothing. With sudden horror, I realized he was dead. I backed up and turned on the light, my hands shaking.

Looking down at Fred, I noticed a bottle of Wild Irish Rose at his side, still half-wrapped in a paper bag. His face looked just the same as always—skin tough and withered, with deep, creased lines around his eyes and mouth. His hair was thin and greasy, his fingernails packed with dirt. He was only thirty-six years old, but he looked like he was in his fifties. Seeing him like that filled my heart with sadness—Fred had been a part of my family since I was just a kid. He was a very sweet man who grew up in a wonderful and loving family. Somewhere along the line, he just got mixed up in the wrong kind of lifestyle. My dad had tried to get him to stop drinking when he first moved in, but it's hard to avoid temptation when you're surrounded by it day-in and day-out.

And now here he was, dead on the floor of his grungy bedroom at far-too-young an age, a testament to the horrors of addiction.

I was about to yell up to Dad, but hesitated. Dad would be devastated by this news. *How could I tell him his best friend just drank himself to death in our basement? Maybe I shouldn't tell him at all, I thought. I'll just leave him here for someone else to find. After all, he wasn't my responsibility. Dad should have known what he was getting into when he invited Fred to live with us.*

After thinking about it deeply for a few moments, though, I realized that I couldn't just let Fred lay there. Someone had to take care of this, and since I was the one who discovered him, it would have to be me. As I walked upstairs to my dad's room, the thing that scared me most wasn't that my father would be angry, it was that he might cry. Nobody had ever seen my dad get choked up, not even me. Fred was one of the few people in the world who made my dad laugh. The last thing I wanted to do was to break his heart by telling him his best friend was gone.

I awoke with a jolt, my eyelids snapping open wide. A light from the next-door neighbor's backyard shone in through the window, and for once, I was thankful that the room wasn't very dark.

Chapter 9 Numb

Everyone was busy getting their day started when I walked into the office at 8:30 A.M. Tuesday morning. Before anyone could stop me, I darted straight to my office and closed the door. Before the door closed, I heard someone saying to me, ". . . <something> . . . lunch today . . . <something> . . ." but I shut myself away before I could see who it was. Stress makes people do strange things and I was not immune.

I was just settling in when Haley called to make sure that I was prepared for the 10:00 meeting. "Linda, remember to say only what is necessary," she reminded me. She sounded nervous about the upcoming day. If anything went wrong, there could be legal repercussions . . . and I'm sure that was the last thing Haley wanted to deal with. Still, I couldn't help but feel like she was trying to tell me how to do my job.

"Haley, we've been over this and I know what to say. Please stop worrying. You're going to make me nervous."

"All right," she said. "Just let me know if you need anything."

I hung up the phone and got to work, trying to ignore the pit in my belly. I ran through my speech several times to find the right tone of voice, pace and intonation. The slightest variation in inflection could make me come across as either emotionally void or too chipper. The more I recited the speech out loud, the easier it became to say, the words losing all meaning and just becoming a script. This did not bode well for my ability to seem compassionate.

The next hour and a half flew by in a blur of normal business, with people knocking on my door to ask questions about their projects, phone calls from other executives with questions about the layoff process, and countless email messages that needed a timely response. Every other minute I'd glance at the clock as it slowly, painfully inched its way toward the hour of reckoning. A few minutes before the meeting was set to begin, Dan stopped in to see how I was doing.

"I'm nervous, but prepared," I told him. "You know, though, I've been thinking a lot about what we can do to help the people who are being laid off. It really feels like we're turning our backs on them."

"Well, we basically are," replied Dan frankly. "I wish there was an alternative, but we just don't have the funding to give them any severance."

"I know," I sighed. "Business is tough. Still, I plan to stop by and talk to everyone we've terminated to offer my help with their job searches. That isn't a problem, is it?"

"No, just make sure they know that you're offering it personally and not as a representative of the company," he warned. "I'm sure the board wouldn't be too happy if they thought their bridge loan was going toward outplacement for the laid-off employees."

"Their generosity is staggering," I mumbled sarcastically.

At 10:00 A.M. I got up from my desk and left my office. As soon as I stepped into the hall, Janet, the woman who'd moved to Austin to be with her Russian boyfriend, was at my side. "Hey Linda, going up to the meeting?" she asked. "I'll walk with you."

"Great," I replied unenthusiastically. I stared at my feet as we walked down the hall to avoid looking in her eyes. We didn't say much on the way upstairs to the third floor. Janet chatted with other employees and I was busy reciting my speech over and over again in my head.

As I entered the room, I nodded to Glen, who was leaning against the wall at the front of the room. Most of the employees were seated at the conference table, engaged in busy talk. I overheard two people talking about an upcoming customer meeting, and I was reminded of the countless little things that would have to be taken care of after this day—after they were both laid off. I'd have to find someone else to cover that meeting.

I looked around the conference room at the twenty soon-to-be-former employees assembled there and braced myself for the speech I was about to give. The sun was gleaming through the windows surrounding the room, spirits were running high, and no one seemed to have any idea that I was about to ruin their lives.

My palms were sweating. I could feel beads of sweat drip down the back of my neck as I ran through the speech one final time in my head. Finally, I lifted my lips into the pleasant-yet-concerned smile I'd practiced in the mirror and I addressed my team.

"Good morning," I said to everyone. "You were asked to join me in this meeting this morning because I need to discuss the state of the company. It is no surprise to you that we haven't closed a deal in more than six months. During that time, the executive team worked endlessly to raise another round of funding from venture capitalists. Unfortunately, the market is not doing well and access to money is limited. The sales team, as well as all of us on the executive team, have tried to close numerous deals that are in the pipeline, but the companies we're reaching out to seem to be fearful of what is happening in the economy."

All eyes were fixated on me. I could see doubt and fear begin to surface on their faces. "We have no indication that we will get funding or close deals, therefore, the company has no choice but to reduce expenses." I removed my hands from the table, sat them on my lap and began rubbing my knuckles in a fast circular motion. "We searched for various ways to reduce expenses—such as eliminating license agreements and travel expenses—but it wasn't enough to keep the company afloat. We have no choice but to reduce staff."

My heart started beating faster and I could feel my throat tighten as I delivered the real message. "Everyone in this room is affected. Your positions have been eliminated, effective today. You will be paid through Friday, and you have until the end of the day to collect your things."

There was a tense moment of silence as my team attempted to comprehend what I'd just told them.

"What?" Janet said, breaking the silence. Tears started to crawl down her cheeks. "This can't be real."

"This can't happen to me, Linda," Sarah said, distressed. "I'm on an H1-B visa. If I can't find a job in less than two weeks, I'll be forced to leave the country."

I turned to Sarah with a look of sympathy. "I understand how upsetting this is," I told her. Then, addressing the larger group, "I'm sure you're all upset, and so am I. You aren't the only people affected. A total of seventy-eight people are being let go . . . including me."

"John and Dan don't know how to run a company and I should have left when I had the chance a month ago," said Jason, my lead product manager. Around the room, upset employees nodded in agreement. I started to understand why I needed Glen there to back me up.

"Team," Glen interjected, "we need to calm down so that Linda and I can communicate the process to you. I'm no longer with the company, either, but I understand that the decision to let me go is not personal. The company had to make some tough decisions to keep the business afloat."

The employees grumbled under their breaths, clearly unappreciative of Glen's tone. I wanted so badly to reach out to them, to tell them how much I empathized with what they were going through, but I couldn't do it for fear of saying something that would put the company at risk. Instead, I stuck to my script and tried to get through the meeting with as little emotion as possible.

"Haley has organized a packet of information for each of you that contains your last paycheck through the end of the week—including any unused vacation owed to you—your insurance form for COBRA and other information," I said.

"You really expect us to walk out this door, pack up all of our belongings and leave the building?" asked Steve.

"You can do it now or by the end of the day," replied Glen. "We have boxes for everyone in the hallway. Your email accounts and network access will be turned off at the end of the day."

"What about all that bullshit about employee loyalty?" asked Mark. "This is unbelievable. Do you think we might do something to the network? After all the time we've put into this company, this is a real insult."

"Everyone, please believe that I know what you're experiencing right now," I said. "I feel it too. All we can do is try to get through this as painlessly as we can. Haley has informed me that I am only authorized to give you your packet after I've collected all of the company's belongings. For those of you that have equipment at home, you will need to turn it in as soon as possible. Of course, Haley and I are willing to answer any questions that you have about benefits, the process or anything else that comes to mind."

As I spoke, I became painfully aware that my words were not making anything better. This was not how I'd imagined the meeting going. I didn't think anyone would be jumping up and down with happiness at the prospect of being unemployed, but I assumed they might give me a little sympathy when they learned that I was leaving, too. But the expressions on their faces told me that, no matter what the circumstances were behind the layoffs, no one was in much mood to sympathize with the management.

"Listen," Glen said, moving to the center of the room. I stepped back to give him the floor, relieved to get out of the spotlight. "No one wanted this, and no one was prepared for it. I know that John and Dan—both of whom are walking out the door with you, by the way—have been agonizing over this decision for a long time.

"The truth is, working at this company has been one of the best experiences of my life. There's more talent in this room alone than I've seen in any other company I've worked for. But we all know the reality of what's going on out there. Companies are shutting down left and right. We had a great product and a great team, but no matter how hard we worked, who's to say we would've been able to last in this economic climate?"

As he spoke, his voice began to quiver and his eyes filled with tears. He raised his finger to say "give me a second" and wiped the tears from his cheeks. It was a dramatic moment that quietly redirected the energy in the room, making it clear to the employees that Glen and I weren't the enemies.

When he collected himself, he continued. "Linda won't tell you this, but I sat in those meetings with her, and she fought tooth and nail for you guys. But in the end, there just wasn't anything we could do. We're in the same boat. I know I wouldn't be leaving if I didn't have to. You guys are the cream of the crop, though, and I'm sure you'll all land on your feet. I'm going to miss being with you every day, and I'm sure Linda will, too."

"I will," I said quietly as I wiped tears away from my eyes.

The mood in the room had shifted. Glen's speech seemed to have gotten through to them. I thought it best to hedge my bets while I was ahead and say as little as possible until the meeting was over.

Soon after that, we dismissed the group. I could feel my coworkers staring through me as they walked past, but I kept my eyes focused firmly on the floor. After they left, Glen and I sat in silence, trying to come to terms with what had just happened.

"Are you okay, Glen?" I asked after a few minutes.

"Yeah, I'm okay. I've been through this before, but it's never easy."

"Do you think you'll have a hard time finding a new job?" I asked.

"I have no idea. I haven't even begun to look yet, but I know the market is not good."

"So they say," I replied. "Well, I guess I should go back to my office, in case anyone's waiting to yell at me for destroying their life."

"Linda, you did a good job," he said, patting me on the arm. "But one word of advice: be careful about what you say behind closed doors. You never know what people will do when they're desperate."

I shuddered at the tone of his voice. Glen was an odd duck. One minute he was making people cry with his passionate speech about how much he was going to miss them, and the next minute he made it sound like the office was filled with murderers. *What exactly will people do when they're desperate?* I wondered.

I was hoping to make it to my office with no interruptions, but of course, that wasn't going to happen. God forbid I should actually have a stroke of luck every once in awhile. As I stepped off the elevator and rounded the corner, I could see groups of employees huddled in tight circles around their cubicles, deep in conversation. One of the first people I saw was Kiley, surrounded by a group of her teary-eyed coworkers. The minute she saw me, she broke away from her group and stepped right up to me.

"Linda, what happened?" she snapped.

The dam that had been holding back my emotions suddenly snapped, and I burst into tears. "I didn't have any choice!" I wailed. "It's just business! Cash flow! Sustainability!" I was jabbering nonsensically.

Kiley stared at me, a tense but empathetic expression on her face. I could tell she had more to say, but out of respect for our friendship she remained calm in front of her coworkers. It was a lot more than I could say for myself.

"Can I speak to you alone?"

I nodded quickly and invited her into my office.

"I thought we were best friends, Linda," Kiley said when the door was closed. Her voice lay somewhere between anger and severe disappointment. "How could you not tell me about this? Or at least give me some kind of hint?"

My emotions suddenly veered from sadness and regret to anger. If she was such a great friend, why couldn't she try to see things from my point of view? "Do you think I wanted to keep this a secret from you and everyone else?" I asked. "Do you think I enjoyed knowing this was coming, yet having to keep it bottled up? Besides, why should you need to know anything about it? You're not even getting laid off!"

"I should know something about it because it affects me, and because we're friends," she said angrily. "I don't know if you enjoyed it or not. But the fact is, you knew that half the company was getting laid off and you didn't say a word to me. Now I know why you've been avoiding me for the last two weeks. What did I do to offend you?"

"Nothing, Kiley," I insisted. "This has nothing to do with you. I'm an executive at this company. You know that I lead with transparency, but there are times that I can't share everything. You of all people should understand that."

"Oh, don't give me that corporate nonsense," she said. "People are freaking out right now. I don't know what to say to them to give them hope."

"I understand their feelings and it's eating me alive," I pleaded. "It's been eating me alive ever since I heard about it last week. I was as surprised then as you are now. This is no picnic for me, either Kiley . . . I'm losing my job, too, you know!"

We stared at each other in silence. Heartbreak was written all over her face. My frustration began to dissipate, replaced by guilt over the way I'd kept Kiley in the dark. I had to speak to stop myself from crying again.

"I'm sorry, Kiley," I said, placing my hand softly on her arm. "I hope you're okay. I know it's going to be tough working here with so many people gone, but at least they aren't shutting the doors. They must have something of value. Maybe this will be the best thing that ever happened to the company."

She sighed, and for a moment I imagined what she must have looked like as a child being disappointed by a parent.

"I know," she whispered.

She gave me a quick hug and walked out of my office. I watched as she gathered her stuff together and went back to her part of the building, never bothering to turn around. The scene was so devastating that it took me some time to realize that everyone in the office was staring at me. As soon as I could move, I closed my door and made my way to my tissue box.

The pattern repeated throughout the rest of the day, with one employee after the next entering my office and asking why they were chosen over other employees who they thought didn't deserve to remain at the company. Some employees understood that it was a business decision and left gracefully. Others were so angry that it scared me to be alone with them in my office. Most, though, were in utter shock and didn't know quite what to say or do. Those were the most difficult people to deal with, because their emotions were frozen.

It was nearly 7:00 P.M. when I finally left for the day. When I exited the building, Frank was waiting for me by the door with Andrew. He wrapped his arms around me and led me to the car.

We drove home in silence, or at least I think we did. I was so lost in my own thoughts that I wouldn't have heard a word Frank or Andrew said to me even if they were speaking. More than anything, I felt awful about how I treated Kiley. I understood why she was so upset, but it killed me to think our friendship might be over due to something that was completely out of my control.

"Oh, by the way," Frank told me as we walked in the door, "Kiley called."

"She did?" I asked nervously. "What did she say?"

"She sounded shaken up, but I think she understands what you had to do."

"What should I do?" I asked. "Should I call her back?"

"Not right away. Give her a little time to let it all sink in first. You both have raw emotions right now. If you call her back right away, you might just end up making things worse."

He was right, of course, but he still had to put in a lot of consoling time before I managed to stop freaking out about Kiley and the rest of the day's events. By the time we stopped talking, I was pretty well exhausted, so I went to bed early. I took a few aspirins from the kitchen cabinet to combat my stress headache and swallowed them with a glass of skim milk. As they began to work their magic on my aching head, I drifted into yet another restless night.

PART 2
TRANSITION

Chapter 10 Hopeful

The past week had been one of the worst times of my life. I was finding it diffi-cult to distance myself from the negative emotions and levels of stress that were taking over. The nights grew longer and I became increasingly more anxious during my sleep.

I woke up early again and looked at the clock. It was 3:17 A.M. I knew I'd never get back to sleep, so I sat on the edge of my bed with my legs curled snug-gly underneath my nightgown, anxiety about work once again dominating my thoughts. For two years, I spent nearly nine hours a day with the people in my office, building relationships through the trials and tribulations of growing a company. The people at Trifinity had become family, and now my time with them was over. Never again would I sit in the boardroom with my team. We wouldn't just magically reassemble at another company. We would never again send each other into laughing fits in the break room or get together for sponta-neous drinks after work.

I'd been breaking into tears at the drop of a hat over the last few days, but none of the tears had been shed for my coworkers. My sadness came from feel-ing sorry for myself. This had all been done behind my back, leaving me feeling blindsided and devastated. *How could I have not seen this coming? How could I not have been included?* Any normal person would have been crying alongside the others, sharing in their pain as a friend. I felt inhuman, lifeless, and alone. Where were my feelings?

I left the bedroom and strolled through the hallway on my way up to the game room. The house was quiet except for the humming of the refrigerator. In the distance, I could hear a lone dog barking. As I walked up the stairs I peered out the oversized window and paused, wondering how many other sleepless people in Austin were doing the exact same thing as me.

I finished climbing the stairs and walked into the game room, pounds of self-pity weighing down on my shoulders. As I slumped onto the couch, I heard my mother's voice in my head, chiding me, "Only the weak of heart sulk in a corner when things go wrong. You're acting like a little girl. What are you worrying for? No one gives a shit about you in this world." Weakness had not been tolerated in my home. You had to be tough to survive my mother's sharp tongue. Her gift for making me feel bad about myself was unparalleled. In some part of her mind, she probably thought she was helping me grow up to deal with the same cruel world she grew up in. All it did, though, was teach me how to freeze my feelings, like an iceberg anchored deep in the ocean. My eternal struggle in life has been to figure out how to melt the iceberg.

Thoughts of my mother tended to evoke anger and resentment in me—the same fuel, fortunately, that often energized me to break out of my box and try a new approach. As I sat alone in the game room staring at the black screen of the TV, I began growing restless. I had such an innate need to always do everything right, to always do what everyone expected of me, to please my superiors, to put everyone else's needs above my own. I had been this way for as long as I could remember, and I was sick and tired of it.

I turned on the TV and flipped through the channels but nothing interesting caught my attention. With nothing better to watch, I selected a fitness infomercial but it was near the end of the program. Another program came on about anxiety and depression and I was just about ready to change the channel when a woman my age appeared and started talking about her problems. She used the word self-pity in her story and it made my skin crawl. I knew I was in a funk, but I was certainly not depressed like these people. They had serious problems.

As I lay on the couch watching a dozen or so people tell their stories, I thought about my own behavior. I'd been moping around the house with the attitude of, "Oh look at me, I'm so miserable and I have good reason to be miserable." Frank and Andrew were very supportive with kind words and hugs, but my negative self-talk overruled. I knew I had to move away from this destructive pattern, but didn't know how. With every ounce of energy I could muster, I forced positive thoughts into my head.

Tomorrow was going to be a new day and a new Linda. Something in me was changing. I could feel it bubbling up in my veins. The feeling was foreign to me—it felt a little akin to arrogance, but without the negativity that accompanied feeling superior to others—and suddenly it dawned on me what it was: confidence. It was an emotion I'd never experienced before, a feeling of self-empowerment, a sudden understanding that I was of value and that I had something to offer the world. I'd always known that I was good at my job, but I had a hard time attributing that to anything inside me. I knew how to play by the rules and do what I was asked to do. This, however, this felt different. *Yeah*, I thought, settling into the new feelings, *I think I can work with this!*

Bursting with sudden, nervous energy, I grabbed a pen and paper and began crafting a plan for handling the layoff on my own terms. *Why can't I help these people in some small way?* I thought. *I don't work for the company any longer. They can't tell me what to do.* Inside, I could feel the layers of fear that had held me down for years beginning to melt. *No one owns me and I don't owe them anything. I will be happy to pack my bags earlier if they have a problem with me lending a helping hand.*

The first and most important step was to figure out what people needed to find a job and what I could do to help. I began jotting notes down on the paper. In marketing, I was responsible for selling a product or a brand. In this case, I decided, the product or brand was the job seeker. *Why can't the same principles apply to a person as to a product? To find a job, people must identify their talents (features), the value they can bring to an organization (benefits), their level of compensation (price) and how to get their foot in the door at interesting companies (launch plan).* I scribbled furiously, getting more and more excited about the idea. If I could successfully market difficult-to-understand products, then surely I could market people. How hard could it be?

A few hours later, I had my plan in hand. I was so eager to get into the office that I opted for the quick-ready program—no shower, quick hair fix, light makeup, casual clothes. I wiggled a pair of earrings into my earlobes and shouted out to Frank as I made my way out of the bedroom.

"Frank, I'm not hungry this morning. I am going to head out a bit early today. Can you hear me?"

"Just a second, love."

"Where are you?" I asked.

"In the bathroom."

Why do I even bother asking? I thought.

A few seconds passed as I collected my things and tossed them into my briefcase. "You done yet?" I called out.

The toilet flushed and Frank scurried out of the bathroom. "I'm right here, jeez," he said, zipping up his pants. "What's the rush?"

"I'm just anxious to get into the office," I voiced assertively. "I'm going to put a plan into action to help some of the people who were let go."

"Really?" he said with curiosity. "When did you come up with this plan?"

"I've been working on it all morning. I couldn't sleep."

"What are you going to do?"

"I'm going to send a message to some of the employees who were let go and let them know that I can help with their résumé, networking, and stuff like that."

"Sounds good, love. If anyone can help them, it's you."

"I hope so," I said. "All right, I gotta run. Give Andrew a big hug for me . . . I'll call you when I get to the office."

✿✿✿

Once at the office, I closed my door and fired up the computer. Instead of being demoralized by the harshness of the fluorescent lights and the drab monotony of the plain white walls, I decided to use them as inspiration. This was exactly why I needed to get out of here. Working at Trifinity wasn't exactly killing me, but I did feel like I was suffocating from a lack of creativity and intimacy in my job. I'd spent months upon months feeling bored with my career, and I suddenly understood why. My job required me to focus on the features and functions of software, when all along I would have been much happier focusing on people.

I pulled the final layoff sheet from my sterile, grey, metal desk and spread it out on the desktop. Next, I opened up my email program and composed a message to the laid-off employees. The message read:

> Hi,
>
> If you need assistance with your job search, please let me know. I am willing to review your résumé, help you network around town or help you prepare for an interview. If I can market products and services successfully, surely I can help you market yourself. This help is being offered by me personally and is NOT sponsored by the company in any way. Since I am still working, I will be available to help you Monday thru Friday during the fol-

> lowing hours: 7:00-8:00 a.m., 12:00-1:00 p.m. and
> 5:00-6:00 p.m. Feel free to give me a ring or send
> an email if you think you might benefit from my
> help.
>
> Linda

I hesitated briefly, contemplating whether to ask Dan for permission. In the end, my independent nature won out and I pressed the send button.

I was feeling fidgety, so I picked up my coffee cup and headed to the break room to get a drink. When I entered the break room, a few people were standing around making small talk. I waited for the coffee to get ready and tried to make myself unnoticeable.

Just as the coffee finished brewing, I heard a recognizable stride making its way toward the break room. It was Dan coming in for his morning brew. He walked in the doorway with a look of forced conviviality, as if he'd just finished a performance and was walking out before a rapturous crowd to take his bow.

"Good morning!" he exclaimed. His voice was much too chipper and his smile too big in light of everything that went down the day prior. "Everybody looks so somber. Cheer up, it's a new day."

If he noticed the undercurrent of resentment in the room, he chose to ignore it. I grunted and turned my back on him to fill my coffee cup. Unphased, he sidled up next to me at the coffeemaker. "Hi, Linda, you look nice today," he said, beaming.

"Thanks," I said, staring at him blankly. It was fine with me if he wanted to act like everything was business as usual, but I didn't have to play along. I did, however, still need him to sign off on my employee assistance plan.

"Dan, do you have a second?" I asked. "I need to speak to you."

"Of course I do. Come on back to my office."

Dan filled his oversized, company-branded coffee cup and then we headed to his office. The only sound in the hallway was made by our feet brushing against the dingy commercial-grade carpet. For the first time, I noticed how depressed the office felt, with its scuffed walls and its almost overpowering quietness.

Dan had a large office with an oversized desk, a round table and a panoramic view of downtown Austin. I'd had the same view once, but awhile back, I had opted to move downstairs to be closer to my growing team. It wasn't like I had moved downstairs because the office was big and made me feel important—the downstairs office was a quarter the size of the upstairs one and it didn't even have a window. It felt like a jail cell. I had moved because I didn't want to separate my team. We had such great synergy, but the only way to keep the growing team together was to change places with sales support. It was just another example of how I'd sacrificed my quality of life for the good of the company.

"What's on your mind?" Dan asked, taking a seat behind his desk.

I settled into the chair opposite him. In spite of my newfound sense of confidence, I was still a little nervous that Dan wouldn't respond well to the memo I'd just sent.

"Well, I just wanted to let you know that I sent a memo to the employees we let go, telling them I'm available to help them if they need it."

Dan put his fingers to his lips in thought. "Okay," he said after a moment. "You know what, Linda, as long as you do it on your own time and still continue to do your job, it's fine with me."

Dan's response caught me off guard. I'd been bracing for an argument. "That was easy," I responded.

"What did you expect? I'm not heartless." He shook his head, mystified that I could possibly doubt his good intentions.

I leaned into my chair with a sigh. "I know you're not heartless, but this whole process sure is," I said.

"Well, you're new to this. It's always tough your first time around," he replied.

"My first and my last, hopefully. I don't know if I can handle going through this again."

He nodded deeply in an approximation of concern.

"Well, I've gotta get going," I said, "I have work to do."

I walked out of his office knowing that I would never interact with him professionally again.

As I left his office, it dawned on me that for the first time since I'd started working at Trifinity, I had absolutely nothing to do. *How should I spend my time now that I'm not a part of the team? Am I still responsible for managing the team until my last day, or can I just do whatever I want? Am I supposed to call Shep to ask him to let me in on some deals? Am I supposed to just call on accounts?* I didn't feel real motivated to plan my future right now, and I had little desire to speak to anyone on my staff.

I returned to my office and fired up my computer. No new email. I contemplated surfing the web, but I barely even knew where to begin, having never had this much free time before. I sometimes read the news online, but I didn't really feel the need to surround myself with more negativity at the moment.

For lack of a more exciting idea, I pointed my browser at Monster.com to see what types of marketing opportunities were available in Austin. In the search area I entered *VP Marketing*. In the location bar I typed *Austin, TX* and hit "go." A few listings popped up for sales, telemarketing and retail jobs. Much to my disappointment, there wasn't a senior position in the bunch. I refined the search by adding quotation marks to *"VP Marketing"* and hit search. No results found. Next, I tried *"Director of Marketing."* Still no results. I played with the keywords for about another twenty minutes using different combinations and testing different cities. It was hopeless. Almost no one was hiring.

As depressing as it was, I can't say I was surprised. Every day, another dot-com company was closing its doors. How on earth would I be able to find a job in this market? Even though I'd been in Austin for many years, I didn't have a lot of friends in the high-technology space. The few friends that I had in high tech had been laid off and were also looking for work. They wouldn't be any help. "What the hell am I going to do?" I whispered, as I closed my eyes and rested the back of my head against the seat.

At lunchtime, Frank came by to take me out for Chinese. The morning had put a damper on my mood and I treated his presence with all the warmth of a lizard in a snowstorm. True to form, Frank took it all in stride. It wasn't so much the loss of the job that had me worried. I'd wanted to get out of marketing for a long time and I recognized that in some ways, I had needed this push to rethink my career. No, the real problem was that several hours after I'd gone out on a limb and offered my services to the company, I had yet to receive a single response.

On the way to the restaurant, I was filled with anxiety about the impression my email might have given people. *I wonder if I came across as condescending, as though I didn't believe they knew how to search for a job on their own? Of course they aren't interested in working with me,* I thought, the voice of my mother ricocheting around my head. *I have nothing spectacular to offer. I'm a marketing person with experience promoting products and services. I don't know the first thing about job placement.*

As we pulled into the parking lot of the restaurant, I shook my head, attempting to clear out the negativity. *It doesn't matter,* I told myself. *The employees are smart, intelligent professionals who have been responsible for finding their own jobs since college. If they need my help, they'll ask for it. In the meantime, I need to focus on my own job search.*

Frank put his arm on my shoulder and smiled. "Let's go eat. I'm starving," he chimed.

"Okay," I said. I opened the door, walked briskly toward Frank and gave him a hug. "Thanks for being you," I whispered. He took my hand in his, and together we walked into the restaurant.

Chapter 11 Faith

From the beginning of our relationship, Frank and I had a tendency to get in over our heads. A few days after the night we had first met, when he "accidentally" left his watch at my apartment, we connected at work via email. He was out of town at a conference so I couldn't just walk over to his cube and give him his watch. When he got back to town he asked me out for a casual, no-strings-attached dinner and I accepted. I figured it would be good to have some male friends in Nashua to hang out with.

Early on, I had no real interest in him beyond being friends—I was only twenty-three at the time, and his head was covered with salt-and-pepper hair that made him look as if he were well into his forties. After talking with him for awhile, however, I learned that he was only five years older than me.

"You're only twenty-eight?" I asked. "Then what's with the . . . I mean . . ."

"The white hair?" he asked. "I don't know. It's been this way since I was twenty-two. I guess I must have seen a ghost!" he grinned.

We met several times after that night and I grew to be awfully fond of him; still, I had a hard time getting over the white hair. When we went out together, people looked at us as if we were father and daughter. I felt like a jerk for making a big deal out of it, but it was pretty embarrassing—I wasn't too keen on being perceived as a trophy wife.

"It is not a big deal," Frank told me when I finally confessed my feelings. "I've always wanted to change it, too. I've just never known how to go about it—I need a woman's expertise."

"What a coincidence!" I exclaimed. "I'm a woman!"

He laughed and I felt relieved that I hadn't hurt his feelings. We immediately hopped in the car and drove straight to Walgreens to pick up hair dye.

We bought a temporary brown dye and went back to his house to roll back the ages. Neither of us had experience with hair dye, but the directions made it sound simple: create the mixture, apply to hair, rinse. Moments later, Frank was seated at the kitchen table with a towel wrapped around his shoulders and I was slathering his head with the goopy brown mixture. As per the instructions, we let it sit for thirty minutes and rinsed.

Frank towel-dried his hair and we stepped back to admire my handiwork. "Hmm," I said, comparing Frank's head to the before-and-after pictures on the package, "well, the good news is that it no longer looks like your hair is going gray. The bad news is that now it looks like its going chestnut."

His hair was no longer black and white. It was now grey with flecks of brown. Whereas before he had looked older than his years, he now just looked like a guy with a bad dye job. We decided we must have removed the dye too soon and headed back to Walgreens to pick up another kit.

Having come to the realization that this was not going to be as easy as we initially assumed, we spent a little extra time scrutinizing our alternatives. The shelves were lined with temporary, semi-permanent, and permanent dyes in dozens of shades from pale brown to black brown. The amount of options was overwhelming.

"Um ... how about this one?" Frank asked, holding up a box featuring a picture of a smiling older man with dark brown hair. A woman who appeared to be in her fifties was draped around his shoulders, sending a clear message to potential buyers that this was the dye to go with if you wanted to drive middle-aged women crazy.

I looked at the box. "This is permanent. I'm not sure we should go with permanent. It sounds a little ... well ... permanent."

"Why not?" he asked. "We liked how the other hair dye worked, we just needed to keep it in a little longer. I want it to last. Permanent seems like a good choice," he declared.

"Does permanent dye work the same way as temporary dye?" I asked, staring at the box in concentration.

"It ... should?" Frank said haltingly.

"All right," I said. "If you're game, I'm game. Let's give it a shot."

We returned to Frank's place and started the process all over again. This time Frank jumped into the shower to rinse off the dye so that I didn't get it on my clothes. As he showered, I flipped through a copy of Reader's Digest that was sitting on the coffee table. Between the MILF-magnet hair dye and his choice of reading materials, I was beginning to wonder whether Frank was indeed as young as he claimed. I did a quick scan of the room—if I saw a bowl of butterscotch candies sitting on a doily somewhere, I was out of there.

The water quieted down and I heard the shower curtain open. A muffled voice came from behind the bathroom door, but I couldn't quite make out what he was saying.

"How's it looking?" I shouted, setting the magazine down on the table.

This time, the message was loud and clear.

"Holy crap!" Frank yelled.

I laughed nervously. "What is going on? Does it look good? Are you going to come out and show me or do I have to keep guessing?"

He joined in with my nervous laughter. "It would appear that we picked the wrong color."

The door swung open and I looked up. My hands shot up to cover my mouth as I gasped in horror. Perched atop his head was a thick layer of hair so black it looked like it could trap sunlight. But that was not the worst part. All around his head, a half-inch strip of black dye traced the outline of his hair from ear to ear. He looked exactly like Count Dracula. No, scratch that. Count Dracula, at least, has some amount of sex appeal. He looked exactly like Eddie Munster.

I could not control my reaction. I burst into a spasm of gut-busting laughter that left me gasping for air. I focused all of my concentration on controlling myself, but the more I tried to stop, the harder it came out. I keeled over and hugged my stomach while stamping my foot on the floor, the pain of stretched muscles shooting through my stomach.

Frank looked at me with a grimace. Clearly, it wasn't quite as amusing from where he stood. *Linda, stop laughing,* I thought. *This poor guy just colored his hair to please you and you are being a total nut. Get a hold of yourself!*

"I am not laughing at you," I gasped, "I'm really not. When I get nervous I laugh uncontrollably. Just . . . give me . . . a second . . ." I said, before bursting into another round of guffaws. Eventually, I managed to calm myself down enough to carry on a conversation. I stepped back and took another look at our handiwork. "We must have left it on too long," I determined, flushing and giggling under my breath.

Frank stood before the mirror, staring at his hair with a look of pure terror. "Oh, my God, what happened to my face? Is this stuff going to come off? I look like I've been mining for coal with my head!"

"Do you think it would help if we matched your eyebrows?" I asked.

Frank looked at me with an expression that was so hopeless and pathetic I couldn't help but start giggling again. As my laughter started ramping up again, he broke into a wide grin, until he finally just couldn't hold it in any longer. We clutched our stomachs and roared together as tears of laughter filled our eyes.

"All right, all right," he chuckled after a few minutes, "let's get serious. Do you know how to get this stuff off my face? I have a meeting tomorrow with an important client and I can't go in looking like I got my hair done by the shoeshine guy."

"Let's see what we can do," I said.

Frank moved to the dining room table. I grabbed a facecloth from under the bathroom sink and doused it with a liberal amount of soap. I then returned to the kitchen and started rubbing the cloth briskly over Frank's face.

"Ow!" he yelped. "You're going to give me a friction burn!"

"Sorry," I said. "I'm trying to be gentle but I'm going to have to really scrub this sucker if we want it to come off." After thirty minutes of scouring his face with a combination of soap and rubbing alcohol, we managed to remove most of the black eclipse.

The next step was figuring out what to do about his hair because it looked absolutely, positively awful. We contemplated the idea of waiting until the next day and getting Frank's hair fixed by a professional stylist, but his early morning meeting made the problem more pressing than it might have been otherwise. Having ruled that option out, we took to the web. A search of the phrase "*hair color disasters*" led us to a L'Oreal hair color removal kit that was available at most major drug stores. We returned to Walgreens for the third time that night and purchased the kit.

When we got back home, we applied the solution as the directions instructed and waited for it to work. After the requisite soaking period was over and his hair had been washed for the third time, we took another look. The black dye was removed, but now his hair was a patchwork quilt of burnt-orange and orange-yellow tones. We thought the black dye job was bad, but now he looked like the leader of a Sex Pistols cover band.

"Should we try to bleach it again?" I threw at him, feeling helpless.

"All right," he said hesitantly. "Let's try it one more time."

"How does your head feel?"

"Well, it's a bit raw, but I think it is okay. Let's get this over with."

Our second attempt wasn't much better so we waited a couple of hours and tried a third time. On the third bleaching attempt, Frank's scalp turned bright pink. We decided to put an end to the chemical treatments for fear that his hair would fall out or he would get third degree burns. He shoved the chair away from the table and stood up. He ran his fingers through his strawberry blonde hair as he walked over to a drawer in the kitchen. He rested his hands on the counter in front of the drawer and looked at me, a determined expression on his face.

"Let's cut it all off," he exclaimed.

"What? We can't cut off your hair."

"We have to. It looks ridiculous."

I left the table and joined him in the kitchen. He opened the drawer and pulled out a pair of medium-sized scissors.

"Congratulations," he said before I could object further. "Your first dye job and haircut in the same evening. I hope you won't ask me to write you a letter of recommendation."

"Har, har," I said, rolling my eyes. I got another towel from the bathroom and we set up a makeshift haircutting station in the kitchen. As I stood over him with the scissors, I began to have second thoughts.

"I can't cut your hair, Frank." My eyes traced his reflection in the sliding glass door across from us. I wondered if anyone had been watching our ordeal from the privacy of one of the neighboring condos. Was the entire complex laughing hysterically at our fumbling parody of a beauty salon visit? A wave of guilt crashed over me for my role in the farce. This poor man had trusted me with his hair and I had ruined it.

As I caught Frank's eyes in the reflection, however, my fears began to melt. I realized at that moment the type of man he was. He had every opportunity to be angry and to freak out on me, but he managed to remain calm and in good humor. He could have asked me to stop laughing, but instead he joined right in. That night his soul shone through his eyes and my heart skipped a beat or two.

"Just give it a shot," he said, smiling. "How hard can it be? And after all, at this point, what have we got to lose?"

I reached around his neck and gave him a tight hug. He reached up and his warm hands clasped mine with tenderness. His touch made me feel safe and loved—a feeling with which I was none too familiar. It scared the living daylights out of me and I pulled back.

He reached for my hands again and brushed them against his lips. I could feel the razor stubble on his face as he skimmed my hands along his cheeks. The pit in my stomach seemed to grow as I thought about him drifting from friend to lover. I pushed his hands away gently and moved back into position with the scissors.

"Shall we?" I asked.

"Wait a second. Let me get a mirror so that I can see what you are doing."

"What, you don't trust me?"

He laughed. "Are you kidding?"

A few moments later he was back in place, staring intently at my reflection in a handheld mirror. As I looked down upon his head wondering where to begin, I tried to think about where my stylist always started. I could not remember for the life of me. I had never cut hair before, not even my own bangs. *Maybe this would be easier if I got some kind of guide,* I thought. *A baseball cap, maybe? It might help me cut a straight line around his forehead. If we hadn't washed off the black dye from his forehead, that might have worked.* I recalled a TV show I'd seen where a woman put masking tape on her hair and then cut under the tape. *That could work, but if I don't get the tape just right it could be really bad. It might actually pull out all of his hair. I'm pretty sure he doesn't want a wax job on his head right now.*

"This is one interesting way to lose your virginity," I laughed nervously.

As I began cutting, Frank's shoulders tensed up. His eyes remained directly focused on the mirror. I knew he was nervous, but he was trying to play it cool out of consideration for me.

Starting at the crown of his head, I began cutting a little bit of hair at a time. I used my fingers to gauge how much I was cutting. I roamed around his head using this method until the cut seemed complete and even. When I stepped back to get the whole picture, however, I discovered that the hair was shorter in some places than others.

"Maybe you could just even it out with some gel," I offered.

"Nothing doing," he ordered. "Keep going."

I sighed and got back to work. After nearly thirty minutes, we were finally done. His hair, which just hours before had been a thick mass of white and black hair, was now bleached blond and about one inch long, all the way around. I could have achieved the same effect much more easily with an electric hair clipper.

"Wow," I exclaimed in shock. "It is short. It is really, really short."

"Holy crap," Frank said for the umpteenth time that night as he examined his hair in the mirror. "I look like I just got recruited into the Army. This head is not meant for short hair."

I stared at Frank for a few seconds, and then shrugged my shoulders. "It looks fine," I said unconvincingly. We'd spent the entire evening working on his hair, and I was ready to be done with the whole miserable experience.

"What makes it look funny is the color," he continued.

"Well, we can always dye it again," I said, chuckling.

"Hmm, not a bad idea," Frank said. "Do we have any left from the first kit we purchased?"

I stared at him in surprise. "Frank, are you for real? Your head looks like a baby's ass! If we put any more chemicals on it I'm afraid your skin is going to melt away. No, let it be for now."

"Will you just put a little bit of the dye on my hair, Linda? It won't hurt to try it. I really would rather not walk into my meeting looking like this."

My gut told me not to do it—I didn't want to do anything else to his poor head. I reached for the temporary dye bottle, but before I could empty it into the sink, he whisked it out of my hands and bounded back to the bathroom. I followed behind him, growing impatient. He stood above the bathroom sink with the dye bottle in his hand, poised to pour the toxic solution on what little remained of his hair.

"What the heck are you doing?" I demanded. "Now you're going overboard."

"If you won't do it, I'll have to do it myself," he said, a wild look in his eye. "Which is it going to be, Linda? You, or me?"

"Fine," I said. "But it's your funeral." I took the bottle from his hand and poured a small amount of the dye on his hair.

"Darn it," he exclaimed as soon as the dye touched his head. "This stuff is burning my scalp!"

"Well, we have to leave it on for four more minutes. Otherwise it might turn into that weird orange color again."

Frank flapped his hands and drew in a long breath of air. "I'll try to leave it on as long as I can, but it hurts."

"I told you so," I said, feeling somewhat self-satisfied.

One thing I can say about Frank, the man has self-control. As much as the dye burned his scalp, he left it on for nearly six out of the ten minutes we planned. We rinsed it out in the sink and were amazed to see that for once, the hair-care gods had chosen to smile on us. The color actually looked good. We were both relieved to see Frank's hair back to a color that could be found in nature.

It was nearly 2:30 A.M. in the morning and we were both exhausted. He asked me to stay the night and I was too tired to argue. He prepared the coffee maker and shut off the lights, and then we meandered up the stairs to his bedroom and snuggled until we both fell asleep.

The next morning, the alarm woke us up at 7:30. Frank stumbled downstairs to make us coffee and I slept in for a few more minutes. When I finally managed to crawl out of bed, I strolled downstairs in the oversized t-shirt Frank had loaned me and staggered into the kitchen. As I soon learned, Frank was useless until he'd had his morning coffee, just like me. Frank poured me a cup while I slowly attempted to adjust my eyes to the light.

We moved into the living room where we sipped our coffee and watched CNN. As the morning light began to creep into the living room, the coffee started to kick in, and the events of the previous night came rolling back into focus. A sharp jolt of unease pierced my stomach as I looked at Frank and realized it was not a dream.

"What is wrong?" he asked.

Holding my breath, I leaned over to inspect his head a bit closer. His whole body tensed up as he looked at me with a worried expression. I brought both hands up to my face and covered my mouth. We were both silent for a moment.

"What is it?" he asked nervously. "Is it the color?"

"No, the color's fine," I said with a nervous smile. "It's your scalp I'm worried about!" His hair was still a bit orange, but what stood out the most were the black scabs underneath. We'd put his head through the wringer the night before, and the scabs were proudly standing out as a testament to that. I couldn't help but start laughing, and soon he joined in with me. There really was nothing else to do.

His meeting went fine despite his hair, and the people at the office got a good chuckle out of his "new" look. I had an amazing time hanging out with Frank. When I took the time to reflect on how much fun we had together and how well we got along, and looked past his hair at his handsome face, I realized I had a serious crush.

That crush led to a full-blown relationship and within months he moved into my place. When February rolled around, he received an invitation to interview for a stellar job in Austin, Texas, with a company called BMC Software, and we discussed the opportunity in great detail. The company was willing to fly me out so we boarded a plane the next week to fly south. I fell in love with

Austin instantly and knew that if Frank was offered the job, I'd have a new home.

Within two weeks, Frank was offered the job. I was so excited for him because it was a great offer, and although I wanted to move to Austin with Frank, my fear began to encroach all other thoughts. If I moved to Austin, I would have to quit my job and rely on him for complete support until I found a job. The thought of depending on another person scared me to death. Frank had to do a lot of persuading to convince me to give notice and move with him. The offer of marriage pushed me over the edge and I agreed. Within two months, we boarded an American Airlines flight for the start of our new journey together.

Meeting Frank changed my life forever. I might still be in New Hampshire today if I hadn't been at the bar one night at the same time as a guy from my hometown who was badly in need of a dye job.

Chapter 12 Encouraged

The office appeared darker and more dingy when I returned from my Chinese-food lunch with Frank. I stood in the middle of the two-story office building looking out the dirty glass windows at one of the engineers loading his car with worn-out cardboard boxes. The execs had relented a bit and had allowed some people more time to collect their things. His face held more sadness than anger and I wondered if he was thinking about what to tell his wife. He sat in his car for about fifteen minutes under the large oak tree as if he were in hiding. I walked over to the window to get a closer look. I feared that he could see me through the glass pane so I pulled the blinds down to hide my presence.

As I peeked through the metal blinds, the smell of dust filled my nose and made me sneeze three times. When I looked out again, he was staring up at the window. He stared at me—or at least in my direction—with intense eyes, seemingly intent to make me feel guilty for an event that I could not control. My heart ached for him because he looked defeated and worried. From my viewpoint, he seemed to have aged ten years from the news of losing his job. I suspected that the pain came from the realization that he was older and knew it would be next to impossible to find another job with so many unemployed people vying for jobs.

I moved away from the window, but could still feel his eyes watching me, blaming me for taking away his ability to support his family. *What was happening to me? How could this guy I hardly knew make me feel such strong emotions?* I ran back to the window to see if he was still in his car, but he was gone. Only an oil spot remained.

I paced the halls with a profound feeling of sadness and loss. Not only were people losing their jobs, they were also losing close friendships with coworkers that they had worked with side-by-side for years. *What was I going to do? What was Frank going to do for work? What were these people going to do for work?* As I contemplated how to cope with all of my emotions, I heard the familiar sound of email entering my inbox.

My fear that no one would want my help was quickly replaced by nervous excitement when a couple of employees responded to my email, taking me up on my offer to help them find another job. As the realization of me helping these people started to set in, so did the panic. *What have I gotten myself into and how am I ever going to help these people?* I thought to myself. I immediately called Frank. I wanted him to know that at least two people didn't hate me and were grateful for any help I could provide. He let me babble on and on to keep me from falling into the trap of second-guessing myself and working myself into a tizzy.

❀❀❀

Drowning myself in helping other people had temporarily made me forget about the upcoming operation. Having a nonviable fetus sitting in my body was painless on a physical level, but the emotional side was another story. I had called Dr. Doss later the same day that we had found out about the baby. He had wanted to wait a week or so after the initial discovery to see if my body would perform its own miscarriage. If it didn't, he would need to remove the fetus and clean out any tissue inside my uterus through a procedure known as "dilation and curettage," or D&C. I gave my body until Thursday. Nothing happened. On Friday, my doctor performed the outpatient procedure and in a few hours I was sent home to rest.

The next day, I was a bit tired and experienced hot flashes and chills on-and-off, combined with a slight headache, but it didn't seem like anything to worry about. With everything that had been going on, it was hard to believe that Thanksgiving would arrive on Thursday, but Frank was incredibly supportive and helpful, caring for Andrew and doing the grocery shopping for all of the Thanksgiving goodies. He also cleaned the house, which allowed me to spend Saturday and Sunday watching Lifetime TV and relaxing on the couch. I cried the whole time because of all the sad movies that Lifetime puts out, but I knew it was a cover for my own personal pain over everything that had happened—Frank's job loss, my having to let people go, my own job loss, and most of all, the loss of our baby.

As Sunday turned into Monday, I woke up feeling nauseous. Normally, my immune system could handle anything. In the entire time Frank had known me, I'd never come down with anything more severe than a headache. When I spent the day unable to keep any food or water down, we both thought that I was coming down with the flu that had been going around. However, that night things went from bad to worse. I tossed and turned all night, sweating through four different nightgowns.

"You need to go to the hospital," Frank said around eight in the morning. "You look terrible."

"I'm fine," I croaked. "It's just the flu."

"Well, let me take your temperature at least," he said. He went into the bathroom and brought back a digital thermometer. Once I saw the results, I understood why I'd been sweating all night—my temperature had risen to 105 degrees.

Frank insisted that we go to the emergency room and drove me to the closest one after getting Andrew ready. I hadn't eaten a morsel of food in almost two days and couldn't keep any liquids down. All I wanted to do was sleep because I was feeling weak. After waiting for nearly two hours, I was ready to walk out the door when the nurse called my name. She collected my vitals and the doctor on call came in a short time later. She also took my vitals, determined I had a virus that would pass in another day or so, and prepared to leave the room.

"See, I told you it was just a virus. Now will you stop worrying about me, love?" I asked with a whisper. "Let's go home. I want to lay down."

"Wait a minute," Frank said. "I have a question for the doctor. Andrew, stay with mommy."

"Frank, let's just go." I knew I wasn't going to get out of there because Frank was not satisfied with the diagnosis.

He put his hand on the doctor's shoulder as she turned to walk away. "In the twelve years I've been with my wife, I've never known her to have so much as a cold. We're not going anywhere until she gets an x-ray."

"I'm sure she'll be fine," the doctor said impatiently. "Make sure she gets rest and plenty of liquids so that she doesn't get dehydrated."

"How am I supposed to get liquids?" I asked weakly. "I can't keep anything down."

"She is already dehydrated," Frank demanded. "We are not leaving until she has an x-ray."

The doctor turned toward me and sighed. "All right," she said. "I'm sure it's just a virus, but I can do a couple more tests if it will make you feel better." She placed her hand on my wrist and took my pulse. She then instructed me to lie down on the examination table. She took my pulse again.

"That's odd," she said. "Stand up, please." She took my pulse again. A look of concern passed over her face. "Your pulse is registering at different rates when you're sitting, standing, and lying down," she said. "That's an indication that you're very dehydrated." And then, as if no one had suggested it before, "Let's order an x-ray."

A nurse came in with a gurney and they moved me to the x-ray room. Within minutes, the x-ray revealed that I was suffering from bacterial pneumonia. One lung had filled completely up with fluid, and the other one was filling rapidly. "You must have an angel watching over you," the doctor said. "If you hadn't come into the hospital when you did, you would have died within a day."

They gave me four shots of a potent, fast-acting antibiotic in rapid succession, one in each arm and one in each leg. My skin began to simultaneously burn, itch and sweat. The itching increased in intensity until it felt like fire. It felt as if someone were holding a giant cigarette lighter to my skin from the inside. I've never felt pain that intense before or since, and that includes giving birth.

Once the pain began to subside, they rolled me to a private room where I stayed for the rest of the day. With much difficulty, three different nurses managed to hook me up to an IV—my veins were so deflated that they had to stab me nineteen times before they were able to insert a neonatal IV into a vein. My body was so dehydrated that it consumed several IV bags full of Ringer's lactate over the course of an hour. It takes most people two hours to get through a single bag. They released me around dinnertime, by which time I was ready to be in my own bed.

"Frank, do you think I got a staph infection as a result of the D&C?" I asked him once we were in the car on the way home.

"That is exactly what I'm thinking. It happens often in hospitals."

"Maybe it was a death wish coming true," I said, part jokingly.

"Please don't talk like that. I could never lose you. I would die."

"What's *die*, Dad?" Andrew asked from the backseat.

"It's nothing you need to worry about little man. It's a big person word," Frank answered.

"But what is it?" he persisted.

"How about we play 'I Spy My Little Eye,' pumpkin?" I interjected without much enthusiasm. I didn't really feel like it, exhausted from the day and ready to crash, but it was better than discussing death with my son. Despite the state I was in—weak and tired—I was sorry I had made the comment at all. Even though I'd felt like I was dying, I didn't want to die. I had my family, who needed and loved me, and even though the last month had been horrendously tough, I knew we'd be okay.

When Thanksgiving rolled around just two days later, I still couldn't eat anything, although Frank made a wonderful Thanksgiving dinner. I recovered fairly quickly. Frank and I decided after this wrenching experience that we should wait awhile before trying to get pregnant again. With our employment situation uncertain, we didn't want to push our luck. The way things had been going lately, it seemed like we didn't have much luck left to push. Besides, with each passing day, it was more and more difficult to keep me from work.

❉❉❉

Throughout Thanksgiving week, I had received several more emails from former employees wanting my help. With each email, my mind raced faster and faster with thoughts about how to help these people. *Will I be able to help them? Am I over my head? Where do I start? What if I can't do anything to make a difference? Will they be upset with me if I don't help them in the right way?* I didn't know. Thoughts travelled through my head searching for answers, but each question lead to the same answer: *I don't know.*

After conducting initial meetings with those who had asked for help, and enjoying our much-needed holiday trip back east, I spent considerable time meeting with former employees off-site because no one wanted to come to the old office. I didn't care about the business development job they'd given me. I suspected I was old news, too, because no one came to my floor seeking any business development help.

Most of the employees wanted help with basic items such as updating résumés, writing cover letters and figuring out how to find jobs beyond *Monster.com*. To my surprise, numerous people wanted to talk about the layoff, and I offered an empathetic ear. I wasn't sure what I was supposed to say so I responded with words from the heart and asked thoughtful questions. It was amazing to me how people just opened up about their feelings because it was something I'd struggled with my whole life. This was the most rewarding work I'd ever done. I wasn't promoting products I didn't care about. I was helping people find the kinds of careers that would improve their moods, their relationships, and their lives.

It was the first time I had been exposed to so many ranges of emotion. Roger was in shock and couldn't quite get past the "why me" questions. Laura's tears flowed like a river every time we met from the overwhelming sense of losing her self-worth. Tad was very angry at the company and at the executives who survived the layoff. Steve, the engineer, was completely hopeless. He felt like he had lost complete control of his life because he lost his job and wife in the same week. The men seemed to have a harder time coping with the layoff than the women. However, the men talked more candidly about their feelings than the women did.

In all, 150 people had been laid off, and I was able to help around 80 of them. After getting over my initial panic, I fell back on my marketing experience to guide these people through the change. I conducted brief meetings with each and reviewed résumés in addition to offering networking advice. I'd had my fair share of experience with networking thanks to my charity experience, fundraising efforts, and speaking engagements at different companies. I didn't keep track of the number of people who got new jobs right away, but I got plenty of positive feedback on the help I offered.

What I had enjoyed the most about the whole process was the people interaction and my ability to help them. They were helping me, too, although I didn't know it then. Through their candid expressions of emotion and speaking from the heart—with no fear of reprisal—they were creating the foundation on which I would become a trust broker. They were teaching me not only that I could be an empathetic listener, but also that I wasn't alone. It felt great to be needed, wanted, and appreciated.

❀❀❀

I finally left Trifinity with little fanfare. We were down to a skeleton crew, and I was looking forward to spending some time at home with Frank and Andrew. My experience helping people with their job searches had gotten me fired up to make a change in my life . . . I just wasn't sure exactly what my next move should be. I figured this period of unemployment would give me a chance to do the same thing I'd been doing for my former coworkers. I'd get to take a good look at what I wanted to do and start to make things happen for myself.

Frank had been in good spirits lately, too. After leaving NomaSoft, he'd kept in close contact with ATX Ventures, the venture capital firm that funded both Mavel (his first startup) and NomaSoft. He had an excellent reputation with ATX Ventures as a talented technology executive who knew how to bring an idea on paper to life. ATX Ventures was a well-respected leader in the Austin business community, providing the seed money for many of the successful companies that formed the backbone of the Austin tech industry. Throughout his initial months of job searching, Frank had met with his contacts at ATX Ventures repeatedly in the hopes that an opportunity would come up where his skills would become necessary. Greg Michlin, one of the partners at ATX Ventures, had approached Frank to ask him if he had any ideas about where the next big wave in tech was going to hit. For Frank, it was exactly the kind of question he'd been waiting for someone to ask him.

Based on the strength of some of Frank's initial ideas, Greg hooked him up with Brock Farrell, an associate at ATX Ventures. Brock's experience was in business and finance, but he had faith that the tech industry would bounce back and he wanted to be a part of the bounce. Greg thought Brock and Frank would make a good team because of their backgrounds. The two met several times a week to brainstorm the next great technology application. Within a month, they identified a real opportunity in the wireless space, developed a business plan, and named their company 3Vocs. They'd presented their ideas to ATX Ventures several times, and despite the partners' growing interest, had been asked to come back with more information.

"I've been doing a lot of research, Linda," he told me one day, "and I think the next big platform is going to be cell phones." We were talking in the kitchen. I'd just gotten back from a run, and I was leaning against the counter and eating some yogurt. Andrew was at pre-K. It had been only a few weeks since I left Trifinity, and I was enjoying the fact that, for the first time in my adult life, I didn't have to be anywhere and no one was watching over me. I was only listening with half an ear. I usually have a hard time paying attention when Frank starts geeking out about technology.

"Oh yeah?" I asked. "So you want to make cell phones? Wouldn't it take a ton of capital to start up a manufacturing business like that?"

"No, I don't want to *make* cell phones," he corrected me. "I want to make *programs* for cell phones. Or rather, I want to provide a way for people to sell programs for cell phones."

"Programs for cell phones?" I asked, confused. "How would you use a program on a cell phone? I can barely send a text message."

"Well, phones are getting more advanced all the time. Someday soon, you could be writing an entire novel on your phone. And I want to create the store that sells you the word processing software you'll use to write that novel."

"I don't know, Frank," I said. "It sounds a little far-fetched to me."

"Well, it doesn't sound that far-fetched to Greg," he said. "We have a big presentation with them on Friday. I think they may finally be ready to give us funding."

"That's great, Frank!" I said.

"In the meantime, I have to spend the day doing some research. Do you want to work together in the game room today? You can work on your business idea while I do my research."

"What business idea?" I asked.

"You mentioned starting a business that provides executive coaching to young women," he said.

"Oh, that," I said. "I wasn't really serious. No one is going to pay for that service. Who pays for those services? Failures?"

"It sounds like a great idea to me!" Frank said brightly. "A lot of people use executive coaches to improve their performance."

"Whatever," I said. "I'll believe it when I see it."

"Well, I think it's a good idea, anyway," he said. "It never hurts to think about it."

We filled up our coffee mugs and walked upstairs to the game room to begin our fun-filled work adventure. We sat down at the side-by-side desks and logged onto our computers. Frank got right to work while I stared at my screen, unsure of what to do.

"What are you working on?" I asked him after a few minutes of watching the shapes on my screensaver float around the screen.

"I'm checking to see if there are any new jobs on Monster," he replied. "I'll need a backup plan in case this 3Vocs stuff doesn't go through."

"Waste of time," I said, shaking my head in disgust. "That website is useless. I've never known anyone who found a job on any of those job boards. The only reason companies set up those postings is to make it look like they're complying with EEOC laws. And then they throw all those résumés in the trash and hand the job to the boss's nephew."

Frank grunted and continued his search. I turned back to my screen and checked my email—nothing but spam. I searched for the latest news to read and quickly became depressed while reading the nonstop parade of tragedies in the headlines. Finally, I navigated to Google . . . not because I had anything to search for, I just wanted to look at something clean and uncluttered.

For lack of a better idea, I decided to follow Frank's lead and do some job researching. *So what do I want to do with my life?* I wondered. As exhausting as the past few months of helping people had been, I'd felt a great sense of satisfaction, so that was where I started. In the search bar, I typed *helping people*. A bunch of links popped up for organizations like the American Red Cross, educational groups, non-profits, tools to end poverty, and page after page about how people's lives are enhanced by pet ownership. I revised my search terms to read *helping people termination*, which mostly gave me links to legal advice for wrongful termination and debt settlements. I tried a couple of other keywords like *recruiting, coaching,* and *counseling,* and those searches were just as fruitless.

"The information I'm looking for has to be here somewhere . . . but how in the heck do I find it?" I wondered aloud.

"Are you searching for something specific?" Frank asked.

"Not really. I'm just typing random keywords like 'coaching' and 'helping people.' I don't want to do family counseling because it's too depressing. Recruiting is a sales job so that will not work. But I'm not sure what to call the kind of help I've been giving."

Frank suppressed a smile as he looked up from his computer. I could tell he was pleased that I was taking his advice about starting my own business, but he wisely chose to keep his motivational speeches to himself for the time being. He thought for a moment and suggested that I try the phrase *career help.*

"Duh, that would make sense," I said, distracted by the need to keep on searching. I typed in the keywords. The top results were links to sites with titles like "Free Career Assessment!" Clicking on one of the hyperlinks transferred me to a web page with a bunch of links to different kinds of personality tests. I clicked on the link labeled "Career Assessment," answered twelve questions in a matter of minutes, and clicked the results button. Some terms popped up that were supposedly representative of what I needed in my next career: expression, harmony, action, and analysis. Following each of these terms was a paragraph explaining what the term meant and why it was an important component of a fulfilling career.

"These assessments are ridiculous," I sighed. "I just took a test to find my ideal career and all I got was a bunch of words that could apply to anyone."

"Those things are like your horoscope," Frank said. "They just tell you what you want to hear."

"My horoscope's a lot more accurate than this bunch of garbage," I replied.

I returned to the search results page and clicked on a few other links that seemed related to career choice. One of the assessments revealed a list of thirteen ideal careers for my personality, including:

- Actor
- Artist
- Advertising Professional
- Community Relations Specialist
- Consultant
- Designer
- Executive Manager

- Marketing Consultant
- Sales--Wholesale
- Teacher
- Trainer
- Veterinarian
- Writer

"These jobs stink. I just got out of marketing. This list tells me nothing," I complained. "It aligns to college degrees, not to the kinds of jobs that people actually do. There's got to be a lot more out there for me than just this. I mean, acting? Really? How many people are making a living doing that?"

"Remember when we were extras in *Hope Floats?*" Frank asked.

"Yeah, what did we get, $57.00 each for two days of work? Is that enough to pay the water bill?"

"Come on, honey, stop being so grumpy. It was fun. You loved it."

"Yeah, I'll give you that."

I paused for a moment and tried to look at the problem from a different angle. I knew that whatever I was looking for, it had to have something to do with careers. I liked the idea of teaching, but "career teacher," only took me to sites for people who wanted to be, well, teachers. *What's another word for "teacher?"* I thought. *Maybe "career coach?"* Jackpot. Within seconds, a ton of links appeared featuring phrases like "career counseling," "career coaching," and "career consulting." This was exactly where I needed to be.

I quickly made my way through fifteen pages of links, avidly reading everything I could about the topic. This was the first time in days that I'd experienced a spark of excitement. I knew the market was overrun with headhunters and job placement agencies, but I had no idea someone could make a living as an independent career consultant. The wheels in my head started spinning as I delved deeper into my investigation.

"Are you finding anything good, love?" asked Frank, breaking my focus. I looked up from the keyboard and blinked, suddenly aware that I'd been hunched over my computer for a long time. I rolled my neck and wiggled my fingers, trying to wake up my sore muscles. "I did," I said. I've been reading about career coaching. It sounds like it might be exactly the kind of thing I've been looking for."

"Career coaching? Is that the same as executive coaching?"

"I don't think so," I replied. "It seems like executive coaching is all about helping people do a better job, while career coaching is more about helping people find the right career and overcome obstacles. It's similar to what I was doing for the people who got laid off at Trifinity . . . tightening up résumés, helping them network, but a whole lot more."

"That sounds perfect, hon," Frank said. "How do you get into doing that?"

"I'm not sure yet, but I plan to find out," I said earnestly. I'd dreamed of the possibility that I could help people with their careers, but until today, I'd assumed I'd have to pioneer the field myself. Finding out that this field already existed was an enormous revelation. Suddenly, my dreams felt like they could actually become a reality.

Chapter 13 Rebound

The days seemed to pass a lot faster now that I had my attention set on something interesting. Frank, Andrew, and the Internet kept me moving forward. Frank was pleased that I'd finally found something to investigate. He wanted me to pursue a career that would make me happy. I fluctuated between being excited and anxious about starting a new endeavor. I'd never run a business before and didn't have any extra cash to rent an office.

When I evaluated my life, which seemed to be happening a lot lately, I felt so lost and alone. In no way had my upbringing prepared me for this. Neither one of my parents had set any kind of example for how to achieve job satisfaction. All they had taught me—my dad while he still could—was how to get by and be happy for whatever paycheck you could get. The little voice in my head—my mom's voice, which was still quite loud in there—kept reminding me that I would never be anything in life. Early experiences had taught me that if you are not an expert out of the gate, then don't bother. I was expected to know how to do things without first being able to learn how to do them.

I had an amazing ability to beat myself up and had mastered the art of negative self-talk. It's not surprising, given the fact that every time I used to try something new I was told, mainly by my mother, that I'd never be good at it. Negative feedback had been given often and still rang through my head. *Your smile looks terrible because you are showing too much teeth. This picture would have been good if you'd used different colors.* Blah, blah, blah.

"Hey, love, I need to go or I'll be late for my meeting," Frank said, smiling as he walked toward me. He reached out to give me a bear hug and held on for a few minutes. "Wish me luck and hope that we get the money we need for this new company," he whispered in my ear.

"Good luck, honey," I yelled as Frank walked away. "You are going to be great. Focus on the problem and how your product will solve it."

❁❁❁

After Frank left to meet Brock for their big meeting with ATX Ventures to present their business plan to the senior team, I tried not to feel too anxious. They had worked diligently for weeks finalizing the presentation for this new venture and I wanted desperately for it to go well. In order to take my mind off of it, I went downstairs after checking on Andrew, who was home for the week since it was Spring Break.

I walked through the kitchen to the laundry room and glared at the pile of clothes sitting there. *Arg*, I growled to myself. *Why am I always stuck doing the laundry when most of it isn't mine. I don't know how we go through so many clothes so fast. I must do three or four loads a day—for a family of three!*

I loaded the washing machine with whites and poured in the blue Tide along with some Clorox bleach. The basin began to fill and soon the clothes were underwater as I wondered about what would happen at Frank's meeting. I was so worried that they wouldn't get the funding because so many start-up companies had folded, and the venture community was not making a lot of investments. A handful of companies had received funding in the last quarter and those companies were already in the portfolio. This was an entirely new idea with no traction or customers.

The hours seemed to pass by very slowly. I decided to give Frank one more hour before texting or calling. Four hours was long enough to present and get an answer one way or the other. However, I was so anxious to find out the results of their meeting that I ended up texting Frank three or four times during the hour, to which I got no response.

The house was way too quite, except for the few noises Andrew made playing Legos. From the sound of it, he must've been playing crash-up derby on my white limestone cocktail table.

"Andrew, are you crashing those Legos on my table? You know they will scratch it."

"No, Mom, I'm not doing that."

"Are you sure?" I questioned.

"Yeah, I'm playing on the floor. Want to play with me?"

"In a few minutes. I need to look for something first and then let's go to the playground."

"Can we go right now? Please. Please. Please," he begged.

"Not right now. Give me some time and we'll go soon."

"Okay, but hurry up," he said eagerly.

I walked into my room and searched my entire bureau for the rosary my mother-in-law bought me for my wedding. It always brought me good luck so I wanted to hold it while I prayed for positive news. The burning sensation in the pit of my stomach was worse than ever. I thought that I'd been controlling my stress levels, but I found myself in a constant panic, tearing up several times a day in secret.

I wasn't handling the quiet very well because it gave me time and space to think, and thinking was not something I wanted to do because I would start dwelling on terrible visions of our future. *We'll have to sell our house. Should I call the realtor right now? Should we sell one of the cars? What if he doesn't get this money? What are we going to do? Would our house actually sell right now? Would we get enough money for it? How much time do we have left before we run out of money? Crap. I don't even know. I need to get a better handle on our finances. Maybe we should move. But I like it here so much. I need to find a job. I'm nuts to think about starting a business. Frank's starting a business. He needs to get a real job. We both can't start companies. We are asking for trouble.* And on and on it would go.

"Mom, can we leave now?" Andrew yelled from upstairs.

"In a few minutes. I'm almost done, pumpkin." I dialed Frank's phone a couple more times but it went straight to voicemail. Frustrated, I started going through the mail pile Frank had sorted on the counter. I stopped when I saw an envelope from Unicare, a provider of healthcare benefits. We had been without health insurance because I hadn't applied for COBRA within the allotted window after leaving Trifinity. Actually, it had slipped our minds entirely until we'd had to bring Andrew to the doctor.

We'd searched endlessly for affordable family medical benefits but with no luck. The cost of enrolling in a new family plan was outrageous. To have major medical with a $5,000 family deductible would cost us about $900 per month. It was the best plan we could find. I considered filling out the application, but couldn't bring myself to do it. *Do we really need these benefits? If Frank gets a job, we'll get benefits from his company. But what if he doesn't get a job?* I stood for a moment with the paperwork in my hand. If something happened to Andrew while we were without insurance, the guilt would be crushing.

I thought about all of the sickness in my family and knew we couldn't live without it. Frank and I both came from families with major diseases. My father had died at the age of fifty with multiple sclerosis and Frank's grandfather had passed of colon cancer. We lived very healthy lives but feared that we might be stricken with fatal diseases ourselves someday. I was surprised by how often my thoughts focused on sickness. It must've been driven by the fear of not having benefits. We'd have to bite the bullet and take on another expense. We couldn't keep going without insurance.

Andrew and I went to the park for an hour and it helped clear my head. I texted Frank a few more times, but still no response. Back at home and feeling bored, I went upstairs to the game room to get on the computer, stopping along the way to pop a movie in for Andrew to keep him busy.

I glared at the computer screen wondering why all of this bad luck was happening to me. *What did I ever do to deserve what life was dealing me?* It had taken so long to build the home and family that I'd always dreamed of and it could all be gone in an instant. The financial struggles of my childhood had decided to come back for round two. I was ready for a fight and determined that no amount of financial stress was going to tear my family apart.

I pushed my thoughts aside and began doing more research on career management. My search was productive because I located a few universities that offered master's degree programs specifically in career development. Despite the fact that all three programs were out of state, I decided to complete three online information request forms. I knew I'd never leave Austin, but was curious about what the curriculum entailed. The university program that most interested me was from JFK University in California. The curriculum appeared to be the most comprehensive of the three programs, and they had an online extension program, which appealed to me because I couldn't imagine sitting in a classroom every day. The classroom option wouldn't have worked even if I desired to attend class because I had to work. In addition, I was unwilling to spend time away from my family at night.

I scoured the JFK site, but it didn't contain a lot of information. I couldn't find a brochure on the program anywhere. It took me a while but I finally located the tuition information and printed the page. I added up all of the fees for a single semester of two courses and realized the program was much too expensive for my tight budget. Besides, the thought of spending money on myself at a time like this seemed selfish.

The thought of going back to school for two years to pursue a completely new career was daunting. How could I think of self-improvement when we were still uncertain about whether or not either of us would ever get another paycheck? I was uncertain as to whether I would like the new career option anyhow. As I was considering my options, I heard the downstairs door open. "Honey, I'm home," Frank called out. "Honey. Are you upstairs?"

"Yes," I shouted. "I'm searching on the Internet for career stuff. I can't believe that you didn't call me at all. I called you about five times and sent you tons of texts."

Frank walked up the stairs and came into the room with a huge smile on his face. He was so easy to read, which was one of his character traits I liked the most. I never had to guess how Frank felt and he didn't play any games. He wore his heart on his sleeve and today it was shining brightly.

"Sooo . . . ?" I asked nervously. How did the meeting go?"

"The board gave us $1 million in seed money."

"Oh my God!" I screamed, leaping up from my seat. I threw my arms around him and gave him a gigantic hug. "That's so great, Frank!"

"I know," he said, laughing. "This is exactly what I've wanted to do, Linda. Start a company from the ground up. And I think it's a really promising one, too. Someday, people are going to be doing everything from building their stock portfolio to making movies with their cell phones, and they're going to need software to do all of that."

"Well, I'm proud of you," I said. "And happy that at least one of us is finally going to be earning a steady income again. Have you talked about salaries yet?"

"Yep," he said, his smile widening. "It looks like I'm going to get a base of somewhere around $185,000, plus a bonus that will put me over $250,000 and tons of stock options."

"Yes!" I shouted, throwing my arms around him again. He laughed, and suddenly the months we'd spent agonizing over our finances simply melted away.

"I've wanted this for so long, hon," he said. "This could really be the start of something big."

"I hope so, Frank," I said. "We must have been on the brink of using up all of our cash."

"Let's not talk about that. Let's celebrate with a bottle of wine," he cheered.

Over a bottle of Stags Leap, Frank told me every detail about the meeting. They had decided that Brock would be the CEO of the company and Frank would be the Chief Technology Officer, responsible for product direction and development. Frank was most excited at the thought of starting something from scratch. This time around, it would be his vision and talent that brought a brand new product to market in a hot field.

Frank's excitement about developing the product was tempered somewhat with apprehensiveness about starting the firm with Brock. In the short time they'd spent working together, Frank discovered that they both had very strong personalities. He and Brock had already locked horns on a few occasions over product direction, and the company wasn't even formed yet.

Frank was so sensitive about his last experience at NomaSoft that he questioned his own ability to make good decisions about people. Generally, Frank and I both shared a knack for reading people, but his confidence had been shaken. We could only hope he and Brock had been on edge due to the stress of fundraising, and that things would settle down now that they'd closed the deal.

I knew that Frank was a brilliant technologist and I trusted his instincts when it came to building viable products. Still, I didn't hold any delusions that it would be a walk in the park. It was a miracle that the company even got seed money in this economic climate. If ATX Ventures thought Frank's idea was worth investing $1 million into, then there must've been some potential in it. I could at least have faith in that, because venture capitalists were a lot stingier with their money now than they had been at the height of the boom. On the other hand, the economy was in bad shape and the odds seemed especially stacked against tech start-ups. I only hoped he could keep it going long enough to get us back on stable footing.

"Are you guys going to get a benefits plan?" I inquired.

"No, Brock decided he doesn't want a plan and that was one of our points of contention," he replied.

"You are kidding!"

"No, he wouldn't budge. At least I have a job."

"That guy is an idiot. Arg."

"Let's focus on the positive. I have a job and we can stop worrying," he said cheerfully.

"I can't believe how close we were to using up all of our savings. Another two months and you would have been forced to sell your stock," I said to him, trying to sound optimistic, yet realizing how precarious the situation was. Only time would tell.

❁❁❁

In the following weeks, Frank and Brock hit the ground running, renting an office space in downtown Austin and assembling a staff of some of the best and brightest professionals in Austin. (One of their hires was my former Director of User Experience, Candice Crane. After Trifinity, I was glad to see her land in a role where her contributions would be greatly valued.) Frank was going to work every day again from 8 A.M. to 6 P.M. Things were looking up, and for the first time in months, I was starting to think that maybe our period of unemployment would prove to be nothing more than just a bump in the road.

PART 3
TORN

Chapter 14   Uncertain

"You know what today is, hon?" Frank asked, plopping down next to me on the couch.

"What's that?"

"It's Andrew's first day of kindergarten," he answered.

"Of course I know that silly . . . duh," I replied teasingly.

Time had passed by so quickly. Spring had turned into summer, which had passed by in a blur. Since Frank had secured funding and was earning a steady income again, I had decided to enroll for the online master's program at JFK University. It was one of the best decisions I ever made, despite the time commitment it would involve—roughly thirty hours per week. In addition to completing coursework, several short-term freelance marketing gigs had come my way, enabling me to make a bit of money to contribute to our expenses. My days were filled with working, typing school papers, and hanging with my family. It didn't leave me much time to start a career coaching business, but I made a bit of headway. I named the company *The Ginac Group*, even though it would be a solo practice. I was thinking toward the future. I also designed my website and wrote a brochure to describe my services.

Frank had continued to build up 3Vocs . . . or at least, he was working hard to make sure it didn't come crumbling down prematurely. Frank's fears about Brock had come true. Almost every day, Frank would come home with some story about him and Brock getting into an argument over how the company should be run. Frank wasn't alone in his annoyance—most of the employees at the company were unhappy with Brock's authoritarian management style. Once again, Frank was forced to stand by and watch his ideas being mismanaged into the ground while feeling powerless to stop it. He had taken the day off for Andrew's first day of school and was relishing the break after almost five months without a day away from the office.

"Of course I know what day it is, silly," I said again. "Where is the camera so that we can capture this experience?" I walked over to the wine rack above the counter in the kitchen where we usually stored the camera in one of the cubbyholes. "Never mind. I found it."

"Put it in your purse so that we don't forget it," Frank said. "And can you check to see if Andrew is up yet? I need to use the bathroom."

"Of course you do," I said.

I went upstairs to wake up the little man and found him sitting in the middle of his queen-sized bed. He had already put on his khaki shorts, deep-green shirt and brown leather belt. He looked up at me with a big smile, rosy cheeks, and big brown eyes and I nearly started crying. He looked all grown up in his school uniform. I grabbed his white tube socks and sneakers and kneeled near his bed.

"You look so cute, Andrew. Want me to put on your socks and sneakers?" I asked.

With as much seriousness as a little boy can muster up, he responded in a mature-sounding way, "No, thank you. I want to do it. I'm big now."

"Yes, you are a big boy now." I rubbed his thick brown hair and gave him a big kiss. "Come downstairs when you are done and I'll make you waffles with butter."

On my way downstairs, I picked up the loose Legos lying all over the rug. It never ceased to amaze me how quickly an only child could make such huge messes. I noticed Frank's coffee cup on the counter, so I picked it up on my way to the coffee pot to pour us more hazelnut java. Opening the fridge with one hand, I pulled out the half-and-half. With the other, I opened the freezer and grabbed two waffles. I put the waffles in the toaster and filled our cups with creamer.

"Andrew," I called out, "come and eat breakfast. We need to leave soon. Aaannndddrrreeewwww!"

"Mom, I'm right here."

I looked down to see him standing right next to me. "Oh, I didn't see you standing there," I said, surprised. "Let me take a look at you. Alright, little man, I need a picture before we leave. Let me get the camera." I made him stand in five or six different poses and then rushed him through breakfast and the ritual teeth-brushing routine.

Frank was taking an extra long time coming into the kitchen, and that could mean only one thing—he was still in the bathroom. I had never met anyone with bowels so efficient. At one time, I actually thought Frank had serious bowel issues or even colon cancer due to the number of times he can go in one day. At a general visit with my doctor, I asked her what she thought might be wrong with him and she replied that he was perfectly normal. To my surprise, I learned that most people poop two to three times a day. Great for him, but he spent a lot of time in the bathroom every day.

"Frank, are you done yet?" I yelled out. "We need to go or Andrew will be late. Let's go."

Frank appeared and we scurried Andrew into the BMW. We drove through the rolling hills of Barton Creek to the school, which was only four miles from our house so the commute was brief. Once at the school, we took pictures of Andrew from the time he got out of the car until we dropped him off at his kindergarten classroom. The teacher let us stay for a few minutes, but it wasn't nearly long enough. I looked at my watch as a way to console my sense of loss. We had spent the entire summer together and it had been so wonderful. Today would be a short day, though, so we'd see him soon.

When we came back to pick him up later on, Andrew was chattering happily with some of his new friends. It made me proud to see him so comfortable with other kids his age. I'd always known he was a sweet kid, but he'd grown up with Olivia, his private nanny, and had only attended pre-k for one year. I thought it might take him some time to adapt to being around so many other kids. Thankfully, he seemed to be right at home. As soon as he spied me, he ran up and threw his arms around my waist.

"Mommy! Daddy!" he said excitedly. He turned to his new friends. "This is my mommy and daddy," he said proudly. The other kids did not look impressed. They'd clearly seen mommies and daddies before.

"How was your first day, little man?" I asked him as we walked out to the car.

"Good," he said. "I'm hungry."

"Well, you're in luck," Frank answered. "We're just about to get some lunch."

We loaded Andrew into the car and drove to La Madeleine, a favorite local spot for business meetings. The tables were filled with guys in jeans and polo shirts scratching diligently on yellow notepads while they ate. No one took a real lunch break anymore. The competitive nature of business around Austin had gotten so intense that if you broke for lunch, you'd likely find yourself without a job when you got back to the office.

"So, as long as I'm on this career coaching kick, let me ask you a question," I said to Frank after our lunch arrived, going into "coach" mode.

"Shoot," he replied, biting into his ham and cheddar sandwich. Next to him, Andrew poked at his own ham and cheese as if he were checking its reflexes.

"Andrew, eat your food and stop playing with it, please," I pleaded with him.

"I don't like it. It has that yucky white stuff on it."

"No it doesn't. I asked the lady to make it plain for you. Let me see it."

I picked up the sandwich and opened it up to inspect the bread. Both sides of the croissant were covered in mayonnaise. "You are right, Andrew. Your sandwich has mayo on it. Mommy will wipe it off and it will taste better."

After the sandwich had been cleansed with a handful of napkins, I gave it back to Andrew for consumption. "I don't like it! It tastes funny," he insisted.

"Andrew, can you please eat your sandwich? Mommy took off the mayonnaise."

"No, I don't like it," he asserted again.

"Frank, could you take it up to the counter and get another for him?" I urged.

"There's a long line. Let's just have him eat it," Frank said.

"Forget it, I'll just do it myself," I said, annoyed. The noise of the busy lunch crowd was starting to get to me, and I couldn't help but think, *Why do I always have to take care of everything?* I shifted out of my chair and went to the counter to try and find someone who would listen to me. In less time than it had taken to argue about it, I returned to the table. "All set. They'll bring out another one ASAP."

"Thanks, Mom," Andrew replied. "I love you."

"I love you too," I responded with a silly face. "Now, color the picture for me, please, so I can hang it up on the pantry door."

"Okay, back to us," Frank said.

"Well," I started, not stopping to sugarcoat anything, "now that you've had a few months to think about it, what do you think really happened at Noma-Soft? Was it really all Ken's fault, or do you think you deserve some of the blame?" I had intended to approach this calmly and use Frank as my "coaching" guinea pig, but since my ire had been triggered, my tone wasn't very friendly. Furthermore, ever since Frank had announced his resignation, the circumstances surrounding his break with Ken had been hazy. I couldn't help shake the feeling that there was something he hadn't told me, and it had been building inside me until this moment, when I decided I needed to ask about it.

"Wow," he said, raising his eyebrows. "Harsh question."

"Well, you acknowledge that you have a strong personality," I said. "I know everyone agrees that Brock's impossible to work with, but I'm sure you're not real timid about telling him when he's wrong."

"Is this about Brock, or is it about Ken?"

"Or is it about you?" I countered. *This isn't going quite like I wanted it to,* I thought to myself. *Maybe I should've opted for a quieter environment to have this conversation.*

I looked over at Andrew, who was making a maze out of the crayons and sugar packets. "Andrew, stop playing with everything. Your sandwich is fixed so let's eat up," I said, annoyed.

"It still tastes funny," he said.

"You have to taste it before you know if it tastes funny," I answered.

Andrew tentatively took a bite of his sandwich. Seemingly unscathed, he continued to nibble at it as I turned my attention back to Frank.

"I'm just saying that you might need to ask yourself some deep questions if you hope to make sure this doesn't happen again," I said pointedly. "You've got to admit, the whole situation seemed a little suspicious. It's not like you were part of a massive layoff like I was at Trifinity. What do you think honestly happened?"

"I don't know, Linda," he sighed. "I think at the end of the day, I just didn't fit in. I wasn't part of the culture. I didn't go out drinking with the guys after work every night because I had a family to come home to."

"Well, you could have gone out with the team," I said.

"That's true," he agreed. "But I didn't want to. I wanted to spend my time with you and Andrew. I don't need a personal relationship with my coworkers."

"Well, then, maybe it's because Andrew was there every evening," I offered. When we'd moved from the suburbs to Austin a few years before, we'd decided to keep our nanny, Olivia. She was a widowed sixty-seven-year-old grandmother who had been with us since Andrew was one year old, and replacing her would have been like replacing our own flesh and blood. The only trouble was that our new home was a forty-five minute drive from where Olivia lived, which was too far to go twice a day, every day. For a brief moment, I had considered quitting my job and staying at home until Andrew was old enough for pre-K, but quickly ruled that option out. Like most modern families, we needed more than one income to sustain our lifestyle. We had finally decided that Olivia would drive to Frank's office, which was about halfway between our place and hers, to pick up and drop off Andrew.

The problem with this solution was that Olivia had to drop Andrew off at 5:15 P.M. every day because she cared for her grandchildren in the evening. In the dot-com world in which Frank and I worked, leaving early was unheard of. We had settled on an uneasy compromise in which Andrew stayed at Noma-Soft from 5:15 until Frank was ready to come home. The arrangement had always made me feel somewhat uneasy. Frank wasn't exactly working in a company full of family men, and I often doubted that they were as comfortable with having a kid running around the office as Frank claimed they were. *What did they say about Frank when he wasn't around? Did they think he was a pushover? For that matter, what did they say about me? Did they assume I was a bad mother because I chose to work late?* We had found a work/life balance that worked for us, but I realized at the same time that it didn't fit into the stereotypical "corporate" mold.

"Nah, I doubt that had anything to do with it," Frank said. "Everyone adored Andrew. He was very good in the office and didn't make a lot of racket. Besides, it was only thirty minutes a day."

"Yeah, well, what people say to your face and what they think are two different things," I replied.

"Spoken like a true people person," Frank said, then adding, "Damn. I hope it's not this hard for all your clients!"

Me, too, I thought to myself. *It wasn't like that with the employees at Trifinity. What just happened?* Then it hit me—I had been able to get Frank to at least start thinking about the circumstances surrounding his departure from Noma-Soft, but had slowly transitioned from "coach" mode to "wife" mode. Then I made a mental note to myself: *Don't try this at home.*

❁❁❁

As Frank and Brock worked on building 3Vocs, tensions between them continued to mount. I tried to put his issues out of my mind because I was terrified of what might happen if we were both unemployed again. I had secretly continued hunting for full-time work, even though I knew I'd be miserable if I went back to a marketing job. The job market in Austin was horrible and the unemployment rate hit a record high. And just when we thought it couldn't get any worse, along came the terrorist attacks of September 11th to put the last nail in the coffin of the economy.

Tonight, however, was not the night to worry about the dismal state of the economy or job hunting or Frank's personality problems with Brock. It was October 2001, and Frank and I were going on our first date night in what seemed like forever. For as long as Frank and I had been married, we'd always made it a priority to have a date night once a week, giving us a chance to spend time alone without worrying about jobs, bills or Andrew. The pressures of starting a new business had made it difficult for us to keep to our regular schedule, though, and I was really looking forward to being alone with him. Tonight was our chance to bring a little romance back into the marriage. We had planned a night on the town, starting with cocktails at Mezzaluna and dinner at Sullivan's Steakhouse. I arranged a babysitter and planned to take a cab downtown at 6:00 P.M. to meet Frank at the restaurant.

Around 4:00, I stepped into the walk-in closet in our bedroom to pick out my outfit for the evening. My dress selection wasn't large, but I had a few sexy ones that I thought might get me in a date-night mood. I ended up choosing a frilly, deep red, flamenco-style dress with a slit to show off my legs. It was one of my favorite special occasion picks. Not only did it ooze sexiness, but the color looked great against my pale skin and chestnut brown hair. To complement the dress, I chose a pair of strappy gold heels and two tasteful gold bracelets. The outfit put me in the mood to paint the town red . . . literally.

After choosing my attire, I set the mood by lighting four candles in the bathroom to get the aromas flowing around the room. Since childhood, I've always found the slow, meditative process of getting ready incredibly satisfying. To me, getting dolled up was an art form that deserved careful attention. The ceremonial act of styling my hair and applying makeup almost put me in a meditative state. If I had to describe what I love about it, I would say it was the ritual aspects of preparing myself. They make me relish every moment and lose all track of time.

As I stepped into the shower, the radio was playing my favorite song in the whole world, "Dust in the Wind" by Kansas. I stood still, allowing the hot water to soak over me. I shaved and exfoliated my body, using a pumice stone to smooth out any rough edges on my feet. Afterwards, I moisturized all over with an orange-scented lotion that made me feel extra feminine.

I turned on my vanity mirror and set it to evening while I sat down to apply my makeup. Sitting in front of the mirror, I noticed the fine lines starting to appear around my eyes. My features still made me look youthful, and most people guessed my age ten years younger than the actual. This was good for my ego, but Frank—looking older than he was with his white hair—didn't enjoy being perceived as a sugar daddy or a cradle robber.

I opted for mysterious and appealing eyes for this evening's look. Slowly, I prepared the canvas with the help of a proper base and used neutral tones to achieve a less prominent matte style. I piled the mascara on my upper and lower lashes, being careful not to smudge any on my skin. To amplify my eyes even more, I applied black eyeliner to the inside rims of my eyes.

I smiled in the mirror to see the apples of my cheeks and applied the blush in small circles around my cheeks. Frank loves my eyes and lips, but I believe my cheeks are my best feature. I love countering them with lots of blush because it makes me look youthful and radiant.

The canvas was almost complete except for lip design. I wanted to achieve full and sensual lips that Frank would find irresistibly kissable. My lower lip was slightly bigger than my upper lip. My upper lip was well-formed with a strong cupid's bow, which make-up artists have called the true power of beauty. To me, they're just lips. With the right lipstick and shine, they completed the picture. Slowly and meticulously, I caressed my face to ensure the powder and blush had settled.

My hair was almost dry when I turned on the blow dryer. Within minutes, the curling iron had circled my head and twenty Velcro rollers sat tight on my head to give it height and natural curl. As they settled, I twirled my way into the bedroom and slipped into the dress, allowing the silk to slide up my legs. The dress didn't require a bra to be worn with it, but I wore one anyhow because I felt awkward without one.

Standing before the mirror, I pulled out the Velcro rollers and tossed them onto my bureau, shaking the curls free with my fingers. I modeled in front of the mirror and inspected the final picture, giving myself a few minutes to make any final adjustments. Finally, I spritzed on a bit of perfume and waltzed out the door feeling beautiful, just in time for the cab.

❀❀❀

I arrived at Mezzeluna a little after 6:00 to find Frank waiting for me by the door.

"Hey there!" he said, walking toward me as I exited the cab.

"Hello, handsome," I responded in my sexiest voice, wrapping my arms around him in a tight squeeze. I slid my hand down his back and around his hip bone as we walked into the restaurant.

"You look hot!" he whispered in my ear.

"Thank you, love," I purred.

"Where do you want to sit?" he asked.

"It doesn't matter to me, as long as I'm near you."

The restaurant was a bit crowded—Thursday nights in downtown Austin are always hopping with thirty-somethings making the social rounds. As we walked in, a table of attractive men near the entrance gave me the once-over, staring at me with a look they should have reserved for the single women. Although it was secretly flattering to know my preparations were being appreciated, I was annoyed for Frank's sake. He's not the type who gets off on having other men leer at his wife, but thankfully he's learned to deal with it since I do attract attention. Otherwise he'd be in arguments often.

We sat down at a corner table in the bar section and a cute waitress with a nose ring and a thick blue streak in her hair came over to take our order. Lora, according to her name tag, welcomed us and took our drink order. We ordered two glasses of the '94 Stag's Leap Cabernet Sauvignon, our favorite wine and also the one we had offered at our wedding. When she left, I reached across the table to caress Frank's forearms.

"How was your day?" I asked. "Any more drama with Brock?"

"Ugh," he said. "I knew I should have trusted my instincts on this one. Brock has this irritating need to control every aspect of the business."

"Oh," I said vaguely. I really didn't want to hear about Brock and kicked myself for opening the subject. The waitress returned minutes later with our glasses of wine.

"Before we get into the work talk, let's toast to a wonderful night on the town and to the fact that you are employed and I'm starting a business," I said as we clanked our glasses in the air. "I have one more thing to celebrate, too," I teased.

"And what would that be?"

I stared at him for a while with a big smile to increase the anticipation. "I got my first grade from JFK University for my first big test in the Master's Career Development Program," I said, pausing for effect. "I got an A!"

"Linda, that is terrific news!" he said. "This is going to be so good for you. I'm so happy for you, love. You finally get to chase something that you love."

I turned my head away for fear that tears would roll out of my eyes. Frank's unconditional love and support still made me uneasy. Those things were so foreign to me growing up that even after almost ten years with Frank, I had a hard time opening up and accepting his love, or for that matter, feeling like I deserved it.

"Tell me what's going on at 3Vocs," I said, changing the subject.

"Nothing I really want to get into," Frank said, taking a sip from his glass. "Technical stuff. Brock wants to add more features to the product that I don't think are necessary."

"Huh," I said. "Why does he want to do that? Are they necessary?"

"Not based on the focus group research the team conducted. He just thinks they're needed," he responded.

"Well, his ideas must be coming from somewhere. Do you really think he's just pulling them out of the air? Maybe he read an article or a customer suggested the changes."

"No, Linda. That's not what happened," he said, with a sigh of exasperation. "Why are you always on someone else's side?"

"I'm just trying to understand, Frank," I said calmly. "I'm not on his side."

"Well, my team designed the product with a set of features based on customer input, and now Brock wants to eliminate those features and include features that customers are not interested in. I've been doing this job successfully for so long I could do it in my sleep. I know what is needed to put out a commercially viable product that generates revenue and grows companies. Most companies overengineer products and don't focus on what's important. That is not me. We've been butting heads at every turn. I can't take it much longer. It's interfering with the team, too."

"What does the team think?"

As Frank told me about how the entire team was on the same page, with the exception of Brock, negative thoughts about Frank began to enter my mind. I couldn't help but wonder if something was wrong with him. He seemed to have personality conflicts no matter where he worked. It was so hard to imagine him not getting along with anyone because he was always so accommodating and strove to please his family all the time.

I went through the motions of listening to him account for the details of his day, but wasn't really hearing what he was saying. Lately, I seemed to be tuning out his voice more and more. Part of me didn't want to hear any more negative news about the economy or people's troubles. I envisioned myself putting electrical tape over his mouth because I wanted to turn down the volume on negative talk.

I loved talking to Frank, but he was doing all the talking while I did all the listening—again. This had been a recurrent trend recently. The thought of sitting in an office with other people struggling with their careers suddenly scared me. *Would I ever find those mini-outlets that allowed some element of positive energy to flow through my life?*

My moment of self-doubt about Frank went away as I stared at him across the table. Despite getting those feelings on occasion, they were always fleeting. I couldn't help but love him. He was one of a kind—a man who actually said what he meant and did what he said. I might've described it as him being too honest, but I didn't really believe there was such a thing. All he ever wanted to do was create something game-changing, but he tended to be too trusting and always thought everyone else's intentions were as good as his. He didn't expend energy on becoming the perfect culture fit because he was too busy driving change in the organization and achieving goals. He's still that way.

"This is ridiculous," I said as I shook my head in disbelief. "I can't believe you're in this situation again. The job market is even worse right now than it was when you left the last company. I'm hearing it from everyone." I looked around hesitantly, making sure no one was looking at us. I put on a plastic smile to hide our discussion from the other people in the bar. Even though I didn't know anyone there, I didn't feel right having such an intimate conversation in a public place.

"The rest of the team said they would quit if I left," he responded proudly.

"Great," I said. "So you told everyone at work that you were thinking about leaving before you talked to me about it? Are these theoretical conversations or have you made up your mind?" I was starting to feel pretty angry. *How can he be so cavalier about this?*

He hesitated before answering. "It is nearly impossible to have a private conversation when everyone sits in the same room," he said, referring to the open space at his office. "I need to make up my mind about what to do," he finally replied. "I wish you and I could work on something great together because as a team we are unstoppable."

"Great," I said sarcastically. "Well, I appreciate you letting me know in such a timely fashion. I certainly don't deserve more than a day's warning that you're leaving your job." I waved Lora over. When she arrived, I mustered up enough class to unclench my teeth and paint a smile on my face. "Bring us a bottle of Stag's Leap, please. This is going to be a long night."

As she scurried off to get our bottle, I took a large sip from my half-filled glass of wine, suddenly on a mission to get drunk. I was surprised at how tipsy I felt after just the one glass. Before gulping the last bit down, I lifted my glass and held it up to Frank in a toast. "To an uncertain future. May it not end in divorce," I muttered.

Frank looked taken aback by my comment. "What are you talking about? Why would you say that?" he insisted. "It's not funny. We are not going to ever get divorced! You're the best thing in my life."

"Am I?" I spat. "Then why do you keep doing this to me?" Despite the escalation of our discussion, only Frank could tell how upset I was getting. We were still being quiet enough not to garner attention, and I was expertly controlling my facial expressions.

"Doing what?" he asked.

"'Doing what'?" I mimicked. "You know what. Pushing me into this constant state of uncertainty, that's what. You said you wanted to start your own business, and I supported you. And now that you've gotten the ball rolling, you've decided you want to quit this company, too? You know how anxious I get with anything involving finances, Frank. And yet you keep putting me into this situation in which I have to obsess over every last penny. I can't keep going through this endless cycle. I need stability." I knew I wasn't being nice, but I'd met Frank downtown to have a relaxing date night, not hear about how he was about to thrust us into more uncertainty by voluntarily leaving a perfectly good job. For me, any job that brought in income right now was a good job, and he was about to ruin that.

"Linda, I know how hard this is for you, but you've got to believe I'm not doing any of this to hurt you. This is a learning process. It's better that I get out now before I'm too invested rather than when it's too late. We're not going to get divorced. We're not going to lose our house. Everything is going to be okay."

"Well, one thing's for certain," I said. "There's no way I'm going back to school now."

"What are you talking about?" he asked, shocked. "Of course you're going back to school. You need to embrace this opportunity and run with it. Don't worry about the finances. We'll be okay. You've always wanted to do this and now is the time."

"What do you mean 'don't worry about the finances'? We can't afford it right now, Frank. It would be selfish of me to put my needs first."

"You of all people have never put your needs above others," he said. "You help people way too much and let them walk all over you. You're one tough lady, but you have a heart as big as an ocean."

"Well, I appreciate you saying that," I acknowledged, "but I just can't make a decision right now. We're going to have a lot to figure out before I can commit to spending any more money."

"It's just money, Linda," he said. "We'll work it out. When you're running a successful business, you'll be happy you took this time to get your degree."

"How can you be so optimistic?" I protested. "What indication do you have that things are going to turn out all right?"

"Well, what indication do you have that things aren't going to turn out all right?" he countered.

"I'm just being pragmatic, Frank. You seem to have this rose-colored view of the world, as if you can just keep stumbling through life and the universe will take care of you."

"Well, it's taking care of me tonight," he said, grinning like a schoolboy. "Did I tell you how beautiful you look?"

"Don't try to sweet-talk me. It's not going to work, buster."

Frank placed his hands on mine. I resisted the urge to draw away from him. "Come on, honey. Let's have a good time," he said. "I'm sorry for springing the news about the company on you, but let's try to enjoy our date."

I looked down at my lap, frustrated. I closed my eyes and breathed deeply to center myself. Focusing on the sound of my heartbeat and the feeling of the blood rushing through my body, I managed to drown out the sound of the restaurant. Taking slow, steady breaths, I pushed my anxiety away and looked up into Frank's eyes.

"Okay," I said quietly. "Let's start over."

Frank leaned forward for a kiss to seal the deal. I somewhat reluctantly tilted my head up to meet him. As I breathed in his scent, I began to feel calmer. *Screw it*, I thought. *If this is the last hurrah, we might as well go out with a bang.*

After drinks, we moved on to a wonderful dinner at Sullivan's Steakhouse. We stayed there for hours, chatting about the ideas I'd been coming up with for my business. I was reminded that Frank and I always had such great brainstorming sessions when we managed to get time alone together. He had always been a great sounding board and that night he helped me expand my scattered thoughts into full-blown ideas.

After dinner, we dropped into the local Speakeasy club for live music, followed by dancing on the roof. At two o'clock in the morning, as we stood under the vast, Texas sky, Frank took my hand for one final dance. As we moved across the floor under a blanket of stars, I was overcome by a sense of romance that had felt absent from our lives lately. He spun me around the dance floor and stepped in to squeeze my waist seductively. It was intoxicating. Before the song ended, he cupped my face with his hands, kissed me slowly and whispered that he would love me forever.

Chapter 15 Worried

I woke up in a daze, wondering whether it was day or night. I turned to the clock—the glowing red light told me it was 4:45 A.M. Once again I couldn't sleep, even though I'd gotten to bed at a decent hour the night before. I rubbed my eyes with my knuckles and pulled them away. The light peeping through the window from the streetlamps outside revealed that the tops of my hands were smeared with black mascara. *I must have gone to sleep again without removing my makeup,* I thought, getting out of bed and padding to the bathroom.

In the bathroom, my suspicions were confirmed—I had been crying in my sleep again. I wet a Kleenex in the faucet and wiped the skid marks from my face as I replayed my latest nightmare in my mind. Concerns about money always triggered dreadful memories from my childhood. No matter how hard I tried to erase those stressful memories from my mind, they always found a way back.

In the dream, I was around eight or nine years old and standing in the kitchen speaking to my mother. She was the prettiest woman I had ever seen, with ivory skin, a perfectly shaped nose, dark brown eyes, and a wavy main of chocolate brown hair.

"Linda, can you go to the store for me?" she asked. "We need a few groceries for dinner."

"Alone?" I asked, surprised. The store was only about a five-minute walk away from our house, but my mom had never before trusted me to walk all the way there by myself.

"Yes, you can go alone," she smiled. She tore a piece of paper out of a notebook and wrote several items on the list and handed it to me, along with a fun-

149

ny looking book. I opened the book—it was filled with colorful coupons that looked like Monopoly money.

"What are these things?" I asked

"It's special money for food."

"I've never seen you use these before."

"They're new," Mom said, looking out the window. "We'll be using them for a while."

I was so excited to be going to the store alone that I skipped all the way there. Once inside the store, I pushed my shopping cart through the aisles with determination, feeling like a real grown-up. When I had collected everything on the list, I pulled up to the cashier and unloaded it onto the counter, just like I'd seen Mom do so many times in the past. The cashier smiled at me and I blushed, feeling nervous and excited to be handling the entire transaction by myself. I pulled the special money out of my pocket—it had dollar amounts on it, just like regular money—and I counted it a few times to make sure I had enough to pay for everything.

Behind me, two older-looking ladies stood in line, waiting to put their food on the black conveyor belt. I turned around and gave them my biggest smile. One of the ladies smiled back and said, "It is a big responsibility shopping all by yourself."

"Yes, it's my first time. I even figured out how to use this special food money," I said proudly, showing them the coupons.

"That's nice, sweetie," she said in a patronizing tone. She turned her head and started whispering to the grey-haired lady behind her. I strained my ears to hear what they were saying over the chimes of the cash register. "Can you believe it?" the woman I spoke with whispered. "Sending someone so young to the store with food stamps? It ought to be a crime."

"Her mother is probably too drunk to leave the house, the poor kid," the gray-haired woman added.

At the mention of food stamps, my face went from flushed-with-excitement to burning-with-embarrassment. I had heard the words "food stamps" before but I didn't even really know what they were. All I knew was that they were something most people weren't proud to be on. Looking back, I now realize those women must have been miserable people to speak that way in front of a young child, but at the time, all I felt was mortification.

"Hey there, little one, can you give me your special money? We're all done," the cashier said.

I could feel the tears starting to well up inside me, so I kept my head down as I handed the cashier the book of money. She tore out what she needed and handed the book back to me with a compassionate smile.

The old man with the crooked back who bagged up the groceries patted me on the head as I walked away from the register, destroying whatever feeling of maturity I had when I first entered the grocery store. Who was I kidding to think I was a grown-up? I was just a stupid little kid who had been tricked into running errands my mother was too lazy to do herself. My face aflame, I pushed the cart away from the register and shuffled behind the other shoppers toward the door, feeling as if all eyes in the store were upon me.

I pushed the shopping cart through the parking lot, across the busy main street and turned up my road with tears streaming down my face. When I opened the front door of the house, a haze of sweetly-scented gray smoke wafted out. Three of my parents' friends sat at the kitchen table. The only one whose name I knew was Haley—she sat right next to my mother. Haley had blonde hair, big shoulders and bug eyes that made her look like she was in a perpetual state of surprise. Next to her sat a man who was attractive in a Magnum P.I. kind of way. He had a mustache that hid his mouth and wore a brown leather vest. Standing near the stereo was a stalky, tall man with a big belly and a huge gap in his teeth. In the dream, their features took on grotesque proportions, as if I were viewing them through a fish-eye lens.

"Can you put the groceries away, Lin?" Mom asked.

"Why can't you do it?" I asked with an edge in my voice.

"What's with the attitude?" she asked, annoyed.

"Nothing," I mumbled.

I walked downstairs and brought the rest of the groceries in from the shopping cart.

"Look at the way she's pouting," Mom said teasingly. "Did you enjoy your trip to the store?" She was always eager to taunt me in some way after she'd had a few drinks in her. Her friends grinned down at me like idiots, having a good ole laugh at my expense. I hated them.

"Yeah, right," I muttered.

"Don't get smart with me, little girl," she said bitterly. "You think you're too great for your own good? Maybe you're too good to eat, too."

My stomach tightened as the hatred swelled up inside my body from head to toe. All I ever wished for was a mother who loved me and I felt like God had made a mistake by putting me in this house. I couldn't tell what I wanted more—for her to wrap her arms around me and give me a hug, or for her to drop dead and get out of my life forever.

"... Linda, what are you doing?"

The sound of Frank's voice pulled me out of my trance. Once more I was back in the present, wiping the mascara from my face in the mirror. In the reflection, my eyes stared back at me intently. At times like this, I often felt like my eyes belonged to someone else, as if they're broadcasting my every move to an overly critical outside observer. My eyes could convey an entire range of emotions without using any words. They gazed disapprovingly at the wrinkles under my eyes and at every tiny bit of fat on my tummy or triceps. They could see right through my forehead into my brain to read my thoughts, knowing how stupid and insecure I felt almost all of the time.

"Honey, why are you up so early?" asked Frank, yawning.

"I had a dream," I replied.

"Was it a bad dream, love?"

"Same ole, same ole," I sighed. "Stressed about money again."

He kissed the back of my head and placed his hand gently on my back. "I'll get us some coffee and I'll meet you on the couch."

"Sounds great," I said. "I'll be right out."

He paused momentarily and repeated a phrase I'd heard an awful lot lately: "Everything is going to be fine."

When I finished removing my makeup, I went out to the living room, trying to shake the negative energy and anxiety from my mind and soul. *It's a new day*, I said to myself. Sitting on the couch before sunrise with a cup of java always seemed to calm my anxious mind. As Frank finished making the coffee in the kitchen, I recited a quote I'd read once: "Faith and fear can't coexist. Choose one."

Chapter 16 Afraid

Weeks turned into months and Frank hadn't found work. He had held true to his word, as well as the others, and had left 3Vocs. He searched endlessly for work, but couldn't get one interview in Austin or outside of the city. I continued to consult on a very limited basis because I couldn't find any marketing contracts. During this time, we used up nearly all of our savings and started to use our credit cards to pay for expenses. It was the spring of 2002, and we were seven months into the longest bout of unemployment we'd ever gone through. After much internal debate, I had taken Frank's advice and continued taking courses at JFK, thinking that his unemployment would be short-lived. Even though it added to our overall debt, I knew if I didn't start trying to make a change now, I might never get the chance again. My schoolwork kept me busy but it was not very challenging. I could already see that there was a lot of room for improvement in the field of career development.

Over the months, Frank and I had developed a fairly regular unemployment regimen. Every day from morning until dusk, we would work in tandem in the upstairs game room, searching for job opportunities in Austin. Of course, I stayed busy with my coursework, too. With each passing day of joblessness, my fear and anxiety increased. I gave Frank points for diligence. He had met with everyone in his network and then some to uncover any potential leads on job opportunities. He was always jetting off to lunches, coffees, and after-work drinks, anywhere that he might be able to get a lead on some full-time or consulting work. To stay fresh, he had started a consulting practice called PMO Corporation and was providing consulting services to struggling, early-stage start-ups in exchange for equity—it seems everyone had run out of money. Under the moniker of PMO, he also picked up some short-term contracts with companies backed by ATX Ventures. Fortunately, and despite the trials and tribulations of his past experiences, he was still respected by the team.

For all his efforts, though, Frank's regular full-time job prospects weren't looking any better now than they did the day he left 3Vocs. On one particularly fruitless day of hunting in May, I brought up the possibility to Frank that he might have to revise his expectations. When it came to opportunities in Frank's career path, Austin seemed to be bone dry. The way I saw it, he had two options: find a job in another city, or take a job beneath the VP level.

"I'm way ahead of you, love," he said. "I've been looking for everything from VP to director to project manager positions. I've applied for jobs everywhere from California to Massachusetts."

"Oh my goodness, I don't want to leave Austin," I said, surprised. "I love it here. It's our home. I meant you should look for jobs in different cities, not out-of-state."

"Well, I don't want to move either," he offered. "I'm doing everything to try and find something in Austin. There's just nothing out there right now."

"How are we doing financially?" I inquired. Due to my money anxiety, Frank was responsible for paying all our bills, keeping track of our expenses, and pretty much everything else that had to do with our finances. When we were doing okay financially, this arrangement worked nicely for me—I never had to worry about where the money was coming from or going to. But now that we had to pinch our pennies, having Frank in charge of the finances was actually adding to my anxiety. For all I knew, we probably had bills piling up for miles.

"We're fine right now," he said. "Don't worry about it."

"How can I not worry about it in this kind of market?" I asked. "The economy sure doesn't seem to be turning around quickly. We have to be using up all of our savings to pay the bills. We must be getting low because it's costing us thousands per month to keep up our lifestyle. How long do we have before we eat up all of our savings?"

"I'm on top of it," Frank protested. "We're doing fine."

"We are not doing fine, Frank. Wake up. You're not making any money worth speaking of and I'm barely bringing in a paycheck. It's gotten to the point where I think we need to talk about reducing our expenses. And, have you forgotten about the tax bill?"

Frank and I had gotten a shock when we sat down to do our taxes earlier that year. We had always kept a separate account for our property taxes but

Frank had dipped into that account when money was low, and now there was nothing left. When the tax bill had arrived, we discovered that we owed $23,000. We managed to get an extension until the end of the year, but it was going to cost us tons in fees. That tax bill put a huge weight over my head every time we discussed our finances.

"Well, why don't you just manage the finances if you know exactly what we should do?" he snapped.

I slammed the screen on my laptop shut. "The way you manage the finances isn't the issue, Frank. I don't know what the backup plan is if you don't get a job soon. I'm not blaming you. I'm just worried. I haven't been able to find work, either. We can't keep living as if we're making good salaries. I don't want to go so far into credit card debt that I can't dig myself back out. I've worked since I was fifteen to have an excellent credit history."

He slumped back in his chair like a defiant teenager being scolded by his mother for staying out too late.

"I hate when you sit like that," I said. "Like your time is too valuable to engage in petty conversation with us commoners."

"I don't know what you're talking about," he said. "I'm just sitting."

"You're sitting with an attitude."

He rolled his eyes and shifted his body into a more relaxed position. "Is this better?"

"No," I said. "Now you're just pretending to be relaxed. But you still have an attitude. It's written all over your face."

"Can we move on?" he asked.

"Fine, let's," I said, irritated. "Let's start by looking at each of our bills and seeing if there's anything we can eliminate."

"I don't know what each individual bill is costing us," he replied.

"You've been managing the bills for the past two years and you don't know how much we're paying for each bill?" I asked.

"I know rough estimates," he protested.

"Well, let's estimate if you don't know exact numbers."

We got out a sheet of paper and started making a list of all our expenses. Between the mortgage, car payments, lawn service, pool service, utilities, Andrew's school, nanny, country club membership, and personal expenses, we estimated that we were spending $24,000 per month. In all, there were over forty expenses listed on the paper, ranging from $99 to $7000 per month.

When I saw the number written down like that, it sent a jolt of fear through my system. "This is completely unsustainable, Frank!" I said. "We can't live like this! Look at this—$4,000 per month for meals and entertainment? We can shave that one down immediately. That is absolutely ridiculous."

"Yeah," he said. "That is a little out of hand. That one's easy. We'll just stop going out so much. What else?"

"What about Tae Kwon Do? That $200 per month adds up." A few months back, Frank had enrolled the whole family in Tae Kwon Do. He thought it would be a fun way for us to spend time together, learn how to protect ourselves, and get our aggression out. I went along to support Frank and Andrew, but there were a lot of other things I would have rather done with my time.

"I've got to draw the line on that one," Frank said. "It really helps me manage my stress. If I can't have Tae Kwon Do, I might go a little crazy . . . and besides, I really enjoy it. It's good for the family. Besides, it's a drop in the bucket. The biggest expense isn't going away, and that's the mortgage. We can clip as many coupons as we can find, but we're still going to owe $7000 per month on the house. And the only way that one is going away is if we sell it."

"No way," I said. "I love this house. This is my dream house. Nuh-uh, we're not selling it. Besides, no one's buying houses in this market, anyway."

"Well, there you go," he said simply. "You don't want to sell the house and I don't want to quit Tae Kwon Do."

As I reviewed the information, I felt disappointed that I had distanced myself so far from the finances. I was completely clueless about our spending patterns. I stared at the paper with my brow furrowed in frustration, poring over endless monthly transactions that should have been stopped months and even years ago. How had we gotten to this point? There was a time in my life when I would have considered $24,000 per year a decent salary. Our car payments alone amounted to more than that in a given year.

"Did you hear that?" he suddenly asked, breaking our silence.

"Hear what?" I asked.

He lifted his head and silenced me with his finger.

"I think I heard the doorbell."

There may have been a time in the not-so-distant past when an unexpected doorbell chime signified that a neighbor had come over to borrow some sugar or a relative had dropped by to say hello. In the modern world, however, where every day was planned down to the minute and families were spread out across the globe, an unplanned visitor was generally cause for suspicion.

"Who would stop over unannounced?" I wondered.

We got up from the table and headed downstairs to see who was outside. When we reached the bottom of the stairs, I looked out the window to see an overweight man with thinning hair and a gray shirt standing on our front porch.

"Who is that? Are you expecting anyone?" I whispered.

"I have no idea. Are you expecting anyone?" he whispered back.

"Not that I'm aware of." I peered out the window to get a bigger view of the driveway. "I can see a truck outside but it doesn't have a name on it," I whispered.

"Why are we whispering?" he asked.

"Oh, shoot." My blood ran cold as I suddenly realized what was going on. "It's the furniture."

Almost a year ago, back when our future hadn't seemed so uncertain, we had ordered a brand new, custom-made master bedroom set that included an oversized king bed, a new bureau, two large nightstands, and a mirror. We had also purchased an additional couch for the downstairs living room because the single couch we had in there right now was getting swallowed up by the cavernous room.

"Oh my God, I completely forgot about the furniture with everything going on," I said, worried. "Should we answer the door? Or should we ignore them?"

"What do you mean?" he asked.

"Well, if we answer the door and accept the furniture, then we have to write a check."

"Okay," Frank said. "For how much?"

I searched my memory bank to try and remember how much the furniture cost. "We owe about $22,000."

"What?" Frank asked, alarmed.

"What do you mean, 'what'?" I responded huffily. "You were with me when we bought this stuff. Why are you acting like you don't know anything about it?" We had been an established customer when we ordered the furniture, which was why we hadn't had to pay in full at the time.

"I didn't mean that literally," he said. "It just took me by surprise. I'd completely forgotten it was coming."

The man in the gray shirt rang the doorbell again. I began to feel a little absurd hiding out two feet from the door. The window worked both ways, after all.

"Well, I'm sure he's seen us by this point," I said. "You should go open the door."

Frank opened the door and greeted the driver cheerfully. After they'd brought all the furniture inside, Frank offered them $100 to help him set it up. For the next hour, Frank and the guys took our bed apart and moved all of the furniture into the guest room on the second floor of the house.

After awhile, Frank and I returned to our computers while the movers continued setting up the new furniture. A few hours after arriving, they finally finished.

"Thanks for all of your help today," I said, signing the final paper work. I cringed as I came to the figure at the bottom of the receipt, but there was no turning back now. I wrote them a check for the full amount and handed it over before I could regret it.

"Thanks for helping me move the old furniture upstairs. You did a great job on setting up the bedroom," Frank said, shaking their hands. With that, he reached in his pocket and, to my astonishment, pulled out two, crisp $100 bills, and handed them to the movers. He walked them to the door and locked it behind them.

"Why did you give them $200 instead of $100?" I asked, flabbergasted.

"Linda, they've been here for most of the day helping us get set up," he said. "I thought they deserved a nice tip."

"$200? That's more than just a nice tip," I argued. "That's like winning the lottery. What do you not understand about our financial situation? We need to be more frugal with our money! It's bad enough that we just spent $22,000 on furniture we don't even really need. The casualness with which you toss away $100 bills astounds me." Frank didn't respond, so I turned my back and walked into the bedroom to try and straighten out the mess the movers had made. He followed behind me, mumbling something I couldn't hear.

"Can you stop mumbling?" I asked, crossly.

"I wasn't mumbling," he complained. "Your back was turned away from me and you couldn't hear me."

I turned around and put my hands on my hips. "It doesn't matter if I'm facing you or turned away from you," I said, spitting fire. "My ears are in the same place."

Frank stared at me with a blank look on his face, the wheels turning in his brain. After a few seconds, he broke into a smile, which quickly escalated into roaring laughter.

"What?" I asked, staring at him with a look of bemusement. "What's so funny?"

He leaned against the wall, shaking with laughter. "Your ears!" he gasped in between laughs. "Your ears are always in the same place!"

"Well, they are," I said, giggling. Now that I thought about it, it did sound kind of ridiculous. He was laughing so hard that I couldn't help but join in, and soon our giddiness floated through the room. Tears filled both of our eyes as we tried to stop laughing.

"Okay, seriously," I said through cracked laughter when we finally managed to calm down. "Look at this room. It doesn't look like all of the furniture will fit."

"Well, let's arrange what we can, and we'll figure out what we need to do after that," Frank suggested.

"Okay, but I'm telling you right now that it's not going to fit. Can't you just look at the pieces and see it?"

"Would you stop giving me a hard time and help me move this stuff?" he said playfully, pulling my body close to his to kiss me. "I love you, you know. Even though your ears are always in the same place."

"Don't try to sweet-talk me!" I whispered teasingly. "Get those dirty thoughts out of your head, mister."

"What dirty thoughts? There are no dirty thoughts here."

"Sure there are. I can read minds, you know," I responded.

"Okay, then what am I thinking smarty pants?"

"You want to get this bed organized and give it a test run."

He smiled. "No, that is not what I was thinking. You can't read my mind. I was actually thinking that we could break it in right now." He had a twinkle in his eyes and a grin at the corner of his lips as he moved his hands to tickle my waist.

"Stopppp," I whined, playing hard-to-get. "We need to get some work done." I covered my waist with my hands to fend off his tickling fingers.

"We don't have any work, remember? We don't work." He pushed me closer to the bed with his hips. He leaned in close and whispered in my ear, "What do you say we make baby number two? Andrew needs a little brother or sister."

"Mr. Ginac, your timing is unbelievable," I gasped. "It is one of your character flaws . . . but I wouldn't want you any other way."

"You ready to stand on your head?" he asked with a sexy laugh. Before I became pregnant with Andrew, we had had trouble conceiving. When I told my mom what was going on, she told me that the women on her side of the family could only get pregnant if they stood on their heads immediately after sex. It sounded ridiculous, but when we finally tried it, I got pregnant with Andrew immediately. If the third time was a charm, we'd have a baby in approximately ten months.

"Well, I guess we'd better get busy," I said. "I'm sure the manufacturing team will want a full report on the functionality and durability of the mattress."

"I suspect you're right," he said, stroking my lower back with his hands. "So, let's make sure we test it appropriately."

"How do you suggest we get started?" I asked.

He laughed. "Oh, I have some ideas."

"Really? Care to share a few of them with me?" My eyes fluttered as I bit his lip. "My imagination is on vacation so you might have to work overtime."

"It would be my pleasure," he purred, as he swept my hair away from my neck.

After we made love, I stood on my head in the corner and tried to think positive thoughts. Maybe Frank was right, and things would turn out to be all right after all. I chuckled to myself. From my perspective, it seemed like our whole world had once again turned upside-down.

Chapter 17 Inspired

Andrew's first year of kindergarten came to an end in June. All signs indicated that he loved school as much as I had when I was young. When we met with his teacher at the end of the year, she raved about his intelligence and his kindness to the other children.

"He's a great kid," she told us. "You two should both be proud."

"We are," Frank said, smiling.

"There's one thing that I'd like to talk to you about, though," she continued. "It's nothing bad, it's just a little unusual. Most kids his age are little bundles of raw emotion. It's not out of the ordinary for them to burst into tears out of the blue or get into a screaming match with one of their classmates over a toy, when they'd been playing together happily just a moment before."

"Oh," I said, worried. "Has Andrew been acting up? That doesn't sound like him."

"Oh, it's just the opposite, actually," she said. "He never acts up. He's the most in-control kid I've ever seen in my entire career. Whenever he feels angry or sad, he takes loud deep breaths and counts to ten to try and calm himself down."

"Well, that's good," Frank said. "He learned how to do that at Tae-Kwon-Do."

"Not necessarily," she said. "For children of Andrew's age, there's a lot of benefit to letting their emotions out. It helps them learn valuable lessons about socialization and it helps us understand what they need. I'm afraid if Andrew bottles his emotions up inside at this age, he may never learn how to express himself in a healthy way."

Her words really struck a nerve with me. If my mom had gone to a single parent conference when I was a kid, my teachers might have told her the exact same thing about me. If there was one thing I never wanted for my children, it was for them to feel like they had to hide their feelings. Frank and I had focused on raising Andrew in a much more open and loving environment than I had been raised in, but clearly he was still picking up some bad habits about how to deal with his feelings. *But how could I teach my son the right way to deal with his feelings when I was often at a loss about how to deal with my own?*

We left the conference feeling proud and confused, yet determined to help Andrew feel more comfortable expressing his emotions. I knew how blessed I was to have such an amazing kid, but after the shock of the teacher's observation wore off, my heart pumped harder and tears started to well up in my eyes. I couldn't fathom having Andrew feel any sadness.

I could tell that Frank was worried, too, as he watched me stare out the car window and whimper as certain songs played on the stereo. Lately I'd been feeling overly emotional. Now, on top of worrying about job and financial stress, I had to stress about thinking my son might grow up to be a monster if I didn't teach him how to share his feelings. *Jeez, it wasn't as if he hid all emotions*, I thought. Andrew seemed like a normal six-year-old to me. He got angry when he couldn't have his way and cried if we didn't give him something. He laughed when we made jokes and talked nonstop. I guess she was talking about a deeper level of expression. I knew this would be a major challenge in my life because I'm not one to express my innermost feelings. I kept everything to myself, then let it out at the wrong time and directed at the wrong person, usually Frank. Ironically, it would be Frank acting as a "life coach" that would start steering me toward emotional maturity.

❁❁❁

At my request, we stopped at the grocery store on the way home. Frank stayed in the car while I went into the store to pick a few things up. I was just about to turn into the aisle for the hamburger meat when I heard my name being called. I turned around to see Kiley headed my way.

"Hi Kiley," I said, feigning a smile. Much as I loved Kiley, it had been months since I'd seen her and I wasn't in much of a mood to play catch up.

She stopped a few feet from me, smoothing back a strand of blonde hair that had fallen in her face. "Where have you been?" she asked, her sharp aquamarine eyes glaring behind her red framed glasses. "I've emailed you several times and you haven't returned my phone calls."

I stepped up and gave her a hug in an attempt to make peace. "Yeah, I know," I said, stepping back. "I'm sorry. I've been so busy."

"Too busy to call me?" she asked, placing her hand on her hip. "I'm your best friend."

"I know, I know," I said.

She crossed her arms over her chest, lifting her eyebrows. "What's going on?"

I sighed and shifted the basket from my right arm to my left, my shoulders straining under its weight. "Nothing is wrong. Actually, everything is really great."

Her eyes thinned as she frowned at me. "How long have I known you? Cut the bullshit, Ms. Everythang!"

"Honestly, Kiley. Things are really . . . really good. Frank is working on a start-up idea and I'm doing contract work for a couple of companies. Neither one of us has to be in the office every day. We actually get to spend some quality time together and with Andrew. Truly, the layoff was the best thing that could have happened to me."

Kiley propped both hands on her slender waist, eying me suspiciously. "Well, girl, as long as you're happy, I'm happy," she finally said. "But don't disappear like that again, okay? Now when are we getting together for a bottle of wine?"

"Anytime," I responded. Truthfully, I missed hanging out with Kiley. I'd become something of a hermit since the layoffs and the thought of some quality girl time was pretty appealing. "Are you free Saturday night?"

"I have a date, but I can bring him, if that's okay," Kiley responded sheepishly.

"Who?"

"Someone you know. Mark."

I searched my memory bank. "Mark who?"

"He worked for you."

"No!" I said. "Mark? Girl, I know you're excited to jump back into the dating pool after your divorce . . . but Mark? He's so serious all the time!"

"You only know him from work. He is so much more. You will love him. He's great."

My mind was racing with thoughts. "I just can't imagine the match."

"Oh, you're just jealous," she responded, giggling. "I'll explain it all later . . ." She fashioned her hand into an imaginary receiver and put it up to her ear. "Call me," she said, then turned and began pushing her cart toward the exit.

"Bring two bottles of wine over on Saturday," I called out as she walked away. "I have a feeling we'll polish off several."

As soon as she was out of eyesight, I darted into the aisle. I glanced up and down the aisle to make sure no one I knew was nearby, and then quickly snatched a One Step pregnancy test off the shelf and put it in my basket, hidden beneath the eggs.

I returned to the car with a smirk on my face. It was great to see my best friend in the store and set a date for fun. "Honey, I ran into Kiley in the store and invited them over on Saturday," I said.

"Oh, great. It's about time you two got together."

"Yeah, yeah, yeah."

As Frank drove us home, I mentally returned to the conversation we'd had with Andrew's teacher. *Was it possible that he would have the same inner conflicts when he was older that I myself felt now?* I had to make sure that didn't happen. I wasn't sure how we were going to do it yet, but I knew Frank and I would have to change the way we communicated if we hoped to live in an open and honest family environment. It might be a lot of work, but I was ready to do it for Andrew's sake. And for the sake of the little brother or sister that I suspected was on the way. The big question was how to do it.

❀❀❀

The next morning, Andrew woke us up bright and early, excited to begin his summer vacation.

"Mommy, Daddy, what are you doing?" he shouted through the door.

"We'll be right out, love," I said, yawning and dragging myself out of the bed.

"I'm hungry," Andrew complained. "Can I have a Fruit Roll-Up?"

"No, it's too early. Hold on and I'll make you breakfast. I'll be right out. Go back upstairs." I grabbed some clothes out of the dresser and walked into the bathroom to get ready.

"But I'm soooo hungry," he whined. "Dad . . . are you in there?"

"We hear you loud and clear, Andrew," Frank said. "We'll be right out." Frank rolled off the bed and pulled his pants and shirt on quickly. He had always been oddly insistent on being completely dressed before attending to

Andrew. Throughout his entire life, Andrew had never seen his dad without a minimum of a T-shirt and shorts. Conversely, Frank couldn't stand it when Andrew roamed the house without a shirt.

"Frank, would you just open the door?" I asked, annoyed by his strict modesty. "It is not going to kill Andrew to see your bare chest."

"I want Andrew to grow up with respect. Guys just shouldn't roam around the house shirtless," he replied. "It's trashy."

"Jeez . . ." I said, shaking my head. "You're his father, for crying out loud. My father roamed around without a shirt and it never bothered me."

"Maybe so, but my mother raised me to be a gentleman."

"Your mother should have been a nun," I laughed. "She had to ask for instructions from her mother on her wedding night. Don't get me wrong, I love your mom, but she makes the Puritans look like Hippies."

Frank laughed as he finished buttoning his shirt. "All right, I'll get Andrew. Are you almost done? I'm getting pretty hungry, too."

I scurried out of the bathroom and spanked Frank on the bottom. "I'm right behind you. Let's go take care of those hunger pangs . . . although I'm surprised you're hungry already. It's so early."

"I'm starving," he murmured. "Your body doesn't work like the rest of mankind. I don't know how you can go so long without eating."

"I just don't obsess about food, I guess."

"Life is unfair," he sighed. "I'm hungry all the time, but I need to watch what I eat. You could eat as much as you want and still stay thin, yet you're never hungry. Most pregnant women eat for two—are you sure you are not starving my baby?" I'd taken the test earlier and confirmed that I was pregnant. Even though our finances were in a sinkhole, we were still paying for insurance and we had both really wanted—and needed—something positive to happen. It may have not seemed like the best time to have a new baby, but we were thrilled to be adding to our family.

"It's probably about the size of a bean right now, Frank," I said sarcastically. "Which means its stomach is about the size of a grain of salt. I will have an extra grain of salt with breakfast if it will put your mind at ease."

We joined Andrew in the kitchen. We hadn't told him about the baby yet. We figured we should wait until the end of the first trimester, just to be safe. I didn't have much desire to explain what "having a miscarriage" was to a six-year-old.

I grabbed a box of cereal out of the cupboard and some milk from the refrigerator while Frank made the morning coffee. I looked at the box of Rice Krispies and was suddenly struck with an uneasy feeling.

"You know, the generic Rice Krispies taste exactly the same, and they're a dollar less a box," I said to Frank.

"Mm-hmm," he answered absentmindedly. It had been weeks since we'd had the new furniture delivered, and we had yet to come up with a serious plan about how we were going to save money. Frank's plan seemed to be that if he didn't talk about it, it wasn't real.

"I'd like talk about finances later," I told Frank as I chopped some banana to go in the cereal. "We need to come up with a plan in case it takes longer than we expect to start making money again."

"Everything is going to be fine," he reassured me. "We'll figure it out."

There were those words again: *everything is going to be fine*. We could be living on the street in a cardboard box and Frank would think everything was going to work out.

"When?" I asked. "All you're doing is pushing an uncomfortable conversation off into the future. You don't live at home with 'Mom' anymore, Frank. She's not here to protect you, and your consolations are just empty words. We need to face this head-on."

"Okay, fine. I know it's something we need to talk about eventually. I just don't think it's as pressing a problem as you think it is. We still have money in the bank. We are not going to crash and burn tomorrow. I promise. Everything is okay."

I lowered my voice. "That's what you always say."

"What do you mean?" He turned his head and looked at me with an irritating look of confusion. He knew exactly what I was talking about.

"Mom, can I have some juice?" Andrew interrupted.

"How about some milk instead?"

"Juice?" he asked again, ignoring my suggestion.

"Fine. Juice," I consented.

Frank grabbed the apple juice out of the refrigerator while I searched the cabinet for a plastic cup. "Andrew, are you taking all of your cups outside to use as toys?" I asked.

"No."

I found an old navy blue Rubbermaid cup and filled it with apple juice and handed it to Andrew. "Now please go sit down at the table and eat your breakfast. Mommy and Daddy have things to talk about."

Frank leaned against the counter, looking at the ground like a wounded puppy.

"I just really hope that I am not going to live a life of financial stress with you," I said, trying to speak quietly. "I had enough stress as a kid dealing with my parents' money problems to fill a lifetime. I don't want Andrew to deal with the same thing, which is why I do not want to finish this conversation in front of him. I think this is the exact pattern that is causing Andrew to bottle his emotions. I'm not sure how to have an unemotional conversation with you when it comes to finances."

I put the finishing touches on breakfast and took my cereal bowl and coffee off the counter.

"I'm going upstairs to eat. I want to be by myself right now," I informed him. Frank's attitude was getting under my skin. If I stayed and ate breakfast with them, I was afraid I'd fly off the handle.

"Mom, I'm still hungry," Andrew complained. "Can I have more cereal?"

"Come on, Linda," Frank said. "Stay down here with us. You might feel better after you eat some food."

"Fine," I said.

I sat down at the table and picked up a spoon. My hand shook as I lifted the cereal to my mouth. Suddenly feeling overcome by everything, I dropped the spoon in the bowl and covered my face with my hands. I took deep breaths, trying to hold back the tears that were gathering in my eyes.

Frank reached over and stroked my hand. "Honey, everything is going to be fine. I love you."

"What is fine, Dad?" Andrew asked innocently, through a mouthful of food.

"Please don't talk with your mouth full, Andrew," I sniffled. "Take smaller bites or you'll choke."

"What is fine, Dad?" Andrew asked again. At such a young age, he already had the knack for being persistent and negotiating until he got his way. Not that different from his mom.

"Whaaaaaaaat is fine?" Andrew persisted.

"Nothing," Frank said. "Mom and I are talking about big people stuff." Then, in a classic Frank distraction move, "Finish your breakfast and we can go buy you a new video game."

Great, I thought, annoyed. *Bribe him to finish his breakfast and reward him for being annoying. Way to impart valuable life lessons to your son.*

"Yessss!" Andrew shouted, pumping his fist. "Can we go now? Let's go to Toys-R-Us." He jumped out of his chair and tugged at Frank's arm.

"Andrew, SIT DOWN and finish your breakfast or we are not going anywhere," I snapped.

"I want Jak and Daxter," he said, sitting down. "It looks so cool. Can I get Jak and Daxter, Dad?"

"Fine, you can get Jaxter Daxter," Frank replied. "Now listen to Mom and eat your breakfast."

"It's Jak and Daxter," Andrew muttered before returning to his cereal.

I didn't even have to look at Frank to know that he was practically turning blue from the effort of keeping his mouth shut. It's not possible for Frank to leave things unresolved. He approached our relationship the same way he approached engineering—when he saw a problem, he wouldn't rest until he found a solution. The problem was that I was just as stubborn, except that I'd go completely silent or run away so that I didn't have to talk. He knew I was angry with him right now, and I knew it was driving him crazy. After about three minutes of eating in silence, he lost the silent game.

"I have a good feeling about some new leads I generated," he offered.

"Great. I'm sure they'll pan out just as well as all your other leads," I snapped sarcastically. "How many times do I have to tell you that I don't want to talk about this in front of Andrew?"

"Talk about what?" Andrew asked.

"Maybe we should talk about it in front of him, Linda," Frank said. "Remember what his teacher said? Maybe we need to start being more open. What kind of example are we going to set if we hide every real interaction behind closed doors?"

"What did my teacher say, Dad?" Andrew asked.

Frank turned to him. "She said that you have a hard time showing your emotions when you're upset about something, Andrew. And Mommy and I both want you to know that it's okay to be upset and to tell us about it. You don't need to close your eyes and count to ten."

Andrew fidgeted with his spoon nervously. "Is Mommy upset about something?"

"Yes," I said. "I am, honey. I'm upset because your dad and I are out of work. We're running out of money and I'm terrified that things are going to be as bad for you as they were for me when I was growing up." I could feel the tears starting to well up in my eyes, but there was no stopping now. "I'm angry with your dad for keeping me in the dark about finances, and I'm angry at myself for secretly wanting to be kept in the dark." Tears streamed down my face as I looked at Frank. "I'm not just scared and angry. I feel paralyzed. I hate living this way. I can't take this kind of pressure every moment of every day. It's driving me crazy. I wake up every morning feeling like a bad person and a bad mother and I'm sick of it. What happened to our life, Frank? You keep saying the economy's going to improve, but when? It's been almost a year! We're sinking further and further into debt, and your only plan is 'trust me!' Well, maybe I don't trust you anymore, Frank. Maybe I can't."

He put his hand on mine and looked into my eyes with a puppy-dog expression and tears. "Honey, it's going to be o—"

"DON'T," I interrupted him, forcefully pulling my hand away from his. "Don't you dare tell me it's going to be okay, Frank. If I hear that one more time, I swear to God..." I stood up and pushed my chair away from the table. "I'm going to our room," I said. "Don't follow me."

I walked briskly to our room, stamping my feet for good effect, and collapsed on the bed, sobbing. I felt completely drained and thoroughly embarrassed to have said such hurtful things in front of Andrew. But it felt good to say exactly what I was thinking and that made me feel even worse. Negative thoughts circled through my mind. *This life isn't working for us anymore. Maybe they'd be better off without me. I don't want to be here. I was destined to be single and alone. Frank needs to be with someone else.* Barely realizing what I was doing, I walked to the closet and pulled out a suitcase. I slammed it on the bed and robotically began filling it full of clothes, as if in a fog. *I need to get out of here*, I thought. *This is all my fault.*

As I stood above my suitcase, still shaking with tears and frustration, a knock came at the door. All I wanted to do was get out of there. The thought of having to pacify Frank right now made me burn with anger. "Go away," I wailed. Behind me, I could hear the door squeak open. I turned around with fury in my eyes. "I SAID..."

But instead of Frank, the only person standing in the doorway was a frightened little boy who desperately needed my love. He stepped into the room cautiously. When he spied the suitcase on the bed, he looked into my face with an expression of such sorrow and confusion that my heart instantly shattered into a million pieces.

"Where are you going, Mommy?" he asked me.

"Nowhere, sweetie," I said, pushing the suitcase aside. I sat down on the bed and extended my arms to him. "I'm not going anywhere."

He tentatively walked across the room and into my arms. I pulled him close and kissed him on the forehead.

"Mommy," he whispered quietly, "would you and Daddy be happier if I wasn't here?"

His words struck me in the chest like a bullet. And at that moment, the months of frustration, the endless fights with Frank over money, my own feelings of self-pity and worthlessness—none of that mattered. The only thing that mattered was the effect our situation was having upon our innocent child. Andrew didn't care how nice our house was, or whether our job titles were commensurate with our experience . . . he just wanted Mommy and Daddy to be happy. And the fact that he felt as if he were somehow responsible for our tension was heartbreaking.

"No, no, no," I whispered, holding him tightly and letting the tears flow. "We would be so sad if you weren't around. You mean everything to Daddy and me, and we love you very, very much. None of this fighting has anything to do with you, okay?"

At that moment, Frank appeared in the doorway. Andrew's comment had deflated my feelings of anger, and when I caught Frank's eye, I gave him a conciliatory smile, which he returned. Right then and there, I made a pledge that I wouldn't quit on my family. Even though it was a lot of work to keep things together sometimes, I knew my life would be nothing without them in it.

"We'll get through this," Frank said as he sat down on the bed beside me and wrapped his arms around Andrew and me. And for once I believed him.

❀❀❀

That Saturday night, Kiley and Mark showed up at our house at 7:00 P.M. with two bottles of Merlot, a bag of tortilla chips and queso. Kiley and I hugged like sisters and then I moved over to Mark and gave him a hug. It felt very awkward on many dimensions. It wasn't simply the thought of Kiley and Mark as a couple. It had more to do with my inability to look at him in the eye because he was one of the employees who had been affected by the layoffs at Trifinity.

I pulled four, crystal, long-stemmed wine glasses from the cabinet and sat them on the counter. Frank uncorked the wine and filled our glasses.

"I'd like to propose a toast," Frank said. "To my wife, the most beautiful woman in the world."

"Jeez, Frank," I said, embarrassed.

"No, it's sweet," Kiley said, then to Mark, "why don't you make a toast to me like that?"

"Because you're not my wife," Mark answered teasingly. Kiley flashed him a flirty look as we clinked our glasses in a toast.

Kiley and I talked so much about the events of the past year that the first glass of wine seemed to be gone in a flash. As I consumed the last sip, Kiley picked up the bottle to refill it. I put my hand over the glass. "Just one," I said.

Kiley looked at me in surprise. It wasn't normal for me to just have one glass of wine, especially during a social event. Her look of confusion soon turned to one of awareness as she burst into a wide smile.

"Oh my God!" she giggled.

"What?" Mark asked, oblivious.

"Congratulations!" she screamed, leaping out of her seat and giving me a hug.

"Congratulations for what?" Mark asked. "Are you quitting drinking?"

"No," I laughed. "I'm having a baby."

"Oh," Mark said. "Congratulations."

We spent the rest of the night talking about the baby, my company plans, and all of the other things that were going on in our lives. Mark and Kiley seemed like a happy couple, and by the end of the night, my worries about things being uncomfortable between Mark and I had faded. When we talked about the layoffs, he told me that no one blamed me for what happened. I appreciated him saying that. It made me feel a lot better about how things had ended.

Frank, Mark and Kiley ended up polishing off four bottles of wine. I was a little envious that I couldn't join them, but I still had a good time. At the end of the night, Frank and I stood in the doorway waving as they pulled out of the driveway.

"Let's go make a baby," Frank whispered, his eyes twinkling.

"We already have one on the way," I said.

"Oh, that's right," Frank said. "Well, let's go make another one."

I laughed and threw my arm around his waist. We closed the door and walked back to the bedroom together, with me feeling happier than I had in a long time.

Chapter 18 Panicked

The morning was crisp and I felt a bit of chill as Frank and I started our four-mile jog on Town Lake. Frank and I had been running together for years, and this morning we had signed up for a short fun run to support cancer research. Frank ran quietly beside me, as I pushed the jogger with Andrew, our arms almost touching as we passed the two-mile marker.

The jog seemed to be taking longer than usual. Occasionally, I turned my head to peer at Frank and see how he was faring. I always run faster than him and it has led to playful taunting between us. Today, he seemed to be doing okay.

We jogged next to each other in silence, our breath feeling heavy in the morning air. When we finally got to the water stop, I downed three snow-cone sized cups of water. Frank's complexion was pale and he was sweating profusely.

"Are you okay, honey?" I asked.

"Jesus, you are fast," he said, glancing down at his watch and fidgeting with a few buttons. "We ran that at an 8:30 pace. I thought pregnancy would slow you down. You could go much faster if you stopped waiting for me."

"Maybe," I said. "I'm not really interested in competing. I run because I like it and it helps reduce my stress."

"Me, too," he said, panting. "Nothing reduces stress better than the impending threat of a heart attack."

"Well, I hope you don't have that heart attack before our black belt testing on Sunday."

"I'm a little bit nervous about you testing for your black belt when you are nearly six months pregnant."

I rolled my eyes and began walking toward the car, feeling stress-free from the run. Six months had passed since our dinner with Kiley and Mark. Frank still hadn't found a job and we were walking on a tightrope. In addition to watching my growing belly, I was busy with school and trying to find clients for my new business so that I could help offload the financial stress from Frank.

Brock had struggled to keep the business afloat after Frank's departure, but was ultimately forced to cease operations because they couldn't get a product built, and following 9/11, there was no new venture capital to be found. There was no appetite for risk. Stuck in a failing economy, Brock had packed up and moved to a new state. Moving from Austin seemed to be a common choice these days for the unemployed.

As I walked toward the car, I began to feel lightheaded and wobbly. Reality set in when I felt a slight cramp in my ovaries. I wondered if I needed to ease up on the aggressiveness of my jogs due to my pregnancy. I pressed my hand to my lower abdomen and waited for the cramp to pass.

"What's wrong, love?" Frank asked, trotting up beside me.

"Nothing. It's just a small cramp in my side. My body must be stretching to make room for baby number two."

"Did you ask the doctor about jogging?"

"I did, and he said it was fine since I've been jogging for years. It's actually good for me."

"All right," he said. "I just want to make sure you're okay."

"I'm fine," I said with love. Because of my miscarriage, Frank had been doting on me this whole pregnancy, and it was getting slightly irritating. It wasn't his concern that bothered me, but rather the assumption that I couldn't take care of myself.

"Let's stop for coffee on the way home," I suggested.

"Are you sure?" he asked.

"Frank . . ." I started, with attitude in my eyes. "I'm getting decaf."

"Okay, okay," he said. He walked over to the driver's seat. "This is what I get for caring," he muttered. "I just want to make sure nothing happens to you or the baby."

"It's just a stretching cramp. It's normal."

Inside, I was petrified that I might lose the baby, but I didn't want to worry Frank. My doctor knew how nervous I was and assured me the whole way that the pregnancy was going very well. *Eliminate the negative thoughts, Linda. It was just a cramp. But, for good measure, start walking instead of running.*

When we got home, I changed into a jean miniskirt—one of the maternity kinds—and a white, short-sleeved T-shirt. Butterflies fluttered in my stomach, but I couldn't tell if it was from the pregnancy or nerves. Over the past few months, my plans for starting a company had solidified, and I was now the official proprietor of The Ginac Group, a career counseling service. The only trouble was that I had yet to get any clients.

That could all change today. Almost a week earlier, Frank had run into Maya, one of his former employees at 3Vocs, and mentioned my new business. He said she seemed very interested in speaking to me and asked for my number. I hadn't yet heard from her so Frank urged me to call her. I was terrified to call because she would be my first official client. *What if it didn't go smoothly? What if I don't ask the right questions? How much should I charge for services? What if she asked me about my experience (or lack thereof)?* Except for the handful of courses I'd taken with JFK University, and the help I gave the Trifinity folks, I had no real credentials to speak about in this field. With all these questions swirling through my head, I decided to just leave it up to chance and wait for her to call me.

❀❀❀

When I woke up the next morning, I didn't get out of bed right away. I stared up at the ceiling thinking about my hesitation to call Maya. It boiled down to being afraid of rejection. I began brooding over what Frank had said and knew he was right. It was typical of me to give up before I even got started. *If I could eliminate my fears, I would be unstoppable.*

Frank has a gift of telling me exactly what I need to hear to warm my heart and get me unsettled enough to take action. I've never been the type of person to wait around and let other people decide my fate. I had finally determined that if I really wanted to get this business off the ground, it was up to me to make the first step. Just as I was about to pick up my cell phone and make a call, Frank walked into the bedroom.

"Want to go upstairs and do some work?" he asked.

"What work do you have?" I asked. I tried to sound lighthearted, but I'm sure he could pick up on the frustration behind the question.

"I need to follow up on a couple of job possibilities. I have plans to meet for coffee with one of my old vendors, and Praba said he might have something for me."

"Who?" I asked. "Probar?"

"Praba. He works for Dazel. I used to work pretty closely with him at NomaSoft. He moved back to India and his division is thinking about hiring a consultant to create training that will help their people improve the software development process."

"Sounds exotic," I said. "Does that mean we'd have to go to India?"

"I don't know. It's worth exploring, anyway. I need to get a job soon, or some contract work, because we are burning through all of our cash, even though we already reduced our expenses as much as we could."

"Oh really? I hadn't noticed," I snapped.

I choked on the rest of my words because I didn't want to start another fight with Frank. Ever since our horrible fight at the breakfast table that one morning, Frank and I had worked hard at communicating more healthily—between us and with Andrew. Actually, Frank stepped up and coached us, often acting as a mediator, using probing questions and making us clarify what we meant. In addition, I read a lot of books and did a lot of research to discover ways of better communicating. It also wasn't hurting that a lot of this was covered in my coursework, and I was having to write a lot of papers on this subject. I did a great amount of self-reflection while working toward my degree.

Already our improved communications had made a world of difference with Andrew. He'd opened up to us in ways he never had before. No longer did he close his eyes and count to ten when he felt angry. Instead, he'd say things like, "Mom, I'm mad at you because I want to play a video game and you won't let me." It often made him a lot easier to deal with. Instead of having to guess at how he was feeling, we knew exactly where he was coming from.

Regardless, it wasn't always easy to maintain perspective when our financial situation was so dire. Frank and I were both tense from the lack of work and income. I landed a few more marketing contracts but not enough to make a difference. Our cash reserves were nearly gone—if we maintained our current standard of living, we would deplete our savings in three more months or less. We continually looked for ways to minimize expenses, but couldn't find any more ways to trim.

By the time I walked upstairs and fired up the computer, I had changed my mind about calling Maya. With a baby on the way and financial disaster looming, I felt like I had no business starting a new company. *Maybe I can find some kind of full-time marketing consulting job,* I thought. *Just something to tide me over until we get through this rough patch.* The thought of getting roped into another go-nowhere corporate job scared the hell out of me, but I knew I needed to do what was best for my family.

I glanced away from my computer and over at Frank, who was sitting at the table with a troubled expression. When I caught his eye, he shook the worried expression from his face, rolled his chair closer to mine, and pulled me into his arms. His warm touch lowered my stress level a bit.

"Sorry to be so irritable, honey," I whispered. "I'm just stressed and confused about what to do."

"About what?" His response was soft and caring.

"Starting this business. I must be a freaking idiot. Maybe I should just try to find another marketing job. That's where my experience is. I have no business selling myself as a career coach," I complained.

"Linda, I want you to start this business," he insisted.

"I appreciate the support, Frank, but this has never been a part of our plan. We always agreed that we'd be a working couple and contribute equally to our future. You know how important that is to me. What right do I have to completely change my career now, when we're at our lowest point? It is going to take a lot of time and money to build a successful business. I don't want to put that kind of burden on you."

"Forget about me," he said innocently. "What do you want to do?"

"Well, I want to start this business. But what I want and what we need are two different things. If you were working, this wouldn't be such a difficult decision."

"Put it out of your mind. I'm going to get another job soon and we'll be fine. We can live off my salary alone, as long as we live very conservatively," he said supportively.

At the words "we'll be fine," my attention started to drift. I just couldn't tap into Frank's boundless optimism. I shifted my seat back in front of my computer and looked away from him. "Be realistic, Frank. Neither of us knows how long it will take for you to find another job."

"Have a little faith," he replied, turning back to his own computer. "I've got it covered."

It was comforting to work in the same room with Frank. When things were going well between us, he was very easy to be around. He knew when I was in deep concentration and allowed me to work silently. In all honesty, he probably appreciated those moments of silence. I have a tendency to fill silence with constant chatter. Every so often, he would reach over and rub my leg or arm to let me know he was thinking of me. Occasionally, without speaking, he'd send me an emoticon on instant messenger to let me know how he was feeling. Sometimes he sent over a simple smiley face. Other times he would be a bit more mischievous and send me a naked smiley-face dancer. It was as close as we ever got to "sexting."

As I stared at the computer screen, I immediately felt bored with my options. The worst part about being unemployed is the boredom. I'd worked at steady jobs for so long that I didn't know what to do with free time. For years, I'd wished for the time to do whatever I wanted, and now that I had it, I was frozen. All I wanted to think about was starting my business, but I was worried about the financial pressure it would put on Frank and our relationship. At the same time, I couldn't bring myself to go through the job-hunting motions anymore. I felt paralyzed with indecision.

As much as I liked to consider myself a self-starter, I'd always wished that some type of divine intervention would come along and magically point me in the right direction. Over the years I'd poured over countless career guides and gotten no closer to figuring out what type of career best suited me. With no clear idea about what type of career would bring passion to my life and make me feel alive, I had remained in the same profession. Year after year, I had taken on more responsibility and earned more money, making it ever harder to extract myself from the grind of promoting products I didn't care about.

Now, I finally had an idea of what I wanted to do—yet I was still stuck. I knew from experience that a job touches every part of your life. It affects your attitude, your relationships, your health, your ability to make decisions—everything. Usually, I'd be the first person to give advice on what others should do with their careers—that's what made me so attracted to the career counseling business in the first place. Why, then, did I have such a hard time answering the simple question, "What do I want to do with my career?" What's the big deal, right? I had found my calling and had a husband who supported my dream, so why was I stalling? *Is it because the nature of the business is so intimate?* I wondered. *Am I afraid that no one will want to work with me?*

The helplessness I was feeling wouldn't subside. I wished I could mute the insecure voice in my head that kept listing all the reasons that starting a business was a bad idea. *It's selfish to pursue your own dreams when Frank is going through his own transition. It'll take too much time to establish a successful business. All that time and money you spent on your education? Wasted. And wasn't your original goal to get to the top of your career ladder? Now that you've reached your goal, you want to throw it all away on a whim?* However, the confident voice in my head continued to whisper competing thoughts. *Don't listen to that party pooper*, it said. *You know how important a fulfilling career can be. You're never going to be happy if you go back to a deadening marketing job.*

Having spent some time working closely with people on their career transitions in the final days at Trifinity, I had seen firsthand how dramatically a person's career happiness affects his or her personal life. Many people whom I'd always assumed had been following their passions were actually deeply unhappy in their careers. They wanted desperately to make a change, but they, like me, were paralyzed by fear. Often, they weren't even afraid for themselves—the biggest concern I'd heard was the fear of disappointing their spouse or family. Time and again, I had talked to people who were unhappy in their careers but felt helpless to change them because of family commitments. It made them feel both guilty and resentful, a combination of emotions with which I could empathize. Those people, like me, had pursued the same line of work because it was where their experience lay, not because they felt called to do it.

As the months had passed by after the layoffs at Trifinity, the people that I had worked with who had quashed their true dreams and remained in the same careers started calling me again. Some of them had told me how empty they felt inside. Some had even begun taking prescription drugs or drinking too much to numb the pain. *Would I end up like that if I didn't make a positive change now?* I wondered.

"I am going to do it!" I announced, as I suddenly became engulfed in a wave of determination.

"I knew you would," Frank reminded me, chuckling.

"But," I continued, "we still need money, and I don't think it's the right time to let my experience completely fall by the wayside. I need to figure out how to use my marketing talent to bring in some income while I build this business."

"That sounds like a great idea," Frank said. "Now, call Maya."

"All right, all right. Stop harassing me," I said as I picked up the phone to dial her number.

He smiled at me. Sometimes Frank was so easy to please.

I picked up my cell phone and walked from the game room to the media room. I stared out the window overlooking the pool, mustering up the courage to make the call. As I punched in the numbers, I thought about how to start the conversation. There was the perky option: *Hi Maya! I have no real experience doing this career coaching thing, but I'd really like to work with you!* Or the desperate option: *My life is falling apart, I want to start a business, and if you don't work with me I may lose my home.* Something told me neither choice was exactly right.

I cradled the phone between my shoulder and ear, wiping the palms of my hands against the sides my shirt to remove the sweat. On the other end of the line, the phone rang a few times. I secretly hoped that she wouldn't answer so that I could just leave a nice message. That would put the ball back in her court. It would then be easier for her to blow me off, saving us both the embarrassment of an uncomfortable conversation. On the fourth ring, however, she picked up.

"Hello?"

Game time, I thought, taking a deep breath and putting a smile in my voice. "Hi Maya. This is Linda Ginac, Frank's wife."

"Oh, hi!" she said in an upbeat voice. So far so good.

"Frank mentioned that you may want to make a career change and I started a business doing just that, so I was checking to see if you might want to go out for coffee and talk about your ideas," I said stiffly.

"I'd love to do coffee," she remarked. "Frank was telling me about the work you did and I've been meaning to call you, I just hadn't gotten around to it. Thanks for taking the initiative."

We set up an appointment to meet at a coffee shop downtown the following Tuesday morning. When I hung up the phone, my heart was pounding—I felt as though I had just tricked the quarterback of the football team into taking me to prom. I jumped over the three stairs leading up to the media room and ran down the hallway back into the game room. "She said yes!" I exclaimed. "We're meeting next week! Oh my God, I can't believe I might actually have a client!" I paced around the game room nervously. "What am I going to say to her about the business? What am I going to wear? I look like a fat cow. Holy crap, she is going to see that I am very pregnant."

"Linda, don't panic," Frank advised calmly. "Just be yourself and tell her your story. She knows it's a new business. I'm sure she'll understand that you're still working out the details. You're not the first pregnant woman who's ever met with a client. You're also very thin, so she won't know how far along you are. Stop stressing!"

"Easy for you to say. You're not the one who has to pitch this thing and then deliver on it. Oh, God, what am I getting myself into?" My chest felt tight at the thought of charging someone for a service I wasn't certain I could deliver.

"You're going to be great," Frank said. "Do some research on the Internet and find out how much people typically charge for career counseling. Someone must publish prices on their site."

"Good idea. Why didn't I think of it?" I asked.

"Maybe you need a business manager," he said, smiling. "My going rate is $150 an hour—upfront and in cash, please."

"Hardy-har-har."

❀❀❀

The following Tuesday I woke up bright and early to compile everything I needed for the meeting with Maya. If I was going to do this, I decided, I was going to do it the right way. I'd spent the previous week putting together a giant binder filled with every resource I could find on career coaching. I had grilled Frank closely about Maya to find out what kind of employee she was—her strengths, her weaknesses, her likes and dislikes. As my first potential client, she could be critical to helping me figure out how I wanted to run my business and how I could sell my services to others. At that point, I needed her as much as she needed me. If I hoped to do this for a living, I needed a success story that I could use to demonstrate the results of my work.

I showed up at the Starbucks at 9:15 A.M., fifteen minutes early for our appointment. Maya hadn't arrived yet, so I ordered a decaf hazelnut latte and sat down at a table against the back wall. All around me, people were typing away at their laptops, looking as if they were immersed in business. I wondered how many of these people were searching for jobs. The customers at this Starbucks alone could keep me busy for months.

A few minutes after 9:30, a woman who I recognized as Maya walked in the door and scanned the tables. When her eyes landed on me, she broke into a friendly smile. I took a deep breath, calming my nerves. *You can do this, Linda*, I told myself. In spite of Maya's friendly appearance, I still had a gnawing fear in the pit of my belly that she was going to leave the meeting thinking I was a fraud. Nevertheless, I stamped those feelings down and tried to project an air of confidence as I rose to greet her.

"Hi, Maya!" I said. "It's so nice to meet you! I've heard so much about you."

"And I've heard so much about you!" she answered. Then, eying my belly, "And congratulations on the baby! How far along are you?"

"I'm due in April."

"That's great," she said. "I'm sure Andrew will be excited to have a little . . . brother or sister?"

"Brother."

"Wow. Surrounded by men. I hope you like football."

I laughed. I liked her already.

Maya stepped away to order a coffee and then joined me back at the table. Her friendliness really put me at ease, so I felt comfortable being honest about the fact that the business was a work in progress. Luckily, she was open to letting me hone my methodology as we went along. "I need some help figuring out the next step in my career path," she said. "Frank says you've already helped a lot of people, and that's good enough for me."

"Well, good," I smiled. "Then let's get started."

Over the next few weeks, Maya and I met weekly to discuss her career. Years of experience in marketing had taught me that almost any product could be sold with the right marketing plan. As I discovered in my work with the ex-Trifinity employees, people are really no different than products in this respect. First, we had to define the need—in Maya's case, and in the case of most job seekers, the need was career satisfaction. Her background was in user-experience design; that is, creating a user-friendly experience for computer software and websites. She wanted to continue down this path, but she wasn't sure if she wanted to hire on to another company or branch off and start her own business.

I was surprised at how natural the role of career coach felt to me. Week after week, I learned so much about Maya. I created a comprehensive talent profile for Maya that encompassed her interests, her values, her hopes and her dreams. We used this profile to determine what the next step would be for Maya to start her own business.

"Wow," she said, as we walked to the parking lot together. "I can't believe we've gotten so far already! If I'm going to start this company, Linda, I'm going to need a lot of help. Would you be interested in helping out with marketing and business development on a regular basis?"

"Absolutely," I said, grinning ear to ear. In less than forty-five days, I'd helped Maya gain a sense of control over her career path that she'd never had before. And she, in turn, helped me realize something important—this was exactly what I needed to do and I'd be a fool to ignore my calling.

PART 4
TRUST BROKER

Chapter 19 Renewed

Frank walked me out to the back patio with a wine bottle and two Steuben wine glasses in hand. He positioned me comfortably at the San Cristobal table, which I had convinced him we needed, and sat in the seat to my right so that we could both have a great view of the pool.

"Are you going to tell me what's going on? I know something is up?" I asked wearily. "You know I can't drink this wine. I'm pregnant."

"You can have one small glass of wine," he reassured me. "The doctors have all indicated that it's safe to have a glass of wine. Besides, why does something have to be up?" He smiled at me in a teasing way, and it felt like a dozen butterflies suddenly flew from my stomach to my heart. *Would I ever get used to his overly optimistic outlook and light spirit in the midst of such unpredictable conditions?*

"You look so beautiful!" he said, grinning and pouring me a glass of Stag's Leap. He hadn't been this attentive in a long while, and it was odd seeing him in such a relaxed state.

"The moon is really bright tonight and makes the pool look very inviting," I mentioned. I've always enjoyed the darkness of night. Tonight was no exception. The backyard was midnight blue and the light radiating from the moon and the candles flickering in the old-fashioned lanterns made the pool shimmer. "If you think a bottle of wine and being romantic is going to stop me from having the conversation about selling the house, you are mistaken," I said in a teasing but serious fashion.

"Can't I just have a nice bottle of wine with my wife?" he asked, getting distracted by a text message popping up on his cell phone. He picked up his phone from the table, looking quickly at the text to identify the sender. As he read the text, I sipped my wine and stared at the wrinkles forming around his weary eyes. *This job-loss experience has aged him,* I thought to myself. But then I felt momentarily guilty, because I knew that I had contributed greatly to his stress levels and it wasn't just the joblessness affecting him.

At that moment, something in the text message made Frank smile from ear-to-ear and I was suddenly curious about the content of the message. "Who texted you and why are you all smiles?" I inquired.

He didn't respond right away because his fingers were too busy tapping on the phone, responding to the mystery text. "Give me a second, love," he said with a huge smirk on his face. I just looked at him, amazed. He never ceased to surprise me with his optimism, even under the most stressful conditions, and now was pretty stressful—we were going on one and a half years of both of us being unemployed. It was one of the things I found so remarkable and frustrating about Frank. He was always positive and in control, with a "never-say-quit attitude," and provided words of encouragement that always made me feel good.

I don't know if it was the few sips of wine or the emotions running high from being pregnant, but my guard was low tonight. My mind started wandering to the life I'd built with Frank. It had not been an easy road for him. Ever since our first date, I had been resistant and always one foot out the door. The thought of someone crushing my heart paralyzed me, so much so that I was always armed and ready for exit with every argument. I fought like a princess warrior so I wouldn't morph into a single personality with no identify of my own.

I pulled my feet up on the chair and held my knees as I rocked the chair slowly and rhythmically. The past had been resurfacing like a time bomb as a result of the graduate work I was doing. I'd procrastinated on several assignments recently because they required me to write personal essays about how my parents had influenced my career decisions. *What would I say?* What I'd learned from them was that it sucks to be a factory worker making minimum wage. They'd had no pride in their work, and I had no fond memories of their employment experience. For days, I had tried to fill the paper with the right words, and the delete button had become my best friend. *Stuck. Stuck. Stuck.* I wasn't experiencing writer's block. The words flowed very easily, but they were intentional and angry, not the type of paper I wanted to submit to a professor. No, I was struggling to find something positive to write about. It was then that

I'd realized I'd never really let go of the past, and that I was still hanging onto the relationship issues I had with my family.

Since I'd been with Frank, I had begun to embrace a more positive outlook on life and my behavior mirrored Frank's more than ever. My appearance had not changed much over the years, with the exception of a few wrinkles and a belly, but it seemed that his wisdom, intelligence, trust, and love were more obvious in my interactions with him, our son Andrew, and with others.

While Frank continued to respond to his text, my mind quickly went over the list of school assignments that were due over the next few weeks. With three courses a semester, my leadership volunteering schedule, increasing client load, and preparing the nursery, I was suddenly overcome with a mild panic attack. *How am I going to manage all of this stuff? Why do I always take on way too much? And how long can we afford to pretend that neither one of us is making any money?*

During our months of unemployment, we had kept telling ourselves, against all evidence to the contrary, that the high-paying dream jobs we were looking for were just around the corner. It was like waiting for a bus that never shows up—the more time you spend at the bus stop, the harder it gets to pick up and walk away. At a certain point, we had stopped worrying about whether or not we had enough in the bank to pay our bills (we didn't) and began putting everything on our credit cards. We had maxed out several cards and it hadn't take long for our interest rates to skyrocket, adding even more to our debt. Eventually, we couldn't even afford to pay the minimum payments due and the interest charges and fees had resulted in higher bills. Thankfully, we'd been able to work out a payment plan with the credit card company, which eliminated more excessive interest charges. Nonetheless, with no steady source of income other than the money I was making working with Maya, and the bit of money we'd gotten from Frank selling some stock, it was nearly impossible to keep up.

"Are you going to tell me what you are texting or shall I check it out myself?" I asked, reaching for Frank's phone.

"I'm done!" he said, moving his phone out of my reach. "Gosh, you have no patience!" He sat back in his chair, arms folded, looking satisfied with himself.

"Go on, already!" I pleaded.

"Love, I know you've been agonizing for weeks about whether or not to put our dream home on the market and take the loss," he started.

"Don't try to talk me out of it because my mind is already made up!" I exclaimed. "I don't want to do it, but we are out of options. We have to call a realtor to see what we can price it at and if it will move. We have to be realistic and we've already pushed it too far."

"Let me finish," he whispered, pulling my chair closer to his so that our knees touched. He looked into my eyes and smiled. "A small miracle came our way."

"What are you talking about?" I wondered out loud, with a curious gaze on my face.

"You are so beautiful. I am the luckiest man alive!" he interjected.

"Thank you, honey! Now stop procrastinating and get to the point, please."

He started telling me about an email exchange he'd had with a friend earlier in the week. His friend had called to inquire about Frank's employment status and told him about a potential contract opportunity at Dell.

"Anyway, he introduced me to the hiring manager and I have an interview scheduled next Monday," he shared with a grin.

"You are kidding me!" I exclaimed, overfilled with a ton of emotion. "Tell me more!"

He told me more about the contract opportunity, which would require him to lead a global eCommerce technology centralization initiative. The contract was for six months and would possibly be approved for another six months if Frank hit the goals. International travel to London, Paris, and Germany was a requirement of the contract. I was so thrilled to hear that he would simply have a job, but when he told me the compensation, I almost fell out of my chair.

"This sounds too good to be true, Frank!"

"Don't start thinking that way or you will jinx it!" he responded quickly.

We spent the rest of the evening talking about how our life would get back on track with this opportunity. It had been so long since we'd spoken of anything hopeful or positive—besides the baby—and it felt good.

❀❀❀

Monday couldn't come fast enough, and the days leading to the interview seemed to take forever to pass. Every day and night since telling me about the interview, he and I prayed out loud to every saint and ancestor that we both could think of to ask for help and assistance in landing this job.

On the night before the interview, Frank was very anxious, and I wasn't quite sure how to calm his nerves because I was a bundle of nerves myself. To pass the time and take my mind off of it, Andrew and I decided to make chocolate cookies from scratch to celebrate Frank's interview. While we were making the cookies, Frank sat at the kitchen table reviewing the job description again to gather his thoughts on relevant experiences to discuss during the interview. He wasn't at the table long before I heard several loud bangs. Andrew and I turned to see Frank walking along the counter and opening and closing drawers.

"Frank, what are you looking for?" I asked, a bit confused.

"The certificate my grandmother gave me. Have you seen it around?"

"What certificate are you talking about?" I asked.

"The one with the five dollar bill in it," he replied, looking like a nine-year-old boy.

"Yes, it's upstairs in the guestroom in my hope chest with all of our other sentimental things." I smiled with great satisfaction because I could locate almost any item, whether lost or misplaced, in minutes.

Frank went upstairs to retrieve the certificate. I knew why he wanted it and was touched by his fondness and love for Grandma Sue, who had passed away years earlier. Around the age of eight, when Frank's parents were going through a bitter divorce, he and his sisters had lived with his grandmother for a short while until things had settled with his parents. It was during that time that his grandmother made him a certificate titled, "The Best Grandson a Grandmother Could Ever Have." She had written him an endearing letter and taped a five dollar bill on the certificate, on which she had written, "Don't spend this because it's a keepsake. For as long as you don't spend it, you will always have money."

Frank needed to hold his certificate and have a special conversation with Grandma Sue about his interview tomorrow. He needed to ask Grandma Sue for help in securing the job and I knew that he'd call his mother next to ask her to also pray for him. I knew in my heart that once the Dell people met Frank and learned about his expertise, he would get the offer.

The next day, Frank interviewed with the team for almost five hours. While he was at the interview, I spent time cleaning every drawer and closet in the house while chanting "he'll get the job" over and over again. I was burning nervous energy, but my nesting instinct was also in full force as the baby was due to arrive very soon. The hours ticked by so slowly. I was a bit worried about the opportunity because it was an individual contributor role. Frank had been an executive for so long I feared that they might be concerned about his ability to roll up his sleeves and do the work himself.

I glanced at the clock nearly every five minutes wondering when Frank would pull into the driveway. At 4:30 that afternoon, I finally heard the garage door opening and I flew down the stairs, through the kitchen, and into the garage.

"Could it have taken any longer? I was going out of my mind," I asked with as much restlessness as a two-year-old. I knew interviews could take hours, but when you are standing on the brink of complete collapse, nothing seems rationale. "How did it go? What did they say?" I asked as we walked into the kitchen and he placed his keys on the counter.

"I got the job, love. I got the job!" he finally blurted out.

"No way! Are you kidding me? They actually told you today?" I inquired in disbelief.

"Yes, I got the job and I start tomorrow," he said triumphantly.

It took me a minute to believe he was serious. "I am the happiest person alive," he said. "I'm making an appointment at the kids' club for Andrew, 'cause we are going to the country club tonight!" Tears streamed down my eyes as I remembered back to when this whole ordeal started. I never could have imagined it would take so long to get back on track. When I regained my senses, I hugged Frank with every fiber of my body and slowly released the ten-ton weight bearing down on my heart.

"Grandma Sue and my mother's prayers came through again," he whispered in my ear.

"Yes, they did," I concurred. "Happy early birthday to you. You got the perfect gift."

"No, we did, hon. We did. I told you everything would be okay," he said.

"I know you did," I replied, thinking that if things continued this way, then everything would be okay.

❀❀❀

It was spring and the dormant grass started to turn a pale green. The flowers along the walkway and around the perimeter of the house began to bloom in colors of red, purple and yellow. I'd spend most days walking around the neighborhood in hopes that the baby would come early. The weight of the baby was killing my back and I was desperate for some relief.

Just three weeks after Frank started working at Dell, we were blessed with another miracle, our baby boy Vaughn. After experiencing so much stress over the past two years, I relished in the bliss of bringing a new person into the world. Vaughn was born on the exact day the doctor predicted and just two days after Frank's birthday. We were thankful for another uncomplicated birth and a healthy baby, despite one minor complication that occurred during delivery but that ended up not being serious. Vaughn decided that he needed to poop while being delivered, and the doctors were worried that he might have inhaled it. Instead of me holding him immediately after birth, they whisked him away to check his airways for meconium. In seconds, the room was full of doctors running standardized tests on him. By the time my doctor cleaned me up, Vaughn was in my arms and out of danger. His airways were clear. I couldn't wait for him to meet his big brother.

It was a blessing that Frank's mother, Patty, flew in from Schenectady, New York, to help us with the baby, but it was also good timing for her. She was going through a very painful separation from her second husband of twenty-five years and was in the process of heavy grieving. The divorce had come as a complete surprise to her and everyone in the family, especially Frank. On the surface, their relationship had seemed so blissful but my intuition told me another story. Frank had idealized his parents' relationship and often told me that he had wanted a relationship just like theirs and had found it with me. In a million years, Frank never would have thought his parents would divorce, and it crushed him to the core.

Unlike my upbringing, and with the exception of his mom's divorce from his biological father, Frank's family life had been akin to the Cleavers. Frank's dad, Tim, was an executive for General Electric in the turbine division and Frank's mom stayed at home caring for Frank and his two sisters. Frank had lived in Schenectady, New York, from birth until the age of eight, and then began a ten-year journey of short stays in various cities around the country, first living with his father in South Carolina, then living with his mother and stepfather. He had lived the life I had always dreamed of, and was fortunate not only to like his family, but enjoy spending time with them. Since they had met me, they had always welcomed me with wide open arms and extended the love and acceptance that I had rarely gotten from my own family.

Frank and I tried to bolster Patty's mood as much as we could. Being able to care for Vaughn was good for lifting her spirits and getting her mind off of what happened, even though she'd often get lost in her own thoughts. She had lost a lot of weight since the separation, too, as her baggy clothes attested. She didn't look like the Patty I was used to, with her perky personality and bright eyes. The only "sparkle" about her was the jingling of her charm bracelets. She must have had thirty charms hanging off of six different bracelets on her arm. I noticed for the first time that she was growing old while my life was just beginning to bloom, and it dawned on me that I didn't want to lose her in my life because she had been like a mother to me. I felt blessed to have someone special who I loved fuss over me and my children. It brought great joy into my heart.

❁❁❁

Patty and I spent tons of time together during her month-long visit, taking Andrew and Vaughn shopping, and hanging out at unique cafés and talking. We also watched quite a few episodes of her favorite show, *Walker, Texas Ranger*, and I hate to admit that I liked it. I managed to complete a couple of consulting projects during Patty's stay. It was the first time in my life that someone other than my husband offered to help me and it was a welcomed relief.

The Ginac Group was starting to pick up momentum at this time, too. I miraculously brought on a few new coaching clients without meeting them face-to-face. All of my new clients were referrals from those that I'd helped from Trifinity. I was amazed that people were so willing to pay for my services without meeting me. It dawned on me that getting referrals would be an excellent way to grow the business at my pace.

During my first pregnancy, work had been my first priority. I had devoted countless hours to building wealth for others while sacrificing my own personal time with my family. Following the hard lessons learned at Trifinity, I decided to never put work first again. My family was and would always be my first priority, and I would not compromise my personal happiness for wealth.

Patty booked a flight back to New York the first week of June, and I dreaded her departure. She had to get back home to move her belongings from the house she shared with Tim to her new home. I begged her to stay longer, but she couldn't. The thought of being a solo parent during the day—especially with a newborn and after going such an extended period of time with help from others—terrified me. When Andrew had been a baby we'd had the nanny, and up until now, I'd had Frank and Patty to lean on. Now it would just be me, Andrew, and Vaughn. Andrew was helpful, but he spent his days at Barton Creek summer camp having fun with kids his age. I thought of my new sweet boy and panicked. *What if I screw up? What if I don't hold him enough? What if I'm a lousy mother to him?* These feelings were new to me even though this was my second child because Andrew's nanny had started so early with him. I guess I'd just have to adapt and keep moving forward, just like I'd been doing my entire life.

Chapter 20 Committed

There was one feeling that I wished didn't have so much control over my life: *guilt*. In other words, working mother's guilt. If there were a way to eliminate this feeling, I would do it in a heartbeat. It's a feeling that I knew all too well, and every day my guilt seemed to grow larger. I supposed this would be how the rest of my life would go—me being torn between wanting to be a great stay-at-home mother and also a successful entrepreneur.

I hummed a random song to tune out the thoughts floating through my mind about whether to work full-time or not. No matter how hard I tried to drown out the sound of my own thoughts, it never worked. *Where is my will power when I need it?* I thought. I had to decide whether to work more hours outside the house or to start turning clients away. It was a tough decision because we needed the income and I thoroughly enjoyed working, but leaving Vaughn with a stranger filled me with nausea.

I caught a glimpse of myself as I passed the hallway mirror and stopped to adjust my hair. As I did so I began talking to the gal in the mirror. *Your reasons for not wanting Vaughn to be cared for by anyone else are selfish. You don't want to share him. Or, to be more exact, you don't want him to love anyone more than you. Why is it so hard for you to admit this to anyone? You are so afraid that Vaughn will create a bond with someone else the way Andrew did with Olivia.* I shook my head to try and get rid of my thoughts and walked on to Vaughn's room to make sure he was still napping. I stared at the baby decorating themes I had pinned on the wall and decided I would go with the cowboy decor. In my head, though, I couldn't let go of the nanny situation. When Andrew was with Olivia I felt like such an outsider and so unimportant. The jealousy was overwhelming and I certainly never wanted to feel that my son loved someone else more than me. Beyond the jealousy, I also didn't want to spend a dime more than was necessary because I was focused on paying off debt. Hiring a nanny would be expensive, and it would take us even longer to pay off our debt. On the other hand, though, if I took on more clients and earned more income, we could pay off more debt. Since Vaughn was still asleep, I decided to use the time to get some schoolwork done.

❀❀❀

By the time Vaughn was six months old, he required more and more of my attention, which gave me less time to work on client projects and school assignments. When I would be two paragraphs into a three-page essay, echoes of Vaughn calling for mama could be heard down the hallway. I knew—finally making my decision—that we would need to start the nanny-interview process.

It didn't take long to find a nanny because our housekeeper, whom we'd hired after Frank started at Dell, had recommended her best friend, Margarita. Frank and I had decided that two days a week would be perfect so that I could work without interruption. On most days I would work from my home office unless I had to conduct a face-to-face client meeting.

Three knocks at the door got my heart racing. Frank and I both walked eagerly to the door and gazed through the decorative glass door at a woman standing by herself. We opened the door and our eyes locked onto a tan, round-faced gal with dark brown eyes, wearing a fitted dress and heels that looked too small for her feet. When she smiled, her entire face lit up like an angel. As we talked with Margarita, it didn't take us long to see how caring her personality was. She was shy and blushed often during the interview. I suspected it was because she didn't feel comfortable speaking English, but we thought she spoke very well. Vaughn, who was hanging eagerly on her legs, probably didn't help with her nervousness, either.

We hired Margarita on the spot based on my gut instinct. She provided us with her information and we agreed that she would start the following week. The next day I conducted a background check and called her former references. I was even more thrilled when all of her former bosses told me how reliable and wonderful she was to work with.

With the hiring of a nanny, I decided that I would make my business more official by renting an executive suite, which was only a mile from the house. Luckily, the suite could be rented by the hour and the cost was cheap compared to the benefit of having four walls and a professional presence. It was getting increasingly difficult to have private and revealing conversations with people when sitting at a table in the corner of Starbucks. More often than not, clients would tear up when they told me their stories and too many people would stare. The barista knew me by name, as well as my regular drink, and there was a regular clientele. I suspected a reputation was forming and I would be labeled "that woman who makes everyone cry." With a plan in place, I scheduled several phone calls to meet with clients in my new digs.

✿✿✿

At my new office, I sat in the chair and placed my computer on the desk in front of me. I was the only one in the entire office suite who rented by the hour. My office was furnished with a mahogany desk and a bookshelf filled with executive books and magazines on hunting, travel, and cars. Pictures of hunting trips covered the wall and two fake green plants provided color. This was obviously a masculine office, but the clients didn't seem to mind since most of them were men.

Shortly after I'd gotten settled, Maya walked through the door. I stood up and gave her my usual bear hug. She sat in the chair across from me and we started with small talk about the new office, Vaughn, and the interesting decor in the office. Today, Maya and I needed to develop her corporate sales pitch and presentation. As an introverted creative, exuding salesmanship and confidence during the sales process did not come easily for her. We had to work on everything from how to enter a room with presence and practicing voice inflection during the actual pitch to educating her on the best way to position her services in the mind of the customer and asking for the deal. Eventually our efforts paid off. Not only did Maya start attracting clients immediately, they also happened to be name brands.

✿✿✿

Over the next year, I completed my master's degree and my client load grew consistently, leading me to move from a pay-by-the-hour executive office suite to my very own office. It was a goal that I'd been working toward for months.

I stood nervously on the stairs, looking at the office building before me and feeling a sense of accomplishment. I clasped my hands and entered the building to meet the property manager. The first thing I saw as I walked through the door was an impressive atrium with an artful waterfall. The property manager was standing near the elevator so I walked over and introduced myself. We rode up to the second floor and she brought me to an office with three solid walls and one floor-to-ceiling glass wall overlooking the waterfall. The office was large enough for a desk, chest and round table. I took a deep breath and asked her to send me the sublease. This would be the place where I would continue to change lives.

Within a week, the lease was signed and I moved my home office furniture to my official place of business. I created formal business cards, a nameplate with the company name, The Ginac Group, and set my sights on building a successful company. My oversized, antique, bone-white desk, matching chest, and red-velvet chairs stood out like a diamond in a bull's ass compared to my office neighbors' drab metal desks and plastic chairs. The decorations drew lots of attention and unexpectedly helped me promote my business to office mates previously unknown to me.

On the way home one evening, I drifted off in thought about all of the unique people coming to see me for help with their careers. With every new client, I was exposed to increasingly complex career issues. Daily, I continued to be astonished by their stories and their comfort level with revealing so many intimate details about their work and personal life. Each client's situation was so different, such as the lady who was so miserable as a lawyer that she was crippled with depression, and the man who was in his late fifties and couldn't get a job because of age discrimination.

I thought about one client who had come to see me because he was a workaholic and it was ruining his marriage. He worked around the clock and then some. He worked so many hours at the office that they gave him a cot. However, his performance at the office had suffered as he tried to save his marriage. He was let go during a company downsizing and his ego suffered severely. He was depressed and his wife's desire to get divorced grew rapidly because she couldn't break through to him. He had no job, a wife on the verge of leaving, and very little confidence—his life was a mess. He had lost everything chasing the dream of becoming an Internet millionaire. Fear had burned through my veins at the thought of him doing something crazy like jumping off a bridge. I had been terrified I might not be able to help him get back on track. I couldn't imagine how working with me would turn his situation around for the better. With no clear process, I simply followed my instincts, listened deeply, and responded accordingly. After a lot of work, he joined a company that was not a start-up, started courting his wife again, and started rebuilding his ego.

My thoughts drifted to another client who had founded a tech company in his twenties after dropping out of college during his junior year. He'd taken on the role of CEO and managed to grow the company with the help of venture capital funds. However, all of the money had gone to his head and he was fired by the board after they discovered he'd spent money for his own personal pleasure. He wasn't the kind of guy I'd have chosen to hang out with in my personal time, but he'd seemed sincerely remorseful about his previous professional behavior so I'd taken him on as a client. At the time he'd come to see me, he'd been unemployed for six months and was living off his credit cards. This sounded all too familiar to me and I could empathize with his situation. Word of his misdeeds had spread around the tech community, making it difficult for him to get a job.. Even when he did manage to find a company where his reputation didn't precede him, the lack of expertise on his résumé made him seem inexperienced. In addition to his lack of income, he'd also lost a significant amount of money in the stock market. His marriage was strained, and overdue bills were piling up by the dozens. After my initial shock regarding his unethical behavior, I had led him down a path investigating his motives for spending the funds on personal items, exploring his behavioral patterns, rebranding him, and helping him launch a job search campaign in states other than Texas.

Even though I'd felt ecstatic about the impact I was having in people's lives, I was also terrified and had thought about quitting often. That little voice would pop into my head, telling me that I wasn't good enough to help these people, but Frank's influence and positive energy would break most of these thoughts, and soon I'd found something to focus on during times of self-doubt. "The next Suze Orman, but for careers instead of finance." Every day I would chant these words to myself because it made my dreams real. My will to dream had been buried long ago in my childhood house, but with my newfound passion for helping people change their lives, it had bloomed like a flower and gave me hope. I had stopped dreaming for so long that I had forgotten how powerful dreams can be. I wanted these dreams to transform me from a fretful, worried girl filled with self-doubt into a woman ready to change lives for the better, one career at a time

I was doing everything that I had dreamed of now. I was working in a career that I loved and helping people find work they could be excited about. Every day, I would show up at the office with excitement about the problems I'd tackle that day. As I had become more effective in my job, I realized that I was so focused on the end-result that I was rushing through the actual change process. I had wanted people to achieve their goals and be successful, but I hadn't wanted to risk any emotional exchanges for fear that I would crumble when clients were "live with Linda."

Even though I'd known that many clients were shielding the truth about their reasons for pursuing new work, I'd never brought up my suspicions to any of them. I'd been determined to help them succeed and create new futures without having to break through any emotional barriers. These people had found me for different reasons, but one thing was consistent—they all wanted to find happiness. Some had wanted to change their careers as a result of downsizing, pre-retirement, parenthood, work/life balance, boredom, handicaps, anxiety, or money. Others had been fired from their job for performance or other heinous acts on the job. Many had wanted to learn how to climb the corporate ladder, and others simply wanted to continue learning and growing.

It had dawned on me that every client situation seemed to mirror my life in some small way. I had subconsciously been evaluating my own life through their experiences and had realized that I needed to deal with the past or I'd never grow. Gradually, with each engagement, I had begun seeking to understand people on a deeper level, pushing my own fears aside and working hard to find each person's one single point of failure, whether it was the moment when their dreams of being an actress, singer, or rocket scientist had been quashed; or the time when someone had advised them that they needed to marry up or pursue a specific path because the family expected it. I wanted to unearth and bring to light each person's moment when they had decided to pursue a path that someone else had designed for them, the path that they now could not walk away from because of increasing family expectations and responsibilities.

I had thought that opening up about my own life would be difficult, but I'd been wrong. It had been freeing. Sharing my own personal experiences about career transition had actually helped my clients feel comforted. I was determined to continue helping people move beyond their fear of being idle in career limbo. Once they'd done that, change could and would occur. I knew that when someone left a well-known job for an unknown future, that's when their journey would really begin, but I had to push and get them to that point.

The sound of a horn blaring jolted me out of my trance and I realized that the light had turned from red to green. *Calm down already, jeez,* I thought, looking in the rearview mirror. I turned into our neighborhood and up my driveway, admiring how the soft interior lights made the house look so beautiful in the dark. I pushed the door open slowly, calling out, "Hello . . . I'm home." The smell of eggs and maple-flavored bacon filled my nose. "You already started dinner? Thanks a bunch, love!" Frank was fond of making breakfast for dinner. I think it's because it's the only thing he knows how to cook!

I put my briefcase down and walked over to Frank, who was standing near the island in the middle of our kitchen. I wrapped my hands around his waist. He was so warm. "Did Margarita already leave?"

"Yes, she left fifteen minutes ago."

"Where are the boys?" I asked.

"Andrew is playing a game and Vaughn is napping. You look tired. Was it a hard day at work? Want a glass of wine?"

"Yes, it was an energy-draining day and I'd love a glass of wine."

He poured me a glass of red wine and I prepared the table for dinner, thankful to be home.

"You know, Frank, there are just too many unhappy and lost people in the world. It's not right. Every day, I am bombarded by successful people who pursued the so-called 'American Dream.' These people invested heavily in their education, achieved great levels of success in their careers, married and had children. But, they seem to be the ones in dire need of change because they are the most unhappy, depressed, and angry."

"Sit down, honey. I'll finish getting dinner, well breakfast, ready. Enjoy your glass of wine." Frank put his hand on my shoulder to reassure me that things would be fine. "You know these people come to see you because you are their last hope in finding a career that makes them happy."

It took all of my energy to nod, even though I knew inside that I didn't want to be their last hope. "Yeah, but is it really a happy life they are seeking?" I whispered. "That is something I can not give them." Then, after a minute, "What's interesting is that so many people are hiding their true feelings from the people they care about the most. They are fooling themselves and their family and friends that everything is okay when inside they are dying."

Did everyone do this to some extent in life? I wasn't really sure. Most encounters in my life had pushed me toward believing that people naturally put on a show to mask their problems and hide what's really going on. But what did I know? I could be projecting my own self-doubt and insecurities unfairly onto others. The more time that passed, the harder it became to see other people clearly. I wanted to know what was underneath the façade or lurking behind the closed door.

"Linda, it sounds remarkably familiar."

His comment hit me like a ton of bricks. It wasn't so long ago that I sat by the computer in the middle of the night, wondering why my career and life stunk. I had browsed career site after career site, searching for something to spark my passion. I recalled sending a résumé or two to a few companies that had posted jobs and seemed interesting, and convinced myself that I could do the jobs, but knew that I'd never hear from them because my qualifications were not a perfect match. The lack of response had fueled such a strong conviction in me to stay on my current path in the miserable field of marketing because change seemed impossible.

By some small miracle, I'd made a difficult career transformation. I reflected on the change for quite some time and searched my mind for a secret formula to use on my clients so they could effortlessly glide through their own transformations. There was no magic answer. My successful transformation had boiled down to my dissatisfaction with work, emptiness, and stress. I'd complained about making a change for so long that I was sick of hearing my own voice and wound up having to do something about it. I'd also had Frank encouraging me the whole time, which made a huge difference.

Throughout dinner and the rest of the evening, my mind raced with thoughts of my own transformation, the things I did, and ideas for how I could help others. I reevaluated all of the elements and steps that it had taken for me to make a genuine transition: self-awareness, knowing my strengths and weaknesses, building new skills, establishing common goals, managing multiple roles, resolving conflict, being flexible, developing a new identity, building new networks, facing my fears and being honest with myself. The list seemed endless. It was not a simple, straightforward process.

After spending years earning a master's degree in career development, I felt completely unprepared to help these people make real changes. Although the degree was nice to have for résumé purposes, the program hadn't equipped me with enough skill and knowledge to be effective. The traditional method for career development, which was mostly counseling, struck me as hopelessly outdated. Actually, the biggest thing I learned from the master's program was that there was a lot of room for improvement in the field of career development— and I was determined to be the one making those improvements!

❀❀❀

With things looking up, I decided to throw a garden party at our house. It would be sort of a "welcome back" party to get together with all the people we'd lost touch with since we had stopped working. The party was set to begin at 7:00 on a Friday night. I spent most of the day running errands with Andrew and Vaughn, and by the time we got back at 4:00, Andrew was feeling a little punchy.

"Mommy, I want to play Jak and Daxter," he commanded as soon as we walked in the door.

"Fine," I said. "Go play Jak-a-daxter. You know how to work the PlayStation. Mommy has to get ready for her party."

"You always say it wrong! It's JAK AND DAXTER!" he shouted as he ran up the stairs.

"Hey!" I yelled after him. "Don't take that tone with me you little stinker! I'll come up there and tickle you to death."

"Sorry, Mommy," he shouted down from the game room. "Love you."

I briefly considered giving him a timeout for talking back, but decided it was more trouble than it was worth. I only had a few hours to get everything ready, and I would rather Andrew play his games and be in a good mood for the party than have to spend the next half hour trying to teach him a lesson. Sometimes you have to pick your battles.

I walked into the kitchen, put Vaughn down to play with a few toys and started cutting up vegetables for a vegetable tray. A few seconds later, I heard Andrew yell down from the top of the stairs. "Mom!" he shouted. "It's not working."

"What's not working?"

"The PlayStation! It's not turning on!"

"Well, then just read quietly in your room," I said. I didn't have the faintest idea how the PlayStation was hooked into the TV, and I hardly had time to mess around with it now. Noticing that it seemed a little dark in the kitchen, I reached over and flipped on the light switch, and . . . nothing. I flipped it off and on again. *Strange*, I thought. I walked into the living room and tried another light switch. Nothing. Then the TV. Still nothing. *Dammit*, I thought, *of all the times for a power outage.*

I walked back into the kitchen, picked up the phone, and dialed Austin Energy. After wading through an endless maze of phone menus, I finally got an actual person on the phone. The representative informed me that no power outages had been reported in our area.

"Well, clearly there are," I said, "because our power is out."

"One moment, ma'am," she said as she looked something up on her computer. "It says here that your account is forty-five days past due."

"What?" I asked. "There must be some mistake. My husband paid the bill."

The representative didn't seem too convinced. "Sorry, but it's not paid."

"I'm having a party in a few hours with fifty people and I have no lights," I argued.

She responded using a tone that made me want to reach through the phone and slap her in the face. "If you pay the bill, we can have someone out to your house by 8:00 P.M."

"My party starts at 7:00," I said, annoyed and panicked at the same time. Before I slammed the phone on the base, I heard her tell me she would do her best to help. I immediately called Frank on his cell phone at work.

Before Frank had a chance to even say hello he heard an earful. "Frank, what the hell is going on?" I shouted. "We have people coming over in less than three hours and our power is out because Austin Energy says we didn't pay our bill!"

"I paid it," he said. "Everything's fine."

"Everything is not fine!" I screamed. "We have no electricity! It's your responsibility. Call them up right now and take care of it!"

"I'm in a meeting right now. I will do it when I'm done."

"Why did you answer the phone if you are in a meeting?" I snapped.

"Because it's you."

"Well, you need to take care of this problem and have the power on by 7:00 P.M. or I'm walking out the door. I can't believe you didn't pay the bill. This is infuriating. I will not live through that stress again."

"Honey, I paid the bill. I will figure out what is wrong." A few minutes later, he called me back. "It's fine," he said nonchalantly. "The darned energy company switched bill payment providers and I was sending it to the old provider. I must have missed the notice in the mail.. They said they're going to send someone out soon to take care of it."

"Yeah, right. You probably just paid the bill now," I said, my insecurities rearing their ugly head again.

"No, I didn't. Please stop and don't get yourself all worked up over this. It's not a big deal."

"Don't tell me not to stress out because it's too late for that!" I yelled. "When will they be here?"

"Soon."

"Soon?" I asked through clenched teeth. "Soon as in tonight? Or soon as in sometime in the next two months?"

"Tonight, I assume," he said. "If it's not fixed by the time I get home, I'll call again and bug them about it."

With my nerves on edge and knife in hand, I sliced the rest of the vegetables, although this time with gusto, then went to our room to get ready. By the time Frank got home at 6:00, they still hadn't shown up to turn the power back on. Frank called the electric company again. They said they'd try to get someone out that night but couldn't guarantee it.

"Goddammit, Frank!" I said as soon as he got off the phone. "What the hell happened? Did they really make a mistake, or did you not pay the bill?"

"I paid it, Linda," he said. "Calm down."

"Are we broke, Frank?" I asked frantically. "Is that what's going on? Did you screw up? Are you lying to me? Pull up our account because I want to see that you actually paid it."

"Honey," he said, "it was just a mistake. You are overreacting."

The minute the representative had told me the power was out because we hadn't paid our bill, I'd panicked. Frank's income was a welcome relief, but I couldn't get over the stress of being on the brink of losing everything. Life was better, but money still had to be shifted around each month to make things work. I suspected that Frank had either given them a credit card that had reached its limit, or he hadn't moved the money from our savings account to our checking account in time. Somehow, I didn't know how, but somehow, it was Frank's fault.

"What do we do?" I wailed. "We can't have a party tonight! I will not have all of our friends think we have no money to pay our bills and that our electricity was disconnected! It's embarrassing, Frank. When will we be free from these mishaps? Sometimes I just wish I lived alone and didn't have to worry about anyone else's crap."

Frank pursed his lips and walked out of the kitchen to sulk in front of the TV. Too bad the TV didn't work. Just then the doorbell rang.

"Oh jeez," I said, shaking nervously. "Someone's here."

I walked to the front door and peered out to see Kiley and Mark standing on our porch. I took a deep breath to calm my nerves and opened the door with a wide smile on my face. I invited them in. At that time of year, it didn't get dark until 9:00, so we had a few hours yet before we needed to really worry about explaining the electricity situation. At least, that's what I assumed, until Mark made a beeline for the stereo.

"Hey, how do you turn your stereo on?" he asked.

"Oh," I said, thinking fast. "There's no power right now. The whole neighborhood's out. There was an accident or something." That would do for the time being, but it was only a temporary solution. As soon as it got dark, everyone would see that the rest of the neighborhood had electricity. "Excuse me for a second," I said, smiling.

I walked into the bedroom, where Frank was still sulking.

"Did you call Austin Energy again?" I asked anxiously. "People are starting to get here."

"They said they'll be here tonight," he said.

"How am I supposed to believe a word you say? You told me you'd paid the bill already."

"I'm sorry, hon," he said, as much of an admission of guilt as I was going to get.

"I don't care," I said coldly. "You've ruined the entire night. Now, you can either go outside and figure out how to fix the electricity yourself, or you can stop acting like a baby and come out here and be a host."

Frank's eyes reflected a mixture of anger and intense sadness. I could tell he thought I'd crossed a line, but I didn't care. The entire situation reminded me too much of my childhood, watching my parents' financial problems drive them deeper into misery. Only this time around, it felt like Frank and I were playing the role of my parents. Under these conditions, it was nearly impossible for me to maintain perspective.

I turned and walked briskly back to the patio. More guests started to arrive and as each new couple walked in the door my stress level shot up another notch. In the background, I heard a soft rock song playing on the patio speakers.

"I got the stereo working," Mark said matter-of-factly.

I looked at him, puzzled. If the power was out, then how did . . . ? I turned toward the house and realized the living room light was on. I let out a sigh of relief. And like that, all the anxiety disappeared and I snapped back into my role as perfect hostess. It took Frank half the party and a few tequilas to snap out of his funk, but for me, the minute the power went back on, I was back to my normal self. If there's one thing I've become good at in my life, it's rebounding quickly from anything.

Chapter 21 Blossomed

Frank continued working for Dell, bringing in more money than he ever had before. We slowly started to climb out of the financial sinkhole we'd fallen into, making monthly inroads into the enormous pile of credit card debt we'd accumulated. We began working with Andrew on letting his feelings out, and he, in turn, was teaching us how to be more open with him and ourselves. I was over-the-moon in love with Vaughn, who was such a sweet, loving child . . . quick to laugh and smile and so adorable that people would stop me in the streets to sing his praises. Andrew was a great big brother, always willing to lend a helping hand, and as soon as Vaughn started to enter the toddler stage, he followed Andrew around like a little puppy.

It wasn't just our home life that had improved. Things were going so well at The Ginac Group that I kicked myself for having spent so much time agonizing over starting the business. I couldn't imagine what my life would have been like if I'd let my fears about job security overwhelm my desire to follow my dreams. After years of playing by someone else's rules, I was finally in charge, and it felt great. As someone who'd had to go through a lot of soul searching to find my career path, I woke up every morning with the drive to help others find their calling. My perspective was a great asset for the business. When clients came to me, they didn't get some kid fresh out of college telling them how to deal with career transition. They were getting an experienced adult who had spent her share of time going through the wringer. In a way, I was my own biggest success story.

Across Austin, the effects of the dot-com bubble bursting continued to be felt. The overabundance of unemployed executives was great for my business, but it gave me no pleasure to see how much trouble people were having finding work. I wasn't in business to make money off of people's misery, I was there to help them find rewarding careers that would keep them employed for the long haul. However, I needed to make an income because we couldn't live on one salary. As I learned more about what worked and what didn't in a real-world setting, I had become increasingly disenchanted with the established methodology for career coaching. The cold hard fact was that people thought they knew what they wanted to do for a living, but it wasn't necessarily what they should be doing.

My thoughts about the career industry were interrupted by the chirp of my cell phone. I looked at the caller ID and hit the green button.

"Hi, you!" I answered happily.

"Hey miss everything!" Kiley replied. I could tell from the sound of her voice that something was wrong.

"What's wrong? I hear it in your voice."

"Gosh, you are good. I'll give you that. Mark's company was shut down today and he's out of work."

"Oh, crap! Kiley, I'm so sorry to hear that and will help in any way that I can."

"Let's go for a happy hour, if you can. I really need girlfriend time."

"I'll call Margarita to see if she can stay a bit later, but I'm sure she will be okay. Where do you want to meet? Tias? Or Canyon Café?"

"Let's go to Tias. I'm in the mood for a cold margarita or two."

Within the hour, I was on my way to meet Kiley at Tias Mexican restaurant. I flopped down at my usual high top, my head resting against the wood beam, arms stretched across the table. Kiley sat beside me, close enough that our arms touched. It always felt so good meeting up with Kiley because we simply understood one another.

"How's business going?" she asked.

I shrugged my shoulders. "It's good. I'm thankful that I keep getting referrals. I must be doing something right."

"You are so lucky to be running your own show," she said, the words just rolling out of her mouth like running water.

"It is awesome, but I have my days of stress and loneliness. Let's not talk about me. What happened with Mark's company?"

Tears welled up in her eyes. "They pulled the funding so everyone was terminated. There are rumors that my company is going to have a layoff, too."

"Oh gosh, I'll pray that you are safe. You're always the last one standing, anyhow," I said, trying to sound reassuring. "And Mark will find something in town because he has great skills, although to be honest, I don't wish that stress on anyone. I've already lived through it once and would never want to experience it again."

"Let me ask you something. Why do you think you are so successful with the people you are working with? It's such a shitty job market."

"It's all about the process," I said. "People need to know where they are at, where they are going, and what the destination looks like."

"What process are you talking about?" she inquired as she sipped down her frozen margarita.

I explained that the problem with the career coaching industry was that it lacked process and best practices. I told her that most coaches were tactical and focused on assessments, résumés, and pointing clients to free resources on the web without doing the hard work of truly understanding all of the client's talents and aligning those talents with careers that would bring them happiness and satisfaction.

"I developed a five phased systematic process of career change. It is a holistic and integrated approach, where hours upon hours are spent finding out what makes my clients tick. How can you help someone find a satisfying career if you don't know anything intimate about that person?"

As Kiley waved down a waitress with arms full of colorful tattoos, I thought about all of the experiences we'd shared together. I had so much respect for Kiley. She had never given up and walked away from anything. She was brave and determined. She always tried again and again until she got things right.

"What do you mean by 'intimate?'" Kiley asked sheepishly.

"Not that kind of intimate, silly." I took a deep breath. "It's about really knowing someone on the inside . . . moving beyond the surface information." I wanted her to understand the profound impact that my career could have on people so I shared a client story without revealing any names.

"Why would you work with someone like that?" she inquired.

"It's not for me to judge. People make mistakes, especially when they are flying high. I knew I could help him."

I explained that there was no way he was going to just wipe the slate clean by slapping a plastic smile on his face and floating a résumé around town. Instead, he had needed a realistic view of his reputation, his experience, and the possibilities available to him in the local job market. I told her how, together, he and I had created a customized career plan, and that I had also introduced him to a great financial planner who helped his family develop a plan to overcome their financial troubles and build for the future. Then, after three months of dedicated work, I shared how he had transformed from a depressed egomaniac filled with bitterness and regret to a confident, self-aware executive who was ready to take on the world. He cleaned up his act and ended up securing an executive-level sales job at a publishing company.

"So, my career development process helped him find meaningful work, change his self-image, improve his marriage, and save his home," I said matter-of-factly.

Kiley waited a moment, then said, "That seems like a lot of work."

"It is. We do a lot of work together."

"Lay another story on me and let's order another round! My spirits are lifting a bit hearing about something positive."

I chose a story that hit close to home and resembled the lives of most of our close friends, especially Kiley, because she was always such a workaholic. "So another of my early successes involved a dual career couple that I'll call Tom and Molly. They were a wonderful couple who had been married for twenty years with two children. Molly originally got in touch with me because she was experiencing guilt and anxiety over the competing stresses of raising a family and pursuing her career interests. As so often happens in the battle between home life and work, work was getting the lion's share of her time.

"Tom and Molly each worked an average of seventy hours a week, spending up to forty percent of the month traveling. Molly had reached the point in her career where she had two options: stay exactly where she was and risk becoming obsolete, or keep climbing up the ladder, ensuring that her stress level would continue to rise unabated. When she came to me, she was concerned that moving up the ladder would further lessen the already dismal amount of quality time she got to spend with her husband and permanently quash her chances of successfully raising a family. Her relationship was strained already, so how could it survive the increased separation that was certain to result from a higher-level position?"

"Sounds like half of the people we know," she remarked. "I struggle with that decision all of the time."

"I know. We all do to some extent. It's just the way it is," I said, pausing for a moment. "This was a tricky situation, though, because I had one willing partner and a spouse who felt like he'd been dragged along."

"What did you do? Work them as a couple?"

"Yup. You know how it is from our own relationships. A union of worka-holics can only survive if both members of the couple are on the same page."

As Kiley took a phone call, my thoughts drifted to my time with Tom and Molly. In my regular weekly sessions with them, I had helped them gain clarity on the level of commitment and the number of trade-offs required to sustain a successful dual-career family. We had implemented a career plan that enabled Tom and Molly to maintain the integrity of their careers while building the foundation for a balanced, more fulfilling home life.

I had watched them open up to each other about what they wanted perso-nally and what they were looking for from each other. By the end of our time together, they had made huge life changes that put their marriage back on track. Tom left his job and pursued his longtime dream of starting a winery, and Molly managed to structure her job so that she never worked past six or on the weekends. They also scheduled a weekly date night based on my recom-mendations because I thought they needed time to reconnect.

"Linda, you there?" I heard Kiley asking.

"Sorry, I zoned out for a minute," I said apologetically.

"Tell me the rest of the story," she asked.

"It's all boring, but I'll just say it worked out for both of them."

"Wow. You are really doing something great. I'm so proud of you! I think you deserve to be called 'Mrs. Everythang' now," she said with a caring heart. I loved Kiley for saying that, but knew that we were entering two different phas-es of our lives. Frank and I were back on a path of growth. In her world, she might have to travel that same dual-unemployed road that I'd already been down.

"Kiley, it is only now that I'm beginning to understand what a profound ef-fect my work has on people's lives."

We drank for hours and the guys joined us later for dinner and more drinking. Mark asked if I'd help him with his career change and I wholehear-tedly offered my assistance. They would not accept my offer to help him for free so I insisted on deeply discounting the service.

❦❦❦

I threw myself into the business with gusto, more proud of my work there than I had been of anything I'd ever done in my life. As word started to spread about the results I achieved with clients, I could no longer manage the load alone and knew I'd have to hire someone to help me grow the business.

As the workload increased, it grew increasingly difficult to tear myself away from Vaughn and Andrew. I wanted to be a career woman and a mother. I made a promise to myself that I would never again let my work negatively affect my relationship with Frank or my children, and I had to stick to it. I set strong boundaries for myself. I didn't work past four o'clock unless it was absolutely necessary, and when I got home it was family time. No matter how hard I worked on building The Ginac Group, I never forgot Andrew's heartbreaking question about whether we would have been happier if he'd never been born, and I did everything in my power to ensure the thought never crossed his mind again.

I searched endlessly for experienced coaches, but after conducting at least twenty-five interviews, I decided that I'd have to find someone with great potential and train them my way. The philosophies that some coaches subscribed to astonished me. It was no wonder that career coaching had a bad reputation. I searched online to investigate some of these coaching philosophies because they seemed so farfetched. One guy used a series of ten questions in a repeated fashion over and over again and claimed to select the right career after five cycles. It didn't work on me. Another woman used crystals in a bowl and asked me to select my three favorite ones, at which point she explained what my destined career path should be. Not all of the coaches used methods such as these, but I was simply not impressed with anyone. I was looking for specific qualities.

Frank and I had many discussions about keeping the company a lifestyle or growing it into a "real" small business. The only way to grow it was to hire talent. There were only so many hours in the day, and if I were the only person at the company who could interact with clients, the company would never move past the level of a solo practice. Although I liked the flexibility of not having any overhead, not only did I need someone to help with the workload, but I was getting lonely in the office and wanted someone to collaborate with.

Knowing that I was going to hire someone on, I began compiling a training manual to explain my methodology, filling it with worksheets, exercises, and examples pulled from meetings with my clients. I didn't exactly know what I was going to do with this training manual once I had it finished, other than train one employee, but I continued to revise and update it, knowing that it could someday be crucial to the success of the business.

The purpose of the manual became clear while dining one night with Kiley and Mark, who had become our regular companions on couples' nights out. "I'm amazed that you know how to do all this," Kiley said, referring to my career coaching abilities. "Did you learn it all in grad school?"

"Not really," I said. "It's been mostly trial and error, but my marketing experience has really been a tremendous asset."

"I've just never heard anyone talk about career development like that," Kiley said. "It seems like a really unique approach. I feel like if more people were doing what you're doing, you could really change how people see their careers. Have you ever thought about putting together a career coach training program?"

"That is a very good idea. As a matter of fact, I've been putting together a manual to describe my method and it's nearly one hundred pages already. I just haven't figured out what to do with it yet."

"You should teach a seminar," Mark said through a mouthful of salad. "Like Tony Robbins."

"Yeah, right," I said.

"I think it's a great idea, Linda," Frank said. "I know how much work you've put into developing that program. I think it's time to share it with others."

"Well, I'll think about it," I said.

Later, back at the house, I thought about the conversation further and decided that it was time to start thinking seriously about sharing my program with others who were passionate about career coaching. I thought about how long it would take to create a training manual that would be adequate enough to train people the right way. I sat in front of our library reviewing all of the training courses Frank and I'd taken over the years to find a sample that I could use as a model.

"What are you doing love?" Frank asked as he entered the library. He looked at all of the books surrounding me and took note of the titles.

"I'm reviewing these training books to assess what I'll need to do to create the training program we discussed."

He stared at me in delight. "It is great to see you so fired up about this project!"

Reflexively, my hands moved to my forehead and I rubbed my temples. "I'm not sure where I'm going to find the time to add another project, but I'm stepping in with both feet." The only training program that I'd ever put together was for technical software, and that was very complex and mostly driven by engineering. And then it dawned on me—I had a training program that I'd taken years ago as a marketing executive and had quite enjoyed. I needed to find where I had stored that binder—it was an excellent example of how to format and deliver training.

Over the next month, I pulled together all of the materials I'd used with clients during various engagements. I shook my head in confusion when I had a copy of everything printed in front of me. The stack of paper was nearly an inch thick. I organized the piles of paper into categories based on the process I'd been informally, but consistently, using with clients. Once the sections were organized, I created header pages for each section and edited the content so that it was directed at the coach rather than the client. A slide deck was created to use in the seminars so that people could follow along.

Part of my brain was sorting out how to pull the training manual together so that it looked professional, and the other part of my brain was panicked with fear about finding people to take the course and sorting out where I was going to deliver the training. In the same instant, my phone rang. I tried to ignore it but something kept pushing me to answer it. I stood and raced for the kitchen. "It's probably a client calling to reschedule a meeting," I said to no one in particular. When I got to the phone, I recognized the phone number and answered it quickly. "Hi, Adriana," I said cheerfully. "How can I help you?"

"Hey, Linda," she answered. "I need to change my appointment time and am wondering if you would be available first thing in the morning?"

"I'm not sure. Let me check my calendar. Hold on a second . . . I need to move the phone away from my ear so if you start talking I won't hear you."

"No problem."

I returned the phone to my ear in less than twenty seconds. "I have an opening at 9:00 if that works."

"That is great. Thanks so much. I really look forward to working on my new résumé," she said.

"Great. Me too. I'll see you in the morning."

I felt like warm water had just filled my veins. Adriana's phone call at this particular moment could not be a coincidence. She had an extensive human resources background and I'd been thinking about approaching her to see if she would be interested in doing some consulting work for me. She was very intelligent, had the right background, an energetic personality, and had been exposed to my career transition process twice. The first time was when she had sent her husband to see me for career help. As he had gained momentum in the transition process and moved toward the realization of his career goal, she had figured she needed to get help for her own career.

I spent the rest of the afternoon drafting a memo to send to my entire network about the training program. The memo would be used to solicit interest from ten people who wanted to be trained for free in the area of career coaching. I explained the details of the program and outlined exactly the type of experience, attitude, and personality that would be an ideal fit. Once I was satisfied with the content, I emailed it to tons of people in my network as well as a few association groups that I belonged to. With that, I turned off the computer and went in search of my children and husband.

Everyone was in the pool so I stripped out of my clothes and slid into my favorite blue bikini. When I opened the door to the back patio, I witnessed my three boys dancing on the water fountain just above the pool to the lyrics of a Black Eyed Peas song that was coming out of the speakers. "The last one in is a rotten egg!" I shouted as I ran across the deck and did a cannon ball into the deep end. "Come and get me," I said when I surfaced. We played in the pool for hours, which was exactly how I needed to end the day, spending time with the people I loved the most.

✿✿✿

The next morning we went through the usual routine and I was out of the house by 8:30 A.M. Once again, I thought about Adriana. She would be a great person to invite to the course, and to ask for expert input on my process. It's one thing for me and a select few to say it's great, but what would a wider audience think?

I settled into my office shortly before 9:00 A.M. and quickly turned on my computer, poured myself a cup of coffee, and grabbed Adriana's folder from the office across the hall, which I had added onto the lease a few weeks earlier. Adriana entered the office dressed in blue slacks and a shirt three sizes too big. I looked at her shoes just to take in the whole outfit. I could see a pair of crazy socks hiding underneath that didn't match anything she had on. She had a big smile and the headband on her head barely contained the large mass of black curly hair underneath.

She sat down at the round table and pulled out her array of colorful notebooks and rainbow set of pens. "I am so eager to work on this résumé. It needs a lot of work and I've not updated it in years," she remarked without saying hello. "I can't work for my psycho boss anymore. The man is evil because of all of the morphine he's taking."

"Your boss is on morphine? Is he sick?" I asked in shock.

"He was sick, but now he takes it because he can. His mood swings are aggressive and his rants are becoming more regular. He's swearing at me and tearing my work up into pieces."

"That is not a healthy work environment. Who's managing this guy?" I asked, puzzled.

"He is one of the owners so his brother ignores it. He's grown immune to it," she explained.

"You need to get out of there before your self-esteem is stolen from you or something worse happens," I told her. I opened the green folder on my desk and jotted down the date and a few notes. We continued the session with me asking her lots of questions about her work history. She answered every question in a comedic and philosophic way, which made me laugh many times in the span of fifty minutes. Ten minutes before the session ended, I told her about the new training program, showed her the materials that I had pulled together, and asked her to audit the course.

"I would love to audit this course," she replied instantly. "What you are doing is so interesting and I was going to ask you for recommendations on learning how to do it. I got into HR to help people, but my job turned me into the termination squad. I grew numb to firing people. It was all about protecting companies from lawsuits."

"Well, that is not what this course is about. Come to the office next Saturday at 9:00 A.M. for the first class," I remarked, as I stood up to indicate that she needed to leave my office. Another client was waiting in the hall. I hugged her and wished her a happy week.

❊❊❊

My nerves were on edge because I didn't think anyone would be interested enough to sit in on an unproven course for eight Saturdays in a row. However, by the end of the week, there was no doubt about the interest in the course. Dozens of people had responded to my email and I had selected seven people in addition to Adriana who seemed to have the appropriate background, although I wasn't sure exactly what experience I was searching for. *Should I train only marketing people or open it up to human resource professionals and other types of counselors?* I wondered to myself.

Ultimately, I elected to train a diverse group. I reviewed the eight names on the roster I had created and didn't recognize a single person except Adriana. Three of the people were in human resources, two were organizational development professionals, one was a family therapist, one was a university career center counselor, and the other person was an NLP (Neuro-Linguistic Programming)coach.

The Friday night before the course, I sat Indian style on the floor spreading the copies of the introduction and first module I had made at Kinko's into nine piles. I separated each module with colorful, tabbed, content-divider pages. The book would not be complete for the first class, but I'd explain to the students that each week I would give them new modules to include. However, I wanted the structure of the binder to be complete. Within each section, I used fluorescent yellow card stock to make it easy to find the sections within each module. I crossed and recrossed my legs multiple times because they were falling asleep. With the piles complete, I reached for the Office Depot bag sitting in the corner and pulled out nine, two-inch white binders with the standard three ring holders and plastic-coated covers. With the binders covering my legs, I picked up one and pulled back the plastic cover to see if my cover would slip in easily. I was pleased that it fit like a glove and put the other eight covers in the binders.

Just a few moments later, I slammed one of the binders closed because I realized that I had forgotten to punch holes in the copies I'd made at Kinko's. With an angry scowl on my face, I tossed the binders aside in search of a three-hole puncher. It was going to be a long night pulling together these manuals in the right way. I was mixed with feelings of excitement and nervous energy, and the negative talk kicked in again. *Linda, why are you walking into another thing that you don't know anything about? You are no expert on career coaching. Lots of people have written books about this stuff. Who are you to think you can change it? Do you really want to add this to your plate? What if it works? How are you going to find the time and money to continue developing it?*

I knew I wouldn't get any sleep and thought about pulling an all-nighter, but decided against it when, around 1:30 A.M., the tiredness crept over me. The house was quiet except for the volume of the television program Frank was watching. I walked over to the TV and turned it off. "Let's go to bed, love," I whispered sleepily. He followed right behind me as we walked in silence to the bedroom.

The next morning, Frank put all of the materials in the trunk and the whole family got into the car. We stopped for bagels and coffee before going to my office to set up for the day. I thought silently about the last time I'd been away from Frank on a Saturday for more than an hour and couldn't remember even a single time that had happened. It was going to be strange being without him on the weekend.

We arrived at my office at 7:30 A.M., which I thought was more than enough time to set up a projector and move a few chairs around. I was fortunate to have leased an office with a community training room. Typically, the property management company charges $750 per day for the room, but they let me use it for free because it hadn't been used in so long. I had coordinated with the facility manager to have the doors unlocked in the morning.

When we entered the building, Andrew and Vaughn bolted straight for the indoor garden with flowing water. Oftentimes, the property manager would hide the small alligators and frogs in funny ways so the kids wanted to find them. Frank and I walked to the training room door and pulled the handle, but the door didn't move.

"Oh my goodness, he forgot to unlock the door," I said, a bit panicked.

"Did you remind him before you left yesterday?" Frank asked very calmly.

"Of course I reminded him. I'm not stupid!" I replied as I gave him a dirty look. "Can you please go to the center table and look through the directory for Mark Sims's name and cell phone number? I think it's on the last page."

As he searched for the phone number, I walked around to the side of the training room to test the other door. It was locked, too.

"No answer, love. It went straight to voicemail," Frank informed me.

"What the hell am I going to do? I'm totally screwed because I can't fit eight people in my office. I'm going to look like a fool."

"Please don't panic. We'll figure this out," Frank offered as he stood looking at the door.

"I have an idea. Give me your credit card, please," I demanded eagerly.

"Why, what are you going to do?" he asked, pulling a card out.

"I'm going to pick the lock. There is enough space between the two doors to fit a card. All I have to do is stick the card in the release lock and it should open."

"Are you crazy? What if they have video surveillance, Linda?"

"Well, I have permission to use the room so I'll just explain that fact and then they can call the property manager to verify it." I shrugged my shoulders and grabbed the card from Frank's hand. "Just keep an eye out for me. I don't want other tenants walking into the building while I'm picking a lock."

Frank shook his head but walked toward the front entrance. I heard him telling the kids to be careful because the waterfall was slippery.

"I got it! We are in!" I shouted. "Woo-hoo . . . I'm good. Maybe if I fail at this career coaching business, I can take up another line of work," I said jokingly.

"Yeah, right. Let's just go in and set up for this class and hope that the cops don't come and arrest us."

After a few hiccups with the projector, electronic shades, and sophisticated lighting system, the room was good to go. People started showing up shortly after and Frank and I greeted everyone as they entered the room. After everyone had arrived, I asked Frank to leave so that I could start the course. I almost thought that he planned to sit through the workshop, but he left after giving me a huge hug and reminding me that he'd be back for lunch.

I spent the first few minutes of the course controlling my fear and forcing myself to breathe through my nose. My palms were sweaty but I hoped the class didn't notice. The afternoon passed quickly, and I looked out at the students, feeling a great sense of accomplishment. I had breezed through the curriculum, answered tons of questions, and the students had challenged me in a number of areas. I ended the day thinking the first class was a hit. Many students stayed afterwards and gave me great feedback about the sections that worked well and the areas that needed a bit more polish.

I knew moving forward that I would burn out of steam if I stayed up every Friday night preparing materials for each Saturday class, so I decided to hire an assistant from a temporary placement agency. The next Friday, the agency sent over Rita, a 30-something brunette ready for a day's worth of copying, hole punching, and organizing binders. I explained to Rita what I needed her to do and she took copious notes. We toured the office building and I showed her where the copier room was located. Then I returned to my office, confident that she would prepare the materials that I needed.

I went into my office to prepare for my meetings and heard Rita shuffling papers, which made me think she was preparing to make copies. I conducted business as usual and around lunchtime, went in to check on Rita's progress.

"Rita, what are you doing?" I asked astonished.

"When I stood up to go to the copier, I dropped the manual and paper flew everywhere. I've been putting the manual back in sequential order," she replied.

"Oh, wow. Do you need any help?" I offered.

"Nope, I've got it under control."

The fact that it had taken her almost four hours to reorganize the stack should have been my first warning sign. I thought about calling the agency to ask for another person, but decided against it. It would take too long to find another person and time was running out.

Later that afternoon, Rita came into my office after my client left. "Linda, this copier is stuck. Can you help me? I can't figure out how to get it unstuck," Rita said as she waved her hands carelessly through the air.

I stared at her thinking she was either completely spastic or on drugs. "Let's go take a look," I said. I fixed the copier about four times, but it kept jamming. "Well, this piece of junk is not going to cooperate today so we need to move to plan B." I looked at my watch and saw that it was nearly 4:00 P.M. "You'll have to go to Kinko's to make copies of all this stuff."

"No problem," she replied. "Where is it?"

"It's just down the street. I would go with you but I have to pick up my son from school and take him to Tae Kwon Do class."

"You don't need to come with me. I've got it covered. I'll make the copies and will be here at 7:30 A.M. tomorrow morning."

"That would be great! Thank you so much for getting this done," I told her as we both gathered our things and left the office. I was looking forward to a relaxing evening and full night of sleep in preparation for tomorrow's class.

The next morning, Frank dropped me off at the office at 7:30 A.M. The training room—unlocked this time—was basking in sunlight on this beautiful end-of-summer day. I could see the flowers in bloom for miles through the tinted window on the north side of the training room. I walked confidently through the room, ready to set up for the day. Once everything was in place, I wandered to the bathroom to take one last look at my hair and makeup. I looked at my watch several times along the way wondering where Rita was. I dialed the cell phone number she had given me and left two messages. *Oh my goodness,* I thought. *I hope she doesn't screw this up. That would be a nightmare. Where the hell is she?* I did everything in my power to calm the anger that was building up inside.

When I returned to the training room, several of the students had arrived and grabbed the same spot they had secured the week before. The clock showed 8:15 A.M. and Rita was still not here. I called her several more times but received voicemail again. Luckily, I hadn't completed the module from last week, so I estimated that we would wrap up that section by 11:00 A.M. *If she doesn't show up by then,* I thought to myself, *I can go upstairs and print another original copy and then run to Kinko's during the lunch break.* After taking a few minutes to center myself and push away the stress, I began class, smiling as if everything were perfect.

At 11:00, with no Rita in sight, I scheduled an early lunch and used that time to make copies. Everyone left for lunch except for Adriana, my client whom I had recruited to the class. She sensed that something was wrong—very difficult to do with me—and asked if she could help. When I told her what had happened, she grabbed the materials and charged ahead toward the copier without even the slightest hesitation or thought.

"Let's go put these materials together" she demanded. "And by the way, I'm starting work for you on Monday since I assume your assistant is fired."

"Yes, she's fired, but I can't afford you. I paid her an assistant's salary and could never afford an HR manager's salary."

"I don't care if I have to work for free. You have opened my eyes to a new career path and this is exactly the kind of thing I'd like to do for a living. Pay or no pay, I'll be here on Monday." I just shook my head in delight, knowing that she was just being kind but very thankful for the helping hand. Thanks to the unexpected assistance I'd received, the rest of the day went off without a hitch and I looked forward to the rest of class.

❀❀❀

The office was quiet when I showed up on Monday morning, which was a welcomed relief. I was thankful that I didn't have a client until 11:00 A.M., which gave me time to bang out a few client projects.

I searched through my desk drawer for my favorite pen so that I could make notes about changes I wanted to recommend on a résumé. My thoughts drifted to the conversation with Adriana and I wondered if she was actually going to show up. *There is no way she will show up. That would be so insane. She did seem believable, though. It would be great to have someone like her, but there is no way I could pay her what she was making at her former job.*

At 9:00 A.M., as promised, Adriana walked through the door. In her hands, she carried a pastel folder with a completed job application she had found on the Internet, a Form W-4 and a Form I-9, along with a copy of her driver's license and social security card. I shook my head in disbelief and wonderment at this person.

"Have a seat and let's talk," I told her. "Since I already know your entire background, I don't have to interview you." I stared at her for a few minutes before finishing. She was smiling from ear to ear. I couldn't help but think of the Cheshire cat from *Alice in Wonderland*. I giggled briefly and finished my thought. "I'm getting more work than I know what to do with. I'd love to bring you on board. We'll have to work out some details about compensation, that sort of thing, but I think you'd be great at this and I'd be proud to make you the first official person on my staff."

Adriana almost had tears in her eyes. "Well, that's good enough for me," she said. You better not change your mind on me!"

"Of course not," I laughed. And with that, I had signed my first employee.

Together, we created a list of the things I needed help with. Adriana turned out to be an amazing employee. She was self-directed and very intelligent. She prepared the rest of the manuals flawlessly and turned out to be a valuable asset in the classroom, too. She was a natural teacher and I knew that she would be the person to help me improve this course and take it to market.

Around the fifth or sixth class, Adriana asked if she could start meeting with clients. Excitement and fear filled my veins at the thought of someone helping me manage the extensive client load. My active client list was well over twenty-five, and that was about eight more clients than any one person could or should handle at a time, given the high-touch service and duration of each engagement. Over the past six months, I'd had to take most of my client work home and work on it after the children went to bed because I couldn't get it done during the day. My days were filled every hour on the hour and I didn't take a lunch break. I knew I couldn't sustain this model much longer.

I didn't think Adriana was ready yet because she hadn't yet been exposed to the entire process, but I figured that she was far enough along to get clients started. With only three more classes to go, I knew she would learn enough to always be one step ahead of the client. I also invited her to sit in on as many sessions as my clients would allow to expose her to the process in real time. It was the best decision I ever made. Within three weeks, she already had six active clients and they loved her. Observing Adriana execute the process was exactly what I needed to determine the content and tools that would be needed in the next version of the training program to better prepare coaches out of the gate.

Adriana made me realize that a lot more depth was needed in the program before taking it nationwide. From that point on, we collaborated on every section of the coaching process and she worked relentlessly to pull out the painstaking details of the process that I took for granted. With her assistance, the training evolved from good to great, and we were well on our way to creating the golden standard in the industry.

Chapter 22 Forgiveness

I lay still in the early morning hour, staring at the clock and waiting for the alarm to sound at 6:00 A.M. Outside I could hear a few birds chirping and knew they were sitting on the tree branch just outside my window. As the sun began to rise, it cast streams of light through the plantation shutters. I stretched several times, thinking how good it felt to push my muscles out of hibernation. Two packed suitcases sat in the corner of the bedroom and I did a mental check of everything I had packed for myself and the children to make sure I had everything for our trip. Everything seemed to be good to go.

Frank and I were taking the children on a trip to New England to visit my family in Maine and his family in New York. It would be the first time that everyone met Vaughn in person. I couldn't wait to introduce him to the family and show them how big Andrew was getting. Traveling to see my mother always caused stress for me. Even though we had worked on our relationship over the years, and it had greatly improved, there always seemed to be an invisible wall between us keeping us both at a distance with our feelings and emotions.

Every time we went home, Frank and I would get into the same argument over where we would stay. He always wanted to stay at a hotel because my mother and stepdad, Don, smoked heavily, and I wouldn't budge. Frank had a difficult time being around smoke because of his contacts, but more so, he didn't want our kids to be exposed to secondhand smoke. Unfortunately, the cigarette smoke permeated everything in her house, including the linens. Unlike most homes, where you might slip into a bed with clean sheets and breathe in the scent of bleach or some fabric softener, at my mom's house, the minute our heads hit the pillow we would start coughing from the layers of cigarette smoke infused in the sheets and pillow cases.

Mom and Don knew this and they would try to adjust their routine accordingly. Instead of smoking in the same room as us, they would stand near an open kitchen window or go onto their porch deck. This was great until the drinking would start and all rules would go by the wayside. I didn't make much of it because I'd been around cigarette smokers my whole life. Dealing with the smoking for two or three days wouldn't kill us, or so I hoped.

As I slid out from under the blankets, I swore I could smell cigarettes in the air but it was only my imagination. I nudged Frank a few times to wake him up and headed to the kitchen to make us some Irish Crème coffee. As I poured the coffee, I thought about the many papers I'd written in the pursuit of my master's degree. It's inevitable that a counseling-based course would require students to reflect on their life experiences; so, nearly every paper I'd written involved stories of my upbringing, or more specifically, my relationship with my mother.

With coffee mug in hand, I walked over to the kitchen drawer where I stored all of my completed papers. The green file folder was in the back of the drawer, piled with several phone books. I pulled out the folder and went into the living room to wait for Frank to join me. The papers were organized by time, so I pulled the one on the bottom and began reading until I finished with the most recent paper.

Just as I had remembered them, the earlier stories about Mom were intense and unforgiving. I expected the rest of the papers to be the same way, but reading the papers in this fashion was a shock to my system. I felt an inexplicable rush of adrenaline and gasped as I realized something for the first time: *I forgave my mother on paper.* The first paper read like it was written by an angry twelve-year-old girl, but the last paper took on the tone of a grown, reflective woman with a grounded and balanced perspective.

I sat there drinking my coffee and got lost in my thoughts. *How had this happened? Am I more forgiving because of my age? Is it because I have children? Is it because I experienced my own personal financial stress and can now empathize with what she must have experienced as a young mother? Frank must be rubbing off on me. It has to be a result of being exposed to so many personal and dire client stories. They needed saving in one form or another, just like me. Only I'm not the one being saved anymore, I'm saving them, I'm the ego encourager, the confidence builder, the believer , , , the trust broker. They believed and trusted that I could help them, and in exchange, I put my trust and talent in them to help them grow and break free from their monotonous and life-sucking careers.*

"What are reading, love?" Frank asked me, breaking me out of my semi-trance.

I stopped thinking for a moment and looked directly at Frank. "I forgave my mother. It's here in these papers. You've got to read them later," I told him, adding, "This is going to be an interesting trip."

"Why is that?" he asked curiously.

"I am finally ready to talk to my mother and share my feelings. I've been gridlocked for so long that I didn't care about knowing anything, but I'm very confused now by my own perspective and need answers."

"Wow, honey, that is really great. I knew you would arrive at this point someday."

"Let's get the kids up and head out. This will be an unforgettable journey."

❀❀❀

I leaned back against the green and white vinyl patio chair, letting the sound of conversation and music fill my ears. The night air was cool and waves of goose pimples covered my arms and legs every so often. The sky was filled with brilliant stars and the wind blew through the trees, making a low whistling sound. The children were playing with their cousins in the patch of grass just below the patio deck.

At that moment, I wondered if this would be the perfect time to start a conversation with Mom. Everybody was calm and I'd already had two vodka sodas with orange slices. It wasn't going to happen unless I opened the door. Three days had passed by already, but I was no closer to bringing up the topic than I had been since the moment at home when the revelation had struck me.

I went through the motions of thinking how to best open the conversation. I didn't want to put her on the defensive because she really seemed to be enjoying our visit. Vaughn didn't take to her right away because, I suspected, he could sense that her guard was up; however, he took to Don instantly. I could tell this bothered her, but she was oblivious to her own vibes.

We had done the usual catching up with life and had discussed every family member and how they were doing. I had educated her more on the business because she didn't quite understand the concept of *career*. To her, a job was something you had to do to put food on the table, not something that would define you in any way, let alone make you happy while you were doing it. It didn't surprise me when she asked me if people really paid for that type of service, and she nearly fell off her chair when I answered her questions about how much people paid for the service. Although my fees were not high by competitive standards, it would take her months to afford my services.

"You are quiet tonight, Lyn," she said. She was the only one ever to call me Lyn. "What'cha thinking about?"

I took a sip from my third vodka and felt my confidence bug getting stronger. "A little bit of this and that," I said noncommittally.

"That's not an answer."

I looked at her and decided to jump in. It was now or never. "I read some papers before coming here and they've been on my mind since I left Texas. They were reflection papers about my childhood and life."

"You haven't had the easiest life, I tell you that. But, you've done good for yourself, Lyn. I'm very proud of you." Tears filled her eyes and I knew that we'd both had enough alcohol to let our emotions show.

"Thanks, Mom, I really appreciate that."

"You have two beautiful boys and it's so obvious that Frank loves you."

I looked at Frank and saw that his eyes were welling with tears, too. He knew how difficult it was for me to hear these words from my mother and to be vulnerable with my feelings. "I love her with all my heart," he said as he took my hand. "She is the only woman for me and an amazing mother."

Don looked at the three of us, shook his head in disbelief, and started laughing. "What the heck is going on here? Why is everyone crying?" he asked. Then he laughed some more and said, "You crybabies." At that, everyone broke into laughter and we all wiped our eyes. The weirdness moment passed. "In all honesty, Lyn, your mom has told me everything about her and your father. She's even told me things that she's never shared with anyone. I know that you don't think she was a good mother, but she did the best she could."

I wasn't quite sure what to say to Don. Just knowing that my mother had talked to Don told me that she had regrets about the past. But, my lack of trust in this mother-daughter relationship immediately made me think she had manipulated the stories to suit herself. She had positioned herself as the victim before, never holding herself accountable for her part in any relationship, and I wouldn't be surprised if that's how she had presented it to Don. But I wanted her to own up to her part of the disaster that had ruined my family.

"Your dad was a good man, but when he drank he got angry and did things to your mom that never should have happened," Don continued. I knew he was referring to the physical and mental abuse that had filled my childhood home;

however, I was not surprised by the fire burning in my belly over hearing someone talk about my father in this manner.

"Don, you only have half of the story," I replied as calmly as I could. "My father was not an abusive man and never hurt my mother unless he was provoked to the point of no return. My mother was a bit of an instigator." I looked at my mother and said, "I'm not trying to hurt your feelings. It's what I remember."

"Lyn, your dad shot me, knocked my teeth out, burned my clothes, and more," she confessed with tears streaming down her face.

"I know this because I watched every moment of it," I said. "But, I also witnessed the torturous things you said to him before he'd act out. You crushed him with words that broke his heart and soul. When you tell a cripple that he is not a man any longer and that you've had affairs with his friends, what do you expect?"

"You were too young to understand what was going on Lyn," she answered, but I didn't want to hear it. "Your dad was jealous and always pushing me on his friends because he didn't feel good about himself. He closed down and wouldn't let me get close no matter how much I begged him. He kept pushing me away and would make me feel so insignificant in front of our friends."

"That is not what I remember," I sighed.

"I know it's not what you remember, but it's the truth. You were not around to witness all of our exchanges. You just happened to show up at the pinnacle of our fights, seeing the worst of our exchanges. It wasn't all your father's fault. I'm to blame, too. I know that, Lyn."

"Then you need to stop talking about him the way that you have been," I said, my lips quivering, I knew I was about to lose control of myself but couldn't stop it. The sobs and heavy breathing began as I allowed the pain to escape, and I closed my eyes and thought to myself that I needed to stop crying so I wouldn't appear to be weak. "He is not here to defend himself," I said through my tears. "He was my father and never hurt me or Steve in any way. I don't want my children thinking their grandfather was an abuser."

"I am sorry, Lyn. I know I was a sucky mother to you and Steve. I didn't know how to make sense of my own feelings so I couldn't help you when you were in pain. I can't take it back, but I can go on from here. Don is an amazing father and he is teaching me how to be a better mother. You just need to give me a chance. I love you very much."

"Mom, all I ever wanted was for you to come into my room and give me a hug and tell me you love me."

"I can do that now."

I'm finally coming home, I thought. I smiled and wiped my tears away. "I would love that," I told her.

"I want a hug, too," pleaded Frank as he opened his arms and began wiggling in place to lighten the mood. With those words, we formed a group hug and began laughing uncontrollably. It turned out to be a very good night.

Chapter 23 Growth

So much time had passed and I finally felt light-years away from the insecure and socially anxious girl I'd been only a decade ago. I was the CEO of a successful growing business. I had trained Adriana on how to execute my career development methodology with outstanding results, created a solid referral engine, organized and served almost two hundred clients, proved I could work a room at a networking event like nobody's business, and talked to people I didn't know with ease. Adriana gave me high marks and told me often that I had a special gift for working with people. To me, I was just doing a job I loved.

Realizing the importance of networking in building a business, Adriana and I decided to each join an organization of our liking. She chose to join the Austin Human Resource Management Association and I became a member of the Young Women's Alliance, a long-running networking group for women in business. I'd been hearing about the group for years and had attended a few meetings, but had always been too busy with my job and family to make the time commitment. The YWA was a great place to meet new people, and I soon had more business than Adriana and I could handle, but somehow we managed.

The year ended perfectly with a wonderful Christmas ski vacation at Mont Tremblant, just north of Montreal, Canada. Although Frank's contract with Dell was coming to an end in February of 2005, I wasn't worried because he'd already started interviewing with several start-up companies. Knowing how long the executive interview process takes, I knew the timing would be perfect. Fortunately, two weeks before his contract ended, Frank was offered a Senior Executive Vice President position at Scalable, an up-and-coming software firm.

There was one little catch, though. The position was based in Houston, almost 200 miles away from our Austin home.

"It's a great opportunity, Linda," he said. We were sitting in the game room, having a post-dinner glass of wine. Vaughn and Andrew were safely tucked into their beds down the hall.

"I know it is, Frank," I said, "but I can't move to Houston. For starters, I like it here. I don't want to leave our house after we've spent so much time working on it, and I'd never want to raise our kids in Houston. On top of that, my business is really taking off. I've been working my ass off to establish a solid brand. If we move to Houston, I'd have to start all over again, make all new connections. That would take a long time."

"I don't want to move to Houston, either," Frank agreed. "But you remember what it was like when I wasn't working. I don't want to repeat that experience any time soon. Besides, you know there are very few opportunities in Austin right now. We really can't afford to turn this down."

"Sounds great," I said sarcastically. "So what are you going to do, spend seven hours driving there and back every day? As soon as you get to Houston, you'll have to turn around and start coming back."

"No, of course not. That would be impossible. I'll stay there during the week and fly back over the weekends."

I stared at him in shock. "You're friggin' kidding me, right? So I'd only see you two days a week? And I'd have to raise Andrew and Vaughn by myself? I don't think so, Frank! No friggin' way."

"You won't have to do it all by yourself. We'll still have Margarita."

"Sure, during the day when I'm at work. But I still have to give them their baths, put them to bed, comfort them in the middle of the night when they're having nightmares. I don't know why we're even arguing about this. You know how hard it would be for us if you weren't around. And it's not just that I want you to be here for their sake. I need you here, too. We've barely spent a day apart since we first started dating. I don't think I could handle that kind of separation."

"I know, hon," Frank said. "It would be hard on both of us. But it will only be temporary. The company needs an Austin office, and as soon as I can get it set up, I'll only have to travel every once in awhile."

"Well, how soon is that going to happen?"

"Within a year, maybe sooner. We'll have a few difficult months, but after that, I'll be here."

I sighed and downed the rest of my glass of wine. Frank was right about how difficult it was to find a job in Austin, but the thought of him being out of town five days a week gave me a sick feeling in the pit of my stomach. It had been so long since we'd been apart that I didn't even know if I'd be able to fall asleep without him lying next to me. On the other hand, it was a great opportunity, and the money he'd be making would go a long way toward helping us pay off our debts and rebuild our savings.

"Will you get an employment contract?" I finally asked.

"Yes. With several months of severance."

"Only a few months severance? You should get at least six."

"Linda, I tried to negotiate six, but they wouldn't budge. They moved on base, bonus and options." Frank leaned his head against the back of the couch and stared at the ceiling.

"Fine," I said numbly. "What choice do we really have?"

He leaned over on the couch and kissed me on the lips. "It's only temporary, honey, I promise," he whispered. "It'll be over before you know it. I don't want to be away from my family any longer than necessary. My mission will be to open an Austin office as soon as humanly possible. I'll also figure out how to not work five days a week in Houston over time."

"I'm counting on it," I said.

❀❀❀

When Frank predicted that the Austin office would be up and running in about six months, he was wrong. It took him nearly a year to convince his boss to establish an office in Austin. For nearly twelve months, Frank would board a plane on Monday morning and come back home on Friday night. After awhile, the separation got to be too much for both of us. I began flying out to Houston on Tuesday mornings, would spend the night while Margarita stayed with the kids, and fly back to Austin on Wednesday mornings. Seeing Frank midweek made it more bearable, but I still worried about how his absence might affect Vaughn and Andrew.

It was a welcome relief when Frank finally started the Austin office and signed a lease in the very same office building as mine. He would be located on the first floor in a 3,500 square foot office. It didn't take him long to prepare the office and hire the staff needed to continue building the company. The travel to Houston didn't stop, but instead of him being there five days a week, it was only one or two days a week.

During this time, I compensated for the loneliness caused by Frank's absence by plunging myself into my business and the Young Women's Alliance. When I was asked by the YWA president-elect to apply for the president-elect role, I was in shock. Over the years, I had moved from member to committee member to chair to a VP role. Leading one of the most prestigious groups in Austin would be a great way to give back to the community and it was an excellent way to get more exposure for my company.

"I know you are busy, but you are the best person in the organization to run the group," Michelle told me over coffee at Mozart's, a local coffee shop/pastry joint hangout on Lake Austin. I was busy with my two children, a growing business, running the house on my own, and operating as a board member for YWA. *How would I be able to add another thing to my plate without compromising my commitment to my family?* With five hundred women in the group, someone surely must have been better qualified than me and more available. I contemplated putting it off until next year, when my life wouldn't be so hectic and Frank would be back in town, but the offer was very appealing.

As Michelle and I sat out on the balcony, a soft mist of rain started to fall upon us as the sunset reflected off the water. There were a million thoughts crowding my mind, some of which were, *Frank will wring my neck, but Kiley will cheer me on because she thinks I'm superwoman.* I sipped my hazelnut coffee and stared at the dozen or so people working on their laptops on the faded picnic tables, their conversations blended with the noises of boats docking. "I'll do it," I finally said. "It's a worthy event that benefits at-risk children. How can I say no?"

"Really?" Michelle responded with excitement all over her face.

"Yes, I'll do it. What are the next steps?"

"I'll send you all of the details in an email," she said, hugging me. "Thank you so much. This is going to be the best year yet!"

✿✿✿

The nominating committee selected me and I was officially the new president-elect. In that role, it was also my job to plan the Austin Under 40 Gala, one of Austin's most prestigious events. I spent nearly a year planning the event and the days leading up to the actual gala were hectic. Dozens of people were involved in logistics and my phone didn't stop because everyone needed advice on last-minute details. My co-chair from the Young Men's Business League and I had done a tremendous job of significantly improving the brand, enabling online ticket purchase, increasing the sponsorship levels, and even managing to find a new venue. The invitations had been mailed and the response was overwhelming with nearly 700 RSVPs.

On the night of the event, I could hardly contain my nerves. The idea of speaking in front of hundreds of people nearly made me pass out. I stood near the front of the stage for hours trying to wrap my mind around how many eyes and ears would be focused on my every word and body movement. I scanned the room to see where the four giant screens were placed— two in the back of the room and two on stage.

A cold sweat broke out on my forehead and neck as the program got underway. I'd never spoken in front of such a huge group as this before and was nervous because of it. The largest audience that I'd presented to included thirty people. I had recited the script hundreds of times and memorized every word and pause. I knew that if I could make it through the first minute I would be fine. It typically took me this amount of time to slow my beating heart and speak without quivering lips.

The master of ceremonies commenced the gala and thanked the sponsors, and with angry butterflies tumbling in my belly, I counted down the minutes to my speech. I rested my head against Frank's chest and prayed that I didn't fall while walking up on stage or become paralyzed with fear while speaking.

Suddenly, I heard my name being announced over the loud speaker. Frank was pushing me toward the stage. I made it to the podium without tripping, but remained motionless for what seemed a very long time. My cochair began his speech and I knew that my lines were upon me. I was alone in my head, sweat forming behind my neck and flowing down my spine like a leaky faucet. I inhaled and exhaled a deep breath and began speaking. To my astonishment, the words rolled off my tongue flawlessly and with passion for the cause.

From the moment I stepped onto the stage at the gala and successfully delivered my first speech in front of such a large audience, everything changed. Never in my life had I felt so energized—I'd arrived. What an adrenaline rush it had been to produce such an enormous event and be center stage for the entire evening. My confidence was skyrocketing through the roof. It was the first time in my career that I had taken on something so important and in such a public way. It felt great to be needed, to be respected, and to be thanked for a job well-done. I felt completely amazing and partied and danced into the wee hours of the morning.

✿✿✿

What I didn't realize then was that I had just started down the path of becoming a socialite. This seemed like an unlikely possibility given that I hadn't been born into wealth, didn't have the appropriate background, and didn't make whopping donations to big charities. Throughout the rest of 2006, dozens of emails and phone calls poured in with requests for me to chair signature charity events. Although very flattered by the invitations, I agonized with Frank over whether or not it would be the right thing to do for the family and the business.

"Frank, what do you think about me chairing another event?" I inquired one day.

"Honey, you are a natural and you enjoyed it so much. I think that you should do it again."

"I don't know. I'm so torn. I would love to do something grand but the business would take a hit, because I only have so many hours in the day, and I may miss out on more family things."

"Linda, hire another person so that the business keeps on growing. You have the revenue coming in and you've been thinking about doing it, anyway. Pull the trigger."

"That would certainly help a lot," I agreed.

Things were going so smoothly at home and work. The pace of work was just right, allowing me ample time to be with the kids, travel with Frank, and keep up an assertive fitness regimen. I wasn't sure that I wanted the company to grow any larger because of my freedom to come and go as needed. I took a deep breath and focused on the positive side of hiring another coach. The most attractive aspect of the idea was that I'd have nearly all day to work on the training program. I'd been working on the program off and on for so many months now, so I knew that I'd have to either hire a curriculum person to realize my vision or do it myself.

I threw my hands up in the air. I knew for certain that I was going to hire another coach and I had the perfect person in mind. I had been working with another client for quite some time and he had the perfect profile to be a coach. Actually, several of his assessments indicated that coaching would be an ideal occupation, but he resisted because he didn't think he could do it. My brain started to work on a strategy for leading him to the conclusion that coaching was perfect for him. I felt a bit guilty about steering him in one direction, but knew the outcome would be terrific. He just needed to realize it, too.

It only took a couple of weeks for me to add a third person to the team. Scott was very excited about the idea of becoming a coach and working for me. He told me that he had thought about that career choice often but thought a more traditional job would be better. His heart won this battle and I was so pleased.

Having two people to deliver coaching services freed me up to focus solely on building the training program. With this new focus, I politely declined all of the invitations to chair events, knowing that my attention had to be on work and home. There would be ample time next year to take on more community initiatives.

Chapter 24 Triumph

By 2007, I rarely found time to pause and take a break from everyday life. *Where had the year gone? How had the time slipped away from me?* Finding time to reflect on the past or think about what I wanted out of the future was nearly impossible. My days were packed with work, and this crisp morning in March was no different. The phone rang at the office and I picked it up immediately. On the other end of the line was a friend, Lacy, that I had met at our kids' school. We'd become close.

"Hey Linda," she said cheerfully.

"Hiya!" I replied. "What's up?"

"I just got this frantic email from a friend looking for help. I guess the chair of the Cattle Baron's Ball quit yesterday because the volunteers couldn't stand him and now they have no leadership. Ginger stepped up to help out, but she has no support."

"That's awful. He must have been a real jerk for volunteers to walk out. When is the event and what kind of help does she need?" I asked curiously.

"The event is in May of this year. Ginger needs any help you can provide. I know that you are busy so even the smallest assistance will go a long way."

I tapped my fingers on the table pondering whether or not I should help given my limited bandwidth already. "How much money have they raised to date?"

"Almost nothing! The goal is $150,000 and they have commitments for $25,000. They are desperate for sponsors."

"Holy cow! Have they considered cancelling the event? That is not enough time to raise that kind of money!"

"Yes, but think of all those people who would be without services from the American Cancer Society. It would be devastating. Ginger had pancreatic cancer. Did you know that?"

"Oh, no. I didn't. She looks amazing. How long ago?" I asked, surprised. In my mind, people who had cancer didn't look as healthy and vibrant as Ginger.

"It's been awhile, but she is passionate about the cause. She really needs us. What do you say?"

I wanted to say no because I'd promised Frank after my YWA event that I'd take a break, but I couldn't. "Sure. I'm happy to help. I'm already reading your mind. You want us to assist with fundraising, right?"

"You are good, Linda. Can you come over tomorrow during lunch to make phone calls? I'm inviting about ten ladies over for a call campaign."

I stared at my calendar for the next day and saw all of the meetings scheduled back-to-back from 8:00 A.M. to 5:00 P.M. "Yes, I'll reschedule a few meetings and be there around noon."

I hung up the phone and noticed Adriana standing behind me. "You are going to help with the Cattle Baron's Ball?" she asked with utter excitement.

"Were you eavesdropping on my conversation?" I responded sarcastically.

"I don't have to eavesdrop on your conversations because your voice carries all the way down the hall!" she replied as she sat down at my round table. "Do you know what the Cattle Baron's Ball is?"

"Yes, it's a fundraiser for the American Cancer Society."

"No. It's not just any fundraiser. It's only one of the biggest social events of the year. They are planned all over the country. The one in Dallas raised nearly $2 million last year." The fact that Adriana knew this was no surprise. She was a walking encyclopedia.

"You are kidding me!" I replied in shock. "Oh crap. What did I just sign up for? Frank is going to kill me for taking this on, especially when he just started a new job."

The past several months had been stressful because Frank's company was not hitting its numbers and they'd lost their head of sales to a competitor. The CEO was having a difficult time finding a replacement, so he'd promoted the wrong guy into the role. Frank had expressed his concerns over the decision to promote the current director of sales because he had not been consistent in achieving his numbers, either.

The investors had been very frustrated and called a three-day, hands-on meeting to discuss the status of the company. The outcome of that meeting was very disappointing. They had decided that the company would not be viable long-term and wanted to move down the path of selling it. With this decision, the investors had downsized the operation to a skeleton crew and nearly all of the employees were let go, including all of the executives.

Fortunately, the job market had improved in Austin and Frank had landed in a stellar job in less than a month. I thanked God for Frank landing on his feet so quickly, because the thought of another long sabbatical scared the daylight out of me. He had joined a company downtown called CompassLearning. It was owned by Reader's Digest, an old established company, so I had comfort in knowing that it wouldn't close its doors anytime soon. Frank was excited about the opportunity because it was in the K-12 education space, and the software focused on helping students improve their performance in the classroom.

When I got home that evening, I stared at the back of the door that lead from the garage into our kitchen, feeling knots in my belly before opening it. *But why?* I thought. *There is nothing wrong with me signing up to help a friend in need, plus, it's for a good cause. Margarita helps in the afternoons and Frank can hang with the kids if I have to have after-hour meetings . . . so why not?* My guilty conscience was working overtime. I wasn't satisfied with the quality or amount of time I spent with the kids, but Frank told me that I was too hard on myself. I couldn't invent hours in the day, so signing up for this event would steal more time away from my family. It wouldn't be that much time, though, because I could make phone calls from the office, and if I had to meet someone face-to-face I could do it during work hours.

As I walked through the door, I tried to remember who in our family had had cancer. *Didn't Frank's grandmother die in the hospital with breast cancer? Wait, I think his grandfather had colon cancer. Who else do I know that has had cancer? Jeez, Linda, your grandmother died last year of lung cancer. That's the angle, then. I'm helping in memory of losing our loved ones,* I thought to myself as I stepped inside.

When I got into the house I could hear Frank talking to Andrew about Tae Kwon Do. It was a topic of discussion often because Andrew wanted to quit and Frank didn't want him to. We had all achieved our black belts—I was a first degree, Frank and Andrew were senior second degrees. He wanted Andrew to achieve his third degree belt before taking a break from the program, but Andrew was adamant about stopping because he wanted to play football.

I wasn't completely inside yet when the door flew open from a breeze and slammed against the granite countertop. Frank turned toward my direction. I felt like a teenager walking in the door after curfew. "Hi, love," I said with a smile, hoping that I didn't look guilty.

"I tried calling you on your cell, but you didn't answer."

"My phone was in my purse in the backseat. I didn't want to stretch back to reach it while driving." *Yeah, that's a good one,* I thought. Vaughn ran to me and I picked him up in my arms for a great big hug. "My goodness, little man, you are getting so big. How was school? What did you learn today?"

"Nothing," he responded without a care in the world.

"What do you mean 'nothing?' I need to call your teacher to see what she's teaching you."

"We did centers and I built a Lego ship. Can you come and see it at school?"

"A Lego ship . . . that's cool. Yes, I will come and see it." I put him down and walked over to Frank and Andrew to give them a kiss.

"Tomorrow?" Vaughn asked. "Can you come tomorrow? How about tomorrow? Mom, how about tomorrow?"

"I'll think about it. We'll see. Go play so that I can get dinner started." I patted his behind before he ran upstairs to play.

"Actually, aren't we going to the club tonight?" Frank asked. "The gang is already over there waiting for us."

"Oh yeah, I forgot. Yes, let's go to the club. I need to change my clothes, though, and don't let me forget to tell you about the call I got today from Ginger. Did you make an appointment at the kids' club?" I asked.

"Yes, already done. Maria is working so Vaughn is excited. Andrew wants to stay home and play Xbox."

I couldn't believe that Andrew was already eleven years old. He babysat for us whenever we asked, but I didn't want to overdo it, so whenever we went to the club we always brought Vaughn to the member's kid care. It was a great place for the kids because they had computers, video games, an outside playground, arts and crafts, and lots more. Vaughn always had something beautiful to give us when we picked him up. My favorite gifts were the colorful drawings he made of the family.

"Honey, you ready to go?" Frank asked.

"I'm all set. Let's hit the road. Where is the little man? Vaughn, come on let's go to Barton Creek."

"Mom, I'm right here,," Vaughn said.

"Oh, I didn't see you kiddo. Give me a big kiss." I reached out my hands to give him a great big bear hug.

"Andrew," I called out, "we are leaving. Do you want me to order you a pizza from Papa John's? Andrew, can you hear me?"

"I heard you," he shouted from the second-floor balcony. "Yeah, I'd like a pizza. Just plain cheese and some Sprite," he quickly replied and ran back to his room to finish his game.

"Make sure you have your phone near you just in case I call," I reminded him.

"I know, Mom. You tell me that every time you go out. I have my phone with me."

We packed into the car and listened to music on the three-mile drive to the club. We dropped Vaughn off with Maria and ordered him pasta with butter and shredded cheese. It was his favorite dish. Then we got back in the car to head over to the main club house.

"Hey, before we go in I want to tell you about my conversation with Ginger," I said, wanting to tell him about my decision before we started our evening. I didn't want to risk forgetting to tell him later.

"Oh, yeah. What did she want?" Frank asked.

"She asked me to help do some fundraising for something called the Cattle Baron's Ball. It benefits ACS—the American Cancer Society. I told her I could spare a few hours a week to help out. I plan to do it during work time. It's in memory of the people we've lost ... your grandmother ... grandfather ... my grandma."

He didn't look convinced, but much to my surprise, didn't argue about it. "It's a great idea. I know how much you enjoy volunteering your time to help others."

"Great, honey. Thanks for understanding."

"No need to thank me. I need to thank you for being such a giving person," he said, and that was that.

We got to the main club house and were happy about hanging out with the new group of people we'd met a few months back. It was the first time in our relationship that we had a group of married friends to hang with. Our typical routine consisted of hanging with one couple at a time for dinner and drinks. We had met Carlos and Julie first because they were club members and we always seemed to be there at the same time as them on Thursdays. After running into each other several times, we had struck up a conversation and had all connected instantly. Carlos and Julie had introduced us to the rest of the gang, which consisted of four other couples who had known one another for many years. It had been a bit awkward getting to know everyone because they were a protective group, but Julie had told us that everyone would warm up to us with time. She'd been right, of course, and before we knew it, we had ten new best friends.

When we arrived at the bar, everyone was already socializing with drinks in hand. We heard Carlos talking about an upcoming trip to Vegas and making plans for a cabana. "The Ginacs!" Carlos called out, hugging us one at a time.

We hugged everyone and pulled up two bar stools next to the group.

"Are you guys planning a trip to Vegas?" Frank asked the group. "We love Vegas and go once a year."

Everyone started giggling, but we were not quite sure why. "This will be our third trip this year," said Julie.

"What? Are you kidding me?" I responded in shock. "You've already been to Vegas two times this year? It's only March!"

"We go to Vegas a lot," said Mary. "It is always a great time, too. You guys should come with us. We are going in December. It's my birthday."

"That sounds like tons of fun. I think we may take you up on that offer," I replied.

As the gang continued to drink, laugh, and recount old stories—albeit new to Frank and me—I drifted in thought, not sure how to take in all of the personalities of the group. It was great being here, but I worried about the volume of drinking this group seemed to engage in. I had worked so hard not to become someone who drank excessively because of my past, and the thought of walking straight into a party group sent chills down my spine. It was not as if they were shoving drinks my way. It was casual drinking by any standards, but it was still drinking. I couldn't help but count the number of drinks each person sipped—three, four, five—as the night went on. As the drinks went down, my anxiety went up. I was on guard, just waiting for a fight or argument to break out, but surprisingly, it didn't happen. Each of these couples appeared to have a great relationship, and this thought gave me great comfort.

❖❖❖

Over the next couple of months, I worked tirelessly at the office on the training program and also doing fundraising for the Cattle Baron's Ball. The event was this evening and we'd raised nearly $150,000 in a very short time. It was almost euphoric knowing that three people had come together to save the event from cancellation. Without our help, so many people would have gone without services provided by the American Cancer Society, such as the free prostheses, wigs, transportation, lodging, and more. The lack of services would have devastated so many families.

I'd never been to the Cattle Baron's Ball and was eager to attend the actual event. I'd been told that you don't go to the ball wearing anything on your feet but boots. Frank already owned a pair of boots, but I had to buy a pair. The event would be held mainly outdoors at an exotic ranch, so boots would be appropriate for such an occasion. I wasn't fond of cowboy boots, but paired with my True Religion jeans and a spaghetti strap, black, silk tank, the cowboy chic outfit looked hot.

The American Cancer Society invited Frank and me to sit at their table and we were thrilled to death. It was such an honor, and I couldn't believe that we landed such great seats. We had planned to find a table with open seating and here we were in the reserved VIP section. The night was magical and we heard so many powerful stories about people who had survived and lost loved ones to various forms of cancer. It was an eye-opener to both of us. We had not realized how many people were afflicted by this dreaded disease every year.

We danced until midnight under the starry sky. By the time we left the event, my feet were throbbing in pain from so much foot work on the dance floor in my new cowboy boots. The heat and humidity of the evening had caused me and every other two-stepper to be completely soaked in sweat. It didn't matter, though, because the night was a success and I was having tons of fun being with my man and an entirely new group of friends.

⚘⚘⚘

Frank and I were more excited about life than ever before. The charity event had offered us a nice change of pace. The boys were doing well in school. Frank loved his new job and the company was growing in revenue and employees. It had been years since I'd seen Frank this excited about work. Our credit card debt was nearly gone and our savings account was finally growing again.

The ACS executive team had been so impressed with my involvement and leadership with the Cattle Baron's Ball that they asked me to take over as chairwoman for the next year's ball. It would be the fifteenth anniversary of the Cattle Baron's Ball in Austin, and ACS was hoping to pull out all the stops and raise more money than they ever had before. I thought about it long and hard, and finally decided that I would only do it if they allowed me to bring Frank on as my co-chair. They loved the idea, thinking it would be great for publicity to have a married couple in charge of the ball, and shortly after that, we got right to work.

As I started planning for the ball, I realized that I had underestimated the time commitment required to chair a charity event as large as the Cattle Baron's Ball big-time. It's a full-time job, and I already had one! There was an art and science to producing a charity event. The event needed to be unique and creative while ensuring that the charity realized a profit. For this event to be a success, I was told that for every dollar spent, I needed to receive four dollars in sponsorships or ticket sales. My budget became my best friend.

The entire committee included 145 active volunteers and it was the largest team I'd ever managed. My entire team volunteered to help me plan the event and every day we worked together to coordinate some aspect of the ball. I wanted this event to feel inclusive, so it was important to me that everyone felt involved. If I could make people feel involved, I knew that they would invest more of their time and heart into the cause. Three or four nights a week, I organized meetings at various venues, mostly pubs, with different committees to provide assistance and leadership. In every meeting, I taught the team how to leverage their networks and encourage participation in the ball, whether it be a committee member, sponsor, or attendee. Although I could have handled these meetings solo, Frank wanted to be involved in every aspect of planning the event. This meant that we'd need Andrew to help out with babysitting a lot more than usual. I expected him to overreact to the idea of hanging with his little brother, but he was surprisingly accommodating.

The Cattle Baron's Ball had been losing ground to other events and my goal was to put it back on the map. For the fifteenth year anniversary, I stepped up to raise $500 thousand and planned to achieve that goal by hosting several events throughout the year leading up to the ball. The first of the events kicked off with a Lil' Buckaroos horseshoe decorating party for kids with cancer, followed by an Urban Chic Style show so that the socialites could plan their wardrobe, the VIP Cattle Baron's Party for the big donors, and finally, the Gala Ball.

Every day, I pushed myself harder and harder and worked as many hours as my body allowed in a twenty-four hour period. Even when I was able to fall asleep by 11:00 P.M., my internal clock woke me at 3:30 A.M. Instead of trying to go back to sleep, I viewed it as an opportunity to get a few more hours in before the rest of the house awoke.

The intense schedule that I kept often made me feel a bit fatigued. To counter the tiredness and stress mounting from the approaching gala, I made several massage appointments, but I couldn't relax enough to derive pleasure from them. My brain just wouldn't stop processing the never-ending task list. My inability to relax was also due in part to the discomfort I experienced in by breasts from lying on my stomach. Like my mother, breast swelling and back pain were normal occurrences, especially during my menstrual cycle.

Despite my obligations, I still made sure to spend as much time as I could with Andrew and Vaughn. Andrew was now in middle school, and had grown up to be a charming and handsome young man. He had conquered his early habit of keeping his emotions locked inside, and regularly had honest conversations with us about the things that mattered to him, which just awed me. Vaughn was just as sweet and happy-go-lucky as he had been as a baby.

❁❁❁

When February 2008 rolled around, Frank had an opportunity to fly to San Francisco for a three-day gaming conference. It was important that he attend because he wanted to overhaul the user interface of his company's product and make it more kid-friendly. The company had received feedback that the legacy product was not interesting enough and Frank wanted to bring the company's products into the 21st century. He strongly encouraged me to go with him because he could see how run-down I'd become. The temptation was so strong and I wanted to go, but I still had so much work to do for the Ball. In the end, he and the children ganged up on me and finally convinced me to take a break.

The trip was my first time going to San Francisco, so I wasn't sure quite what to expect. We were booked at the Fairmont Hotel in the historic section of downtown. It was an extraordinary hotel with magnificent architectural features. It was the perfect place to be to enjoy the festivities of the city and take part of the culture.

Frank had to attend the conference from 8:00 A.M. to 5:00 P.M. to fit in everything he wanted to see. I had no interest in walking the streets of San Francisco by myself, so I just camped out in the hotel for most of the time, responding to emails. I did take a break or two to enjoy a facial and cocoa butter body scrub. On the third day, I loosened up a bit and splurged on a two-hour relaxation massage to eliminate the last bit of stress in my neck and back. Frank and I had planned a romantic dinner so I wanted to be completely calm and stress-free.

Around 2:00 P.M., I was greeted by a middle-aged woman with a body shaped similar to a professional rugby player. She greeted me and shook my hand, her fingers stubby and palms a bit rough, which meant that I was in for a mediocre massage. With clipboard in hand, she reviewed my profile to evaluate my needs and asked about the level of discomfort in my neck and back. She left me alone in the dimly lit treatment room so I could remove my clothes. I slid under the white cotton linens, facedown, and adjusted my body for maximum comfort. I placed my head in the cradle, waiting for the masseuse to reenter. Within minutes, I needed to readjust my breasts several times because the weight bearing down on them was very uncomfortable. For a woman with a 34C cup size, I felt like I was lugging around a 40DD rack.

"This is a beautiful old building," I told the masseuse after she'd returned to the room. I typically make small talk at the beginning of massage and taper off my conversation within the first fifteen minutes. She began her warm-up routine, sliding her hands up and down my back, with just enough pressure to cause slight pain.

"Is the pressure okay?" she asked. "Let me know if I need to lighten up."

"The pressure is perfect," I replied, thinking to myself, *I hope she recognizes when my conversation starts to slow down and she doesn't talk to me throughout the entire massage.*

"Are you from here?" she asked me.

"Actually, I'm not from here," I said. "I'm from Austin . . . here with my husband for a conference."

She continued the massage with a few comments here and there, and found the origin of my back pain. She spent a lot of time trying to eliminate the knots with her thumbs and elbows. As her hands passed over my shoulder blades, the discomfort in my chest increased. It was almost impossible to rest because I was so focused on trying to find a comfortable position. She could tell that I was uncomfortable from my constant fidgeting and checked in with me several times, but I told her to keep going. However, after twenty minutes, I told her I needed to turn over because my breasts were swollen from my menstrual cycle. She nodded, understanding instantly. As she resumed the massage, it was all I could do to quash my anxiety. *What the hell is wrong with my right boob? I've checked them several times over the past few months and they've felt fine. They are a bit swollen and feel a bit dense, but that's to be expected during my period. I must have a cyst, but why is only one boob sore? Don't start freaking yourself out, Linda. Just enjoy the rest of this massage and talk to Frank tonight.* The rest of the massage went fine, but I just wanted it to end. My thoughts were consumed with the aching in my breasts, especially the right one in which I could feel a pinching sensation. I was actually relieved when it ended and I could return to the hotel room.

Later that evening when Frank returned from the conference, I was standing in my black Victoria Secret's push-up bra. "Do my boobs look bigger to you?" I inquired.

"They look great to me," he chimed as he walked over to inspect them.

"No, do they actually look bigger? It feels like I had a boob job or something. They feel dense and heavy."

"They look the same to me . . . sexy momma."

"Frank," I said, a bit annoyed. "I'm being serious. Feel them. Don't they feel like lead weights? Feel my right boob, do you feel anything strange?" I asked nervously.

"No . . . nothing," he said, feeling me up and obviously not minding the exercise. "They feel exactly like they normally do."

"Yeah, I've been feeling them all day and didn't feel anything, either. But I broke out in a full-blown sweat today during my massage because my right boob hurt so much. It freaked me out." We talked about what had happened during the massage and decided that I should go to my OB/GYN and have it checked out to put my mind at ease. In the meantime, I tried to enjoy what was left of my mini-vacation and take advantage of the break in my busy schedule.

❀❀❀

The only times I'd been to my OB/GYN's office were for my annual pap smears and during my pregnancies. We arrived home on Tuesday and my doctor's office scheduled me in on Friday of the same week. Anxiously, I walked through the door and noticed that the walls were still covered in an old-fashioned fabric reminiscent of what I'd seen in doctor's offices in the 1970's when I was a little girl. It was like visiting an old-fashioned museum. Even the over-sized pictures of the doctor's two girls were dated by nearly ten years.

"Dr. Doss will see you shortly, Linda. Have a seat. Anything change with your insurance?" the receptionist asked.

"Oh, yes. Let me get my new cards," I said, rummaging through my wallet. I found the cards and handed them to her over the Formica countertop.

Within a few minutes, I was escorted into the back area. "Hop up on the scale for me," the nurse's assistant said.

"Okay, you know by now that I'm not stepping on the scale," I replied. "I barely stepped on it while I was pregnant and don't plan to start now. Trust me, I weigh the same, about 112 pounds or so." She looked at the other nurses for approval and then shrugged her shoulders. It irritated me to no end that I had to be weighed every visit. I found it oddly satisfying to turn down their request for my weight. I'd never owned a scale—ever—because I subscribed to Cosmopolitan Magazine's weight philosophy. I judged my weight by the fit of my clothes, and mine always fit perfectly.

The visit was uneventful. I described my experience in California while the doctor probed my breasts with his long, cold fingers. "No, I don't feel anything," he said. "You are too young to worry about breast cancer," he continued, "but it won't hurt for you to get a mammogram. I'll have the gals call over to the Women's Breast Center to see if they have any openings today."

My mind began to race with negative thoughts. *Did he want to get me in today because he felt something and didn't want to tell me? Do I look that nervous? I thought I was actually acting calm and collected. Don't get ahead of yourself, because he's just trying to be helpful.* "Okay, great. Thanks, Dr. Doss."

Luckily, they had an appointment within the hour so I took it. I'd never had a mammogram before, but the process was fairly simple and quick, lasting only about fifteen minutes. I was instructed to remove my shirt and bra and put on a gown that opened in the front. Once I did that, I was led to the x-ray room, which was rather small and very cold. The x-ray machine took up most of the space in the room, where the radiologic technologist took one breast, positioned it on the platform, and commenced squishing it from here to infinity (and almost beyond) between the platform and a paddle that came down on top of it. After doing the same to the other breast, I was allowed to change back into my clothes and was escorted into the waiting room. As I sat waiting for the word that everything was fine, I ran through my entire family history trying to recall if anyone had had breast cancer in my family. I came up empty.

The technologist retrieved me from the waiting room with good news. "You can go, Mrs. Ginac," she said. "Your x-rays came back clean."

"What does that mean?" I asked, somehow still not relieved. I wasn't sure if they were supposed to give me results or if I had to wait for them. *Are they telling me everything is okay and I'll find out the bad news from my doctor?* I wondered.

As if reading my mind, the technologist replied, "Everything looks good. We'll send a full report to your doctor, who will go over the results with you in more detail, but the radiologist didn't find anything to be concerned about."

You would think that those words would have put my mind at ease, but they didn't. "Are you sure? I really feel like something is wrong. Is this the only test that you perform?"

"One second, Mrs. Ginac. Let me talk to the doctor on call," the technologist said, turning to leave the room. I already knew that no matter what the doctor said, something wasn't right. My gut feelings were almost never wrong. If I walked away without figuring out what was going on with my body then I'd drive myself and Frank nuts, and that couldn't happen. I had to know what was up.

The technologist returned. "The doctor said that we can perform an ultrasound. It's not typical unless we see something on the mammogram, but experience has taught us to listen to the patient."

Again, just like the mammogram, the ultrasound process was quick and painless. I was led to a different room, asked to change, and then waited to be examined. When the sonographer arrived, she had me lie down on the examination table and then scanned my breasts using a hand-held scanning device called a transducer. As I was told before with the mammogram, the ultrasound turned up nothing.

"Well, looks like you're in good shape," the sonographer said, smiling. "It must just be a pulled muscle. You're good to go."

I watched her pull a white paper from a clipboard for the next patient while I tried to process what she was telling me. *How can everything be okay? My body has never felt this way before and I know something is not right.* I wasn't looking for something to be wrong, but I wanted a satisfactory explanation about why my breast hurt. I couldn't let her move on to the next patient, not yet. "I know I'm really harping on this, but I can tell there's something wrong with my body and I want to know what it is. Can you check one more time for me in a specific spot?" I asked, feeling around my breast until I pinpointed the spot where it hurt. "Here," I said, directing the sonographer toward the appropriate spot. "Press here. Hard."

She pressed the transducer into my breast and studied the screen. After about forty seconds of fishing around, she mumbled a bit, recognizing something. "Hmm," she said. "Well, this could be something. It's awfully small, though. I don't know how you could feel something that small."

"I don't know how big it is, but I feel something," I said.

They performed another mammogram, this time concentrating on that one tiny spot, and blowing up the x-ray as big as they could. The doctor looked at it, his brow furrowed, and finally said, "Well, I suppose there could be something there. I doubt it's anything, but we'll recommend a doctor to do a biopsy just to make sure."

"What the heck is a biopsy?" I asked as my head began to spin and my knees started to shake.

"It is a routine procedure to test breast tissue for the presence of cancer cells," she responded. "The procedure can be done in a doctor's office and takes less than ten minutes to perform. I will recommend two doctors that can perform the procedure for you."

I got dressed, picked up the doctor referrals at the front desk, and quickly walked out the door. When I got into my car, I reached into my purse and pulled out my iPhone. Before I even called Frank, I tapped on the Safari browser and typed "breast biopsy" in the Google toolbar. I clicked dozens of links and read pages of information about the procedure. The more I read, the more freaked out I became. *What are the odds that I have cancer the same year I volunteer to chair the Ball? It can't be. Maybe I'm just overly sensitive to the topic because of all of the discussions I've had with people about cancer. It's just at the top of my mind. I'm sure this is just a cyst.* I continued trying to reassure myself it would all be okay, then called the master of reassurance. Frank took the news calmly and told me to come home. We'd get through this.

❂❂❂

The following week, my body lay flat on the doctor's table. I was covered by the typical patient dress, with the exception of my right breast. Frank was sitting in the corner of the outpatient room, smiling at me to calm my nerves. I don't know who was more nervous about the procedure, though, him or me.

Expect for a minor sting from the injected anesthesia, I didn't feel much discomfort during the procedure. The doctor turned on the ultrasound machine and moved the wand around my boob for over a minute. The nurse stood over his shoulder and all of our eyes were fixed on the screen. The nurse removed her glasses several times and it struck me as funny because they're a tool to see better. After several minutes, the doctor picked up the mammogram films and scanned through the ultrasound notes sent over from the Women's Imaging Center.

"I am not seeing anything under this ultrasound," he explained.

The nurse nodded in agreement. "I didn't see anything either." I explained that the imaging center had had a very difficult time finding anything, and told him where he needed to place the wand and push. On his second try, he found the same small mass in an area just below my nipple. Then he said, "This mass is so small that I'm not sure if I am going to be able to get a good sample, but I'll do my best."

This did not give me any assurance that I'd selected the right doctor. In addition to the recommendation from the imaging center, he had come highly recommended by several people at ACS. He explained that he would be conducting an ultrasound guided needle biopsy to pinpoint the suspicious area. Within a few minutes, a very long needle entered my breast to do its job. I closed my eyes and pretended that I was getting an evaluation for a boob job. When he finished, he told me that it would take about a week to get the results of the test. I knew it would be the longest week of my life.

❀❀❀

From the day of my mammogram/ultrasound until I received the results of my biopsy, I frantically searched the Internet looking for information. I learned that cancer didn't hurt, which was one of the major reasons it goes undetected for so long, so from the best I could tell, I probably had fibrocystic disease.

After a very long week, I got the results of my biopsy. I'd just pulled into my driveway a little after 5:30 P.M. when my cell phone rang. I didn't recognize the number but answered it anyway. "Hello?" I said into the phone.

"Hi, Linda. It's Doctor Askew. I received your results."

My heart stopped beating for a few seconds and my body froze in fear of hearing what the doctor was going to tell me. *Everything is fine. It's all good.*

"The good news, Linda," he said, "is that your biopsy tested negative for cancer. But, there were some atypical cells which, ironically, are fairly typical for women."

I suppose that's really good news, I thought to myself, feeling a bit relieved. "Is it just a cyst then? Should I remove it? What does atypical mean?" I asked the doctor, barraging him with questions because I was still confused about what was happening to my body and what he was telling me.

"Well, we did detect a few anomalous cells around the area," he said. "It's not a big deal. Everyone has a few irregular cells. You can either leave it alone and hope it goes away, or you can remove the cyst by having it cut out."

"What do most people do?" I asked, confused about what steps to take.

"Most people leave it alone because they do not want to go under the knife it they don't have to," he responded very casually.

"Well, I want it removed," I said. Since I had first started feeling the pinch, I'd been unable to get massages, and there are few things in this world that can relax me like a good massage. If I had to stop getting massages because of a few irregular cells, then those irregular cells were coming out.

"I have one last question," I said to him. "What are the odds that cancer actually exists when a biopsy comes back negative?"

The doctor replied, "Very small, but it's happened." A chill ran up my spine, which only meant one thing to me. I already knew I had it, and knew that was what the doctor would discover after he removed the tissue.

I shared the doctor's news with Frank and he was elated. He wanted to celebrate with the gang, but I just wanted to hang low. I shared my fear with Frank, but he brushed it off and told me that I had just experienced a major ordeal and was still frightened by the experience. I wanted him to be right, but knew deep in my heart he was wrong.

❁❁❁

The surgery to remove the cyst took place in March 2008, just days prior to the Cattle Baron's Ball fashion show hosted by Neiman Marcus. Frank was very supportive and did as much research as me, probably more, on the topic of breast cancer. The amount of reading I did on the Internet coincided with the rise in my anxiety. I made Frank swear not to tell anyone about the surgery, including his mother as well as the children. People didn't need to worry about me for no reason and I didn't want to get caught up in answering everyone's questions, especially since the Cattle Baron's Ball was only two months away.

The day after the operation, I carried on as usual, happy to have it behind me. Although I was very sore and didn't feel up for a night on the town, I had to attend my own party. Missing out on the very first event for Cattle Baron's would be terrible and I did not want to disappoint my team. Downtime was not an option, and I'd already spent too much time worrying about my health.

I stared at myself in the mirror and focused in on my boobs. "Frank, they are two different sizes."

"Linda, you just had a major surgery. Your breast is swollen."

"Everyone is going to notice. I can't go to this event," I whispered as a tear escaped my eye.

Frank walked over and put his arms around me. "No one is going to notice. You look beautiful. We don't have to go, but I know you want to."

"Please don't hug me too tightly. You are pressing against my boob and it hurts. I don't *want* to go . . . I *have* to go," I complained. I broke from his embrace and opened the medicine cabinet. I pulled out the Advil bottle and shook it until two pills were sitting in my hand. I swallowed the pills and buried my emotions deep inside, mentally psyching myself up. *Tonight, you will prepare yourself for a night of mingling and hosting with the supporters and volunteers of this important event. There is a whole world out there with cancer. You were lucky and just had a cyst removed. Suck it up, girly!* With those thoughts, I mustered up the energy of a seventeen-year-old girl going to her first prom, and convinced myself that it would be a great night.

✿✿✿

When the phone rang, it pulled me out of a trance. I'd been deep in concentration on a difficult section of the training program. I was surprised to hear the phone ring because it was nearing five o'clock in the evening and most calls happened earlier in the day. I suspected it was a prospect calling to schedule an appointment for a free initial consultation.

"Hello, this is The Ginac Group, Linda speaking. How can I help you?"

"Hi, Linda. This is Dr. Askew's office. I need to schedule time for you to come in and see Dr. Askew," the voice said. "When is your earliest availability?"

I had not expected to hear from Dr. Askew's nurse. It confirmed my worst fears. "What's it about?" I asked, feeling very uneasy. The blood was starting to drain from my head and I was suddenly very lightheaded.

"All I can tell you is that he needs to meet with you as soon as possible," she replied.

I made the appointment as my heart started pounding and my hands began to shake. *I thought I'd beaten this thing,* I thought to myself. *What the hell does he need to see me so urgently about? What if I do have cancer?* Even after the room stopped spinning and I regained whatever composure I could, I couldn't shake the feeling that something really bad was about to happen.

I called Frank and told him the news. For the next several days, we tried to carry on as if nothing were amiss, but they felt like the longest days of my life. Frank tried his best to remain positive and optimistic, but his face revealed his true feelings. He was a man walking in a cloud of fear.

The day of the appointment, he held my hand as we entered the doctor's office and assured me that everything was fine. I held my tongue, concentrating on the best outcome. We sat nervously on the edge of our seats in the doctor's private office. I picked up a magazine, and the first page I turned to was a story about an elderly woman with cancer. This didn't make me feel any better.

Dr. Askew walked in, sat down at his desk, and opened my folder. After a few pleasantries, he got right to the point. "It's standard procedure to conduct a more comprehensive biopsy on any abnormal cells we remove from a breast," he told us, "and I have no idea how you knew this, but you were right all along. Your cells tested positive for cancer."

I had no physical or emotional reaction to his words, and I purposely didn't look at Frank for his reaction. I simply said, "Okay. Tell me more."

"It's very early-stage. The type is called HER2+ and ER positive breast cancer. It's the most aggressive form of cancer . . . but, it's the most curable when caught at this early of a stage."

"Stage? How many stages are there?" I asked numbly.

"Many. You are considered stage 1 and this is good news. It is really amazing that you were diagnosed so early on."

I pulled out a piece of paper and pen, ready to outline everything I needed to do to eliminate the problem. The doctor stared at me for a few minutes. "Are you okay?" he asked.

"Yes, I am perfectly fine. Just tell me what the next steps are."

The doctor turned in Frank's direction, which made me look his way, too. I've never seen Frank look so small. His elbows were resting on his knees, with one hand pressed tightly against his forehead and the other held tightly to his stomach. He looked very pale, like he was about to pass out.

"Frank, are you okay?" asked Dr. Askew.

In a very frail and shaky voice, and on the verge of crying, Frank asked the doctor, "Is she going to die?"

"Oh my God! No! No! No! She's not going to die," Dr. Askew reassured him. We've caught this very early, and had it not been for your wife's persistence—had we waited another six months—it might be a different story. But thankfully, that's not the case. This is quite treatable."

There were lots of things I could have said at that very moment, conversations that I had rehearsed in my mind, but instead I just sat there, stunned. "Everything is going to be fine, Frank," I finally said, stealing his favorite line and using it on him. "I love you, honey, more than anything else, and everything is going to be fine." I brushed my hand along his arm to comfort him. I paused, feeling my throat constrict. My love for this man was so deep, so enormous, that it took times like this for me to fully appreciate the breadth of it. In the bustle of day-to-day life and routines, I'd lost sight of just how much he filled my heart. I smiled to give him strength. "Let's get the details from the doctor and go home." He needed my strength.

Chapter 25 Acceptance

I didn't have what you would call a typical reaction to being diagnosed with cancer. Frank was a lot more torn up about it than I was, fearing that he would lose me, but I just saw it as yet another hurdle I needed to overcome. Compared to what I'd endured during my childhood, this would be something I could attack head-on, especially since I had Frank in my corner, and I wasn't about to let it get the best of me. If the years hadn't proved anything else, they had shown that I was a fighter and not likely to give up without a fight. Luckily, I'd happened to catch the cancer at the earliest possible moment. Most people didn't notice anything until the tumor was about the size of a grape, or even a walnut, but mine was about the size of a pea. Time was on my side in that respect, but I was still going to have to go through at least a year of treatment.

My first thought as I began my research on treatment options was that I didn't want to go through chemotherapy. Through my work with the American Cancer Society, I'd seen up-close what chemotherapy does to a person and it isn't pretty. I'd always had a healthy immune system, and I couldn't see how filling my body with near-lethal doses of poison was going to help me get better. These drugs would literally destroy my immune system and make me permanently infertile. If the cancer didn't kill me, something as simple as a fungal infection could! It just seemed wrong to me. There had to be a better option.

I searched endlessly for alternative treatment options and one study in particular caught my eye. It said that estrogen was the chemical that regulates breast growth, so limiting the production of estrogen in the body was one way to inhibit the growth of cancer cells in the breasts. The treatment in this particular study involved a period of radiation followed by drug treatments that basically brought on the onset of menopause. Fortunately, the post-menopausal condition wasn't permanent. Once I was cancer free—which was what I was determined to be—I could stop taking the drugs and return to a pre-menopausal state within months.

I had a briefcase full of clinical studies and felt fully informed when Frank and I went to meet with the oncologist that Dr. Askew had recommended. I had discovered that an oncologist must prescribe the treatments for various forms of cancer, and that the treatments are dictated by the board of oncology. My oncologist informed me that I fell into the category that recommended chemotherapy in addition to using a drug called Herceptin (very effective against my form of breast cancer), and the estrogen eradication treatment. I knew I was in for a battle over my treatment plan.

"Linda, this is the treatment plan that I highly recommend. It has the highest survival rates," she informed me.

Frank, siding with the oncologist, said, "Honey, you should do what she recommends for treatment."

Sticking to my guns, I said, "Look, I'm not worried about losing my hair, but I may want to have another child someday. If I do chemotherapy, it'll kill every chance of that happening. My immune system is strong and I want a treatment plan that won't take it down in the process. If you can't recommend an alternative plan, I'll look for a doctor who can."

"I really would like to you to think about this. It is a very important decision. Maybe you should sit on it and speak to your family," she advised.

"Honey, that sounds like a good idea," Frank suggested. "Let's go home and talk about it."

"I am not going home to discuss this with you. It's my body and my decision," I told Frank as I turned to look at the doctor and stare straight into her eyes. "My mind is made up. Period. Done. It will not change. Either you help me using alternative methods or you refuse to bring me on as a patient. I'm not trying to be difficult, but I know what's right for me." Frank and the doctor stared at me in silence, stunned by the intensity of my decision. Frank's shoulders hung in defeat as he took in my expression. He rubbed his hands together, knowing that I was not going to budge on my decision, the consequence of which could be death, but I was okay with it.

In order to get the kind of treatment I wanted, I had to sign a number of release forms acknowledging that I had refused the recommended treatment plan. Even though numerous studies had shown that the plan I chose was more effective in battling HER2+/ER positive breast cancer, the U.S. medical establishment isn't quick to incorporate new techniques. Having the support of my doctor made a tremendous difference. She finally caved and recommended a better treatment plan than the one I had discovered. She was incredibly supportive and made me feel that I made the right decision.

The first step in my treatment involved surgery to scrape out the rest of the cancerous cells, in essence a partial mastectomy. It was a fairly major surgery, but I wasn't about to let it get me down—I had a big Cattle Baron's event in three weeks and I wasn't going to let cancer get in the way of my life. Throughout the entire ordeal, only Frank and a few close friends and family members knew what I was going through. I chose not to tell my kids or anyone on the Cattle Baron's committee. I shared the news with my team and when they broke down in tears, I asked them not to cry for me. I didn't want anyone's pity. To me, it was just a simple operation with some medication.

Frank and my team thought that I wasn't accepting the news well or dealing with the emotional aspects of being informed that I had cancer. They may have been right on some level, but they didn't really know me well enough. I was an emotional rock when it came to sickness. I'd had lots of experience in this area because of my father's fight with a terminal disease. Dealing with situations like this was when my strength shined its brightest.

I firmly believed that with everything we do in life, from finding the perfect career to healing illness, our minds and attitudes played a huge role in how things work out. I could have sunk into a depression after the cancer diagnosis or used it to get sympathy from the people around me, but I knew I'd only end up hurting my chances for recovery if I wasn't one hundred percent convinced that I was going to beat it.

Ever since I'd felt my first real brush with confidence, back when I started helping people with career coaching, I recognized that life was truly what we made of it. If we sat around feeling sorry for ourselves, our lives would give us something to feel sorry about. If, on the other hand, we woke up every morning and thanked God for the blessings we had been given, He, the universe, or whichever higher power you draw your spiritual strength from, would respond by helping us through the difficult times with dignity and hope.

✿✿✿

After all the time and energy I'd put into planning the Cattle Baron's Ball, the day of the Gala Ball was finally here. It was May 31, 2008, and this final event was the culmination of all the work we'd done over the previous year. We had rented out the Texas Disposal Systems Exotic Game Ranch and Pavilion Complex for the event, a beautiful, sprawling facility that was needed to accommodate the nearly 1,000 guests that would be attending—the biggest turnout in the Ball's history! I had 220 committee members working on everything from decorations to food to auctions to games. My only official job that night would be to be a great host and give a heart-felt welcoming speech. After that, I could let my hair down—hair that I still had thanks to my refusal to follow the outdated guidance of traditional chemotherapy—and enjoy an evening of fun with friends.

A few months prior, I would have assumed that the only thing that would be on my mind the day of the Ball would have been making sure the event went smoothly. However, tonight would be the night that I revealed that I was diagnosed with cancer and going through treatment. This news would come as a complete shock to nearly everyone in the room. Many people would have taken months or years to recover after cancer surgery and treatment, but I knew it just wasn't an option. I had worked hard to get the Cattle Baron's Ball together and I wouldn't have missed it for the world.

It was 4:00 P.M. when Trudi arrived at the house to prepare me for the ball. When she found me in the bedroom, she walked in and gave me a big hug. "Are you ready for me to make you more beautiful than you already are?" she teased.

"You know it. Let's go into my bathroom. I cleared a space for all of your makeup." I sat down on the counter instead of in my makeup chair so that she didn't have to bend over the whole time she applied beauty products to my face.

"You are going to be the most beautiful woman at the ball when I'm through with you," she said proudly.

"I don't know about that," I countered. "But I do want to thank you so much for doing my makeup when I know you have to get yourself ready, too."

"It's my pleasure. I'm happy to do it. You worked so hard on this Ball. It's going to be a smashing success."

Sixty minutes passed before she was done. I could hear our friends talking in the living room with Frank about how excited they were to be attending the Ball with us. I'd booked a limo to drive the six of us to the event and back. It was a long drive and I knew that we would be drinking, so I'd gotten us a very fancy designated driver.

Trudi wouldn't let Frank in the room to look at me, and she wouldn't let me look in the mirror, either, until I was fully dressed. While she packed up her things, I went into the master closet to slip into my shimmery, off-white, spaghetti strap dress and heels. I walked back into the bathroom and Trudi put her hands over her mouth. "You look absolutely beautiful, Linda. The dress is stunning on you."

I looked in the full-length mirror and almost started crying. For the first time in my life, I felt absolutely beautiful.

"Don't tear up or your makeup will run off your face!" Trudi said. I gave her a hopeless look and scooted us both out the door and into the living room.

"Oh, Linda! You look amazing," gushed Dondrea. "You are going to be the most beautiful person at the Ball."

"Thank you," I said. It was good to hear that. Frank and the rest of the gang gushed over me for a few minutes and I gladly soaked it up.

"It's time to go or we'll be late. Let's hop into the limo for some champagne," Frank said. In minutes, we were packed in the limo on our way to the Ball. On the way to the Game Ranch, I only had a few thoughts in mind. One thought was to raise as much money as I could for the charity. The second thought was to thank everyone who had given countless hours and money to make this event a success. And the last thought was for me to have as much fun as a person could have in a single night.

When we arrived, the Ranch looked amazing. It was classy and elegant, and looked exactly as I'd imagined. The volunteers had worked so hard today that it made me want to cry again. When I got out of the limo, I walked around the entire venue checking out every detail. When I had left the Ranch earlier that day, it had been a disorganized mess and now it was a sight to behold. The auction tables were overflowing with oversized themed baskets. The casino was organized and ready for gamblers. The VIP area was staged to have the best view at the venue and everyone would be able to see the large donors having fun and wishing they had donated more. The dining area was set up outside under a white tent and was the size of a football field. Just beyond the tent sat the stage, exactly as I'd imagined it. The stage had never been placed in that location before and everyone had expressed concern that it wouldn't work, but it could not have been better and I knew I'd get kudos for a job well done.

As I walked toward the registration area to check on things, I heard someone calling my name, but wasn't sure who it was. In a second, I focused in on a woman jogging my way waving something in the air. It was Kelly, the chair of reservations. "Linda, Linda! Look at this."

"What is it?" I asked. "Is something wrong?"

"Oh, no. Far from it," she replied, smiling. "I thought you'd want to see this, though. Isn't it great?" She handed me the latest issue of *Your Address*

Magazine (Austin's premier home lifestyle publication), featuring a cover story on the Cattle Baron's Ball. Frank and I were on the cover of the magazine.

"Let me see that thing," I said nervously, anticipating an amazing cover that people would rave over. "Oh my God," I gasped as my hand covered my mouth. I wanted to cry but held back the tears.

"What is it?" asked Kelly.

My eyes were instantly drawn to the bodice of the dress I was wearing in the photo. "This looks terrible. I hate it. Why did the publisher think this was amazing?"

"Are you serious? Y'all look great, Linda," Kelly said. "The article and other photos look great, too. This was a fantastic way to promote the Ball."

"Frank looks great. Not me," I argued self-critically. I stared at the magazine cover for what seemed like an eternity.... *I can't believe how terrible my chest looks. I don't remember my boobs looking so uneven when I looked in the mirror before the photo shoot—everyone's going to be able to tell that I had surgery! Jeez. Well, that is why we're here, right? I'm planning on revealing my cancer ordeal tonight, anyhow.* Finally I said, "Well, it's not all that bad, but look at my chest. Doesn't it look uneven?"

"Are you serious, girlfriend? No, it doesn't! You are way too critical of yourself. Stop it!" Kelly demanded.

"You are probably right," I sighed. I peeked a quick glance down at my bust to see if it looked uneven, but everything looked fine from my perspective.

"Stop looking at your chest. The girls look great in that dress," she said. "Now put that magazine down and get to work. We have a ball to run," then, looking at her watch, "Rats! I need to go. Talk to you later, girlfriend. You look great!"

"Thanks for ruining my night, Kelly!" I responded with laughter in my voice. As she ran off to the registration table to make sure her team had everything they needed for the VIP crowd, I shrugged away my negative thoughts— I still had things to do, after all. I looked toward the entrance and noticed that both reservation tables were packed with people and long lines were already forming. *I hope twenty people are enough to check in over a thousand guests. If not, I'll have to send some champagne out there because the sun is very hot and people will sweat! I need to keep my eye on that line because that could be a disaster if not handled right.*

Frank arrived moments later and I held up the magazine. "Terrific, but I'll have to look at it later," he said. "They need us near the stage. They want to run the program one more time to make sure we have the content nailed."

"Again? I've already prepared my speech and rehearsed it in front of them almost a dozen times."

"Let them do their job, love. They don't want to screw it up. There is a lot of synchronization that has to happen with the videos, presentation, logos, and our speech," he said, smiling as he locked his arm in mine and led the way to the stage.

As the event began, right after the cocktail hour, I ascended the stage to welcome the guests. "Hi, everyone," I said. "My name's Linda Ginac, and my husband, Frank, and I are the co-chairs of this year's Cattle Baron's Ball. How's everyone doing this fine warm night in Texas?"

A huge cheer arose from the crowd, where everyone was dressed up in their finest cowboy boots, rhinestones and whatever everyone else interpreted as attire in accordance with the night's theme. I smiled widely. It was so rewarding to finally see the fruits of our labor come to life. The guests looked great, and it seemed as if everyone was having a good time already.

I started by thanking all the people who had helped make the night a smooth event. Then I told the audience a little about the American Cancer Society and all the amazing work they were doing for cancer patients. Finally, it was time for the hardest part of the speech, the part I'd been agonizing over ever since being diagnosed with cancer a few months before.

"Finally," I began, "I just wanted to say a quick word to let you all know how much this event and this organization means to me." I paused for a moment and then continued. "A few months ago, I was diagnosed with breast cancer." A hush fell over the crowd. At the foot of the stage, Frank looked up at me with tears in his eyes. I hadn't told him I was going to say anything because I didn't want him to worry. He was having a harder time dealing with my cancer than I was, and I hadn't wanted him starting the night out any more concerned about me than he already was. I gave him a loving smile and continued.

"Before I came up here tonight, I debated whether or not I was going to say anything about my own diagnosis. I know this announcement probably comes as a surprise to those of you who I've been working with over the past year. I haven't even told many of my closest friends. But I don't tell you this because I'm looking for sympathy. My treatments have gone well so far and the doctors say there's a great chance that I'll be cancer-free in a year. I'm telling you this because I want you to know how important your donations are to the American Cancer Society, not just for me, but for all the people out there who are living with this terrible disease. The American Cancer Society is leading the charge to find the cure for cancer, but we can't do it without your generous donations. As someone who knows firsthand what an important role ACS plays in conducting research and assisting cancer patients, I encourage you to dig deep in your support for this wonderful organization tonight. On behalf of cancer patients everywhere, I thank you for buying a ticket tonight and I want you to know that you have the power to make a difference. So please, play some games, bid on the auctions, and most importantly, have a great time. Thank you!"

I left the stage to the supportive cheers of the crowd and walked straight into Frank's arms. He squeezed me tightly and whispered, "I love you," in my ear. I held him tightly for a moment, and then we walked together into the crowd, with no other thought on our minds than having a magical night.

And what a magical night it was—the most successful Cattle Baron's Ball Austin had ever seen! We hit a new record in fundraising and I couldn't be more pleased. My committee members took care of everything, so I was able to just enjoy myself, laughing and dancing into the night. I realized that night that despite all the hardship we'd been through, from the layoffs to our money troubles to dealing with cancer, there was no place I would rather have been than right there, letting loose under a beautiful, starry, Texas sky, hand-in-hand with the man I loved.

❂❂❂

A few days after the Ball, I began radiation therapy. Over the course of the next seven weeks I had radiation five times a week—every day except Saturday and Sunday. The radiation didn't make me sick, my breasts barely turned red, and I never missed a day of work or working out. As a matter of fact, I increased my physical activity significantly by training for a half marathon, preparing for the **LIVESTRONG** Challenge ninety-mile bike ride, and building more muscle with a personal trainer. Although a bit tired, I was more determined to live my life as normally as possible. It was the only way I knew how to cope.

Along with the radiation therapy, I had another year of treatment left to go. Every three weeks, I had to spend ninety minutes in the infusion room at Texas Oncology watching an IV bag full of a drug called Herceptin slowly drain into my body. Herceptin was an amazing drug that went into your body and clinged to the cancer cells, allowing your own immune system to literally eat them alive. I also received an injection of a drug called Zoladex, a common drug used in treating both breast and prostate cancers, that shut down my ovaries and effectively put me into menopause. On top of that, I was also taking a drug called Femara that stopped the body from producing estrogen through other pathways outside of the ovaries. I had regular bone scans, PET scans, and MRIs to check my progress. It was a huge time constraint and I hated all of the appointments, but I had no choice.

As far as keeping my cancer a secret, the cat was pretty much out of the bag after the Ball. I still managed to keep the news from Andrew and Vaughn, though. I knew what it was like to live with a parent with an illness, and I refused to put them through the kind of pain that I went through with my father. As long as I continued to show signs of improvement, there was no reason to make them live with the constant stress, fear, and feelings of instability that accompany having a sick parent. When the time was right I would tell them, but I couldn't predict a specific timeframe. My heart would tell me when the time was right so I'd just have to wait for that feeling to emerge inside.

❉❉❉

Sitting in a cancer room was very uncomfortable, and not just because I was the only one with hair receiving treatment. It was so difficult to look across the room during every visit and see the many different faces, ages, and races of people impacted by cancer. The Ball had passed and I'd done my part to help, but I knew it still wasn't enough. Billions more dollars would be needed to fund research to find a cure for cancer. I prayed that I would be able to see a real breakthrough before my death.

I shook my head in sadness. I was tired of visiting this place and recognizing someone newly diagnosed every few weeks. The severity of my situation had grown stronger the closer I came to the end of my treatment. I realized how fortunate I'd been with the success of my treatment plan. It could have cost me my life by opting for a plan that was not proven and recommended by the oncology board. *Maybe by putting myself out there and being a test subject I will pave a new path for people. Chemo is so harmful to people and eats your body from the inside out.* I didn't regret my decision, but it shook me to the core to think that death could have been just around the corner. I would have lost out on seeing what growth I'm capable of, my son's growing up, and more.

I had worked through so many painful experiences in my life, and I'd finally reached a point in my personal growth where I felt prepared and ready to break past the final barriers that were holding me back from a path of authentic discovery. I'd always dreamed of a life in which I could be vulnerable to love, emotionally available, and free from shame. This was normal for most people, but it never was for me.

Having cancer brought me closer to my family and helped me discover a level of strength and compassion in myself that I didn't know I possessed. I found myself taking stock of what was important in my life and learning how to focus more on the present. My conversations with the people around me became more intimate, and I found myself sharing parts of me that had laid dormant for most of my life. I knew that the only gift I needed in life was the love of my precious husband, children, family, and friends. Having cancer helped me to really live.

❁❁❁

After one year of treatment and many scans later, Frank and I went in for my final exam with the oncologist. I sat on the examination table and he sat next to me, squeezing my hand. The doctor came into the room carrying my charts and we both looked up at her with expressions of hope. Her face was inscrutable, the unreadable mask of someone who delivers life-changing news on a regular basis. She sat down in a chair across from us and looked up at me. Every second seemed to be multiplied by ten as I waited to hear what she had to say.

"How do you feel?" she finally asked.

"Great," I said, "I feel great." Then, anxiously, "Should I?"

She smiled ... a positive sign ... unless it was a smile of compassion, the kind of smile you give to a child who doesn't understand how the world really works. ... She looked down at her chart. "Well, we've taken a look at the tests, and it appears—I think you should still keep taking Femara to be safe—but it appears, from everything we can tell, that you're cancer free. Congratulations, Linda."

Frank burst into tears of joy and threw his arms around me, clutching me as tightly as he could. I laughed giddily. In that moment, I suddenly felt all the weight of the last year drop off of my shoulders. Across the room, my doctor beamed, her poker face finally gone. I'm sure it wasn't very often that she got to deliver good news.

"You did it, baby," Frank said. "I'm so proud of you. Now what are we going to do to celebrate?"

"First things first," I laughed. "I want a massage."

"I'll book some massages for us this weekend. Let's go to the club tonight after work. This is such a huge milestone." Frank took my hand and we walked out of the cancer center with our hearts nearly bursting open.

The parking garage was dark except for the light where cars entered and left this building. I was certain that tears would flow once I was out of the presence of the doctors—there was no reason to hide my feelings. Frank was staring at me intently and I looked away from his gaze. We stood in silence for several minutes in front of my car holding hands. Slowly, I lifted my arms to embrace him. We hugged at the car for what seemed like several minutes and when I looked up at him, his eyes were filled with tears.

"What are you crying for? This is exciting news."

"I know how hard this experience was for you. I'm so happy that you are cancer-free," he revealed. "I was so scared that we might get bad news and that I'd lose you. You are my whole life, Linda."

My throat was so constricted with emotion and love for this man. "You are my husband and you are supposed to say that. I love you too, honey."

He cupped my face and gave me a slow kiss. "Everyone loves and cares about you."

"Everything turned out fine," I said. I smiled and looked away, hoping my expression looked authentic.

"Are you okay, love? I can't believe you are not jumping up and down with this news," he said.

"Give me some time, Frank. I am overwhelmed with emotion and it will take me some time to process everything." For the past year, I'd done exactly what had been expected of me during the treatment program. I'd worked out diligently and had read numerous books on how to live cancer-free. I'd been the best mother, wife, and friend I could be. Some people waited a lifetime to have the kind of love that I shared with my family; but somehow, I didn't feel worthy to have this much fortune. "Give me a kiss," I told Frank. "I want to get back to the office and put this behind me."

I knew that I could trust Frank with my heart and soul. He was completely and unconditionally in love with me, and I with him. The years had been tough on us emotionally, and at several points in our relationship I had wanted to run away. The financial and job stress we'd endured weighed heavily on my heart and pushed my thoughts to the past. I didn't want to go through life feeling disconnected and not caring about anything. Having Frank and the boys had truly transformed my life. They had helped me bloom in every way imaginable, as a woman, mother, entrepreneur, fitness buff, and more. It was time to let my heart speak instead of my head. Now I just needed to do it.

Frank got into his Yukon and I hopped into my BMW. We waved to one another before going our respective ways. As I drove along the highway back to my office, I expected the tears to flow freely but they didn't. It was so unusual for me not to cry because I was so sentimental and emotional. I couldn't even watch *Little House on the Prairie* without crying. When an employee shared something painful going on in their life, I'd be the first to spill the tears. I could hardly complete a session with a client without crying because their story touched me so deeply.

I'd forgotten my sunglasses and had to squint my eyes slightly so I wouldn't be completely blinded by the sunlight beaming through the windshield. I reached my hand across the center console and cranked up the music on the radio. Then I opened all of the windows, including the sunroof. I grabbed the steering wheel and deliberately pushed my foot on the gas. I ignored the speed limit and passed several cars in the right lane without a care of being caught by the police. I held my breath as I pushed my foot harder on the pedal, and soon I was driving 85 mph in a 40 mph zone.

Without warning, giggles consumed my entire body as I sang the lyrics to "Sweet and Low" by Augustana. I didn't understand where the laughter came from, but suspected that it was my body's way of saying, *I'm trying to let go and be happy.* I wondered if it was possible to cry without having real tears stream down my face. I certainly felt like crying, but something was blocking me from shedding the tears and letting them flow. Maybe it was the fact that I had business to conduct at the office and I didn't want anyone to see my red, puffy face. I knew deep down that that was not the case, though, because the minute I walked in the door, a bunch of red, puffy faces would stare me down, waiting expectantly for the news about my prognosis. Giggle after giggle, I knew that my body was experiencing the physical reaction of tears.

I couldn't help but wonder if I was slightly crazy. *Who laughs when most normal people would be crying with joy and happiness over being cancer-free? I'm really losing it. Why can't I cry for myself? I should be overwhelmed with tears. I should blow the rest of the day off and do something joyous.* But all I could think about was getting back to the office and getting work done. I'm fairly certain it had to do with pent-up anxiety. It's not the first time I'd laughed at inappropriate moments when I should have and would have rather had expressed anger or sadness. It pissed me off and I tried not to laugh, but the more I tried not to laugh, the more I did. *People are going to look in my car and think I am crazy or drunk. Who cares? I would certainly find it odd to see an attractive woman speeding on the highway, laughing hysterically by herself with music blaring out of the windows. Linda, slow down because you are going to hurt someone! No, I'm speeding all the way back to work.*

As I turned into the parking lot of my office, I turned down the music and closed the windows. I looked in the rearview mirror and saw the same reflection I'd seen for years. I wished I knew what to say to the woman looking back at me. *Someday you will be ready to let the floodgates open.*

Chapter 26   Resilient

By 2009, The Ginac Group was growing in clients faster than we could handle, and we had officially launched the career management training program, whose classes were filling quickly with students from across the nation. One wall in my office was covered in thank you cards from clients who had changed their lives with our help. After years of building a solid reputation in the community as a solo practitioner, I was thankful that I'd achieved a new level of success where clients were no longer asking for me by name. Most prospective clients no longer expected to work directly with me, but with a coach at my firm. The word "Ginac" was no longer simply my last name, it had become a brand. To top it off, a prospect came into the office one day and guessed at what my last name stood for. His guess was: **Get IN A C**areer. The team loved it, so we started using that slogan when people asked the coaches what Ginac stood for. I felt like I'd finally reached the top of my game and was ready to take my business and life to the next level.

The cancer was behind me, my kids were doing great in school, and Frank was doing amazingly well at CompassLearning. The company had separated from Reader's Digest with the help of an equity firm and had regained the freedom to innovate again. Within a year, several of Frank's products won national awards and he was fully engaged in the business with the confidence he'd had in years past.

My thoughts were no longer focused on what I hadn't achieved in life. I was quite satisfied with what Frank and I had built and sustained through all of our trials and tribulations. With Andrew and Vaughn getting older, I was ready to take on the world and fulfill my goal of building a national company.

Unlike so many people I'd met over the past decade, I'd found my passion and had a newfound confidence that made me feel whole in ways that I could never have anticipated. After everything was said and done, I wanted nothing more than to help every single person I could to find that kind of deep and fulfilling happiness. But, how? It was time to grow again . . .

Frank suggested that I meet with a local rock-star, start-up lawyer for advice on raising money for my business, so I did. The Ginac Group was a service company focused mainly on delivering career transition services to end users. With the addition of the career management training, I didn't want to dilute the brand. Building a company to train and certify career coaches was a very different business model and one that could scale quickly. Carmelo had worked for many international law firms and had a solid reputation in the community. Our discussion led to him taking me on under a contingency arrangement (I only had to pay if he was successful in helping me achieve my fund-raising goal!). With his assistance, we approached the fund-raising process with discipline, focus, and rigor. I created a new business plan and presentation and pitched to dozens of investors across Texas well into the summer of 2010 with no luck. We met plenty of people masquerading as angel investors who hadn't invested funds in years. We made a giant list of people and firms of those we thought would be great partners, and spent our time accordingly. We encountered a few more bad apples along the way and tossed them aside.

During the process of being rejected ten times over, I wanted to throw in the towel more times than I could count, but Frank would not let me give up. Frank's mantra became "Keep on knocking, keep on asking, and keep on calling until the investor actually says 'yes' or 'no.'" I have always known that persistence and perseverance are two traits you need to be successful, but I was struggling to believe that I could raise money despite all of my recent success. I often went to bed feeling defeated and ready to throw in the towel, but in the morning, I'd always find the energy to devote one more day to achieving my dream.

Having a positive outlook on life went a long way to keeping my team's spirits alive. If I'd given up, I'd never be able to say that I did it. After fourteen months of traveling to four states and numerous cities, and meeting with dozens of potential investors, I'd finally raised a series A round with a small handful of prominent local angel investors who believed in me and the opportunity to invest in a proven career management system.

❁❁❁

On New Year's Eve day around 2:00 P.M., we were sitting at the Tejas Bar at Barton Creek when the final investor's money was wired into my business account, which saved me from having to let go of most of the team that I'd hired with the hope that I'd actually pull off the financing. It was a huge load off my shoulders. I looked at Frank in disbelief. "We got it," I said, smiling. "We got the funding! I still can't believe it."

As always, Frank was the optimistic one. "I knew you would, love. You did a fantastic job," he smiled.

"It's because of you, honey. I hope you know that. I never would have done it without you."

"That is nice of you to say, but it was all you. I just never let you give up."

"Let's go hang with our loving and supportive friends. I could really use a huge celebration. Tonight, let's not make any resolutions that have to do with our careers, fundraising, or business. This year, let's focus on making more couple friends, going on more trips with the kids, and taking in the Austin music scene," I said with a huge smile on my face.

"It's a deal," he replied as we clinked our glasses to the wonderful news and the New Year.

Frank and I had booked a guestroom at Barton Creek. We wanted to spend the night alone with no kids. We knew we would be consuming much champagne, too, and didn't want to drink and drive, especially on New Year's Eve. The kids were safe with Margarita at our home, and I'd bought them tons of traditional New Year's hats and whistles so that they could have fun, too.

Sometime after midnight, we left the celebration and staggered through the brisk night from the grand ballroom to the hotel and conference center. My feet hurt so much from dancing that I had to remove my shoes. Instead of walking through the paved walkway, Frank and I decided to take a shortcut through the manicured golf course. The cold grass ticked my feet and I spread my arms wide as I looked up at the moon. "Thank you for everything, God. Thank you for my life. Thank you for Frank. Thank you for my children. Thank you for sending amazing angels to look over me," I effused. Suddenly I stopped and my knees fell to the ground.

"Honey, what are you doing?" Frank asked me. "Are you sick? Let me help you up. You are going to ruin your dress. People are going to see us if we stay here."

"So, let them look. I don't care if someone sees me sitting on the greens."

"Come on, honey, let's go to the room."

"I can't breathe," I responded, panting frantically.

"What's wrong with you? Are you in pain?" Frank asked, his face panicked.

I shook my head to indicate I had no physical pain. However, all the pain and anguish that I'd been suppressing during the last decade suddenly bubbled to the surface. The fortress I'd put up around myself—all of my strong defenses—came crashing down as the tears I'd held back for so many years burst out of me, streaming down my face and stinging my eyes. For the next twenty minutes, as Frank helplessly stood by, I knelt on the grass, clutching my gut and sobbing uncontrollably. I didn't care about anyone passing by and staring at me. I sobbed for all the sleepless nights I'd spent worrying about money, all the anxiety I'd felt during those endless years of unemployment, and all the pain and terror and hatred I'd had to endure as a child. I was finally letting it out.

The next day, New Year's Day 2011, I took a long-deserved break. Stretching out on the couch with Frank, we watched reruns of *The Office* and a few Lifetime Movie Network original movies. As we lay there, I thought about my journey through life up to that point, and Frank's and my journey together. We'd come so far and had grown in so many ways. In working with Andrew to express his emotions, we'd become so much more open as a family. I'd taken great strides in learning how to trust, and Frank and I no longer had the kind of fights that would send me into a tailspin of fear and doubt. Vaughn had never even really known those times. He'd grown up in a world where he felt free to express himself, knowing that his concerns would be met with compassion and empathy.

The release from the night before had felt horrible yet liberating, and I realized that it was the first time in a long time—or maybe the first time ever— that I'd let my guard down and allowed myself to be vulnerable and honest. I wasn't the rock that everyone depended on all of the time. I was just a person. And when all was said and done, I was still okay. I was alive. I had a wonderful family, supportive friends, and a career that was more rewarding than I'd ever thought a career could be.

I felt the start of a smile warm my face. It felt good to be in this place and I knew that my journey of self-discovery was just beginning. It would be from this point forward that I could learn and experience new things about myself and others. I'd learned to trust myself, and with that came a new ability to help others trust themselves.

As I thought about these things, I looked into Frank's eyes. This big, strong, funny, handsome, perpetually positive, and unbelievably supportive man had been right there by my side through all of it—the bad times, the worst times, and what was our current and hopefully our future situation, the great times. We'd been through so many difficult moments together, but every night when we turned out the lights and went to bed, regardless of how angry or worried we were, I always felt safe knowing that he was by my side. For someone who'd grown up without the faintest concept of what safety and trust meant, it was a giant leap forward for me. I knew that through our love, we were giving our children a much better platform for happiness and success in life. We weren't perfect—no one was—and that was okay. For the first time in my life, I was exactly who I wanted to be.

I am Linda Ginac, far from perfect, and perfect in every way . . .

www.ingramcontent.com/pod-product-compliance
Lightning Source LLC
Chambersburg PA
CBHW031946090426
42739CB00006B/101